OHIO

OHIO

A History

Walter Havighurst

UNIVERSITY OF ILLINOIS PRESS

Urbana and Chicago

First Illinois paperback, 2001
© 1976 by the Walter E. Havighurst Testamentary Trust
Reprinted by arrangement with the copyright holder
All rights reserved
Manufactured in the United States of America
P 5 4 3 2 1

Originally published by W. W. Norton & Co., Inc.,
and the American Association for State and Local History
in The States and the Nation bicentennial series.

Library of Congress Cataloging-in-Publication Data
Havighurst, Walter, 1901–
Ohio : a history / Walter Havighurst.
p. cm.
Originally published: New York : Norton, c1976.
Includes bibliographical references and index.
ISBN 0–252–07017–8 (pbk. : alk. paper)
1. Ohio—History. I. Title
F491.H4   2001
977.1—dc21   2001027666

Contents

Illustrations

OHIO

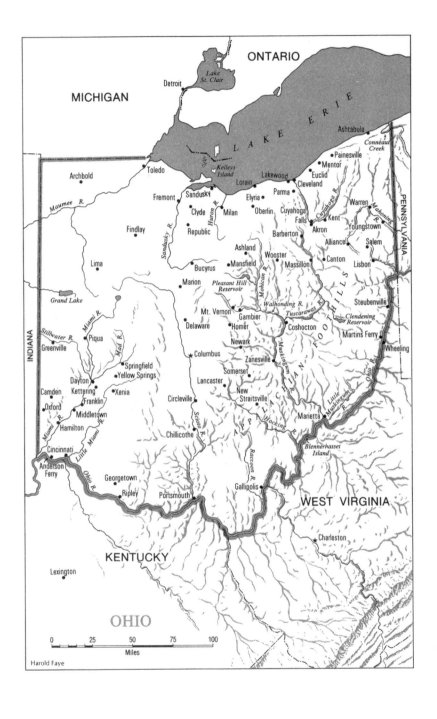

ONTARIO

MICHIGAN

Detroit

Lake
St. Clair

L A K E   E R I E

Ashtabula

Conneaut
Creek

PENNSYLVANIA

Archbold

Toledo

Painesville

Kelleys
Island

Lakewood

Mentor

Euclid

Cleveland

Warren

Mahoning R.

Fremont

Sandusky

Lorain

Elyria

Parma

Maumee R.

Clyde

Huron R.

Milan

Oberlin

Cuyahoga
Falls

Cuyahoga R.

Kent

Findlay

Sandusky R.

Republic

Barberton

Akron

Youngstown

Alliance

Salem

Lima

Ashland

Wooster

Massillon

Canton

Lisbon

Bucyrus

Mansfield

Grand Lake

Marion

Pleasant Hill
Reservoir

Mohican R.

A P P A L A C H I A N   F O O T H I L L S

Steubenville

Mt. Vernon

Gambier

Walhonding R.

Tuscarawas R.

Clendening
Reservoir

Miami R.

Delaware

Homer

Coshocton

Martins Ferry

Wheeling

INDIANA

Stillwater R.

Piqua

Mad R.

Newark

Zanesville

Muskingum R.

Ohio R.

Greenville

Columbus

Springfield

Somerset

Little
Muskingum R.

Dayton

Yellow Springs

Kettering

Xenia

Lancaster

Marietta

Camden

Franklin

Circleville

New
Straitsville

Hocking R.

Oxford

Middletown

Miami R.

Hamilton

Chillicothe

Scioto R.

Blennerhasset
Island

Cincinnati

Little Miami R.

Raccoon R.

Anderson
Ferry

Ohio R.

Georgetown

WEST VIRGINIA

Ripley

Portsmouth

Gallipolis

KENTUCKY

Charleston

Lexington

OHIO

0   25   50   75   100

Miles

Harold Faye

1

Flag-Shaped State

When all is told, Ohio is at once North and South; it is also—by grace of its longitude and its social temper—both East and West. It has boxed the American compass.

—R. L. Hartt

*O*HIO, shaped like a wind-rippled flag, rolls westward from the Allegheny Mountains. The northern counties, bordering a long, straight shoreline, are almost as level as Lake Erie. In the south, hill country frames a serpentine river. Some of the state's rainfall plunges over Niagara on the way to the cold Gulf of St. Lawrence; more of it flows to the tropic Gulf of Mexico. Yet there is no visible divide. Topography made Ohio a spacious, open, inviting realm. Geographically and historically it lies in the mainstream of America.

Two centuries ago it was a forest wilderness. Five Indian peoples—Miami, Shawnee, Ottawa, Wyandot, and Delaware— some fifteen thousand altogether, left the land unchanged. Beyond a few brush villages and ragged cornfields, the only sign of their possession was a path through a thicket and a charred circle beside a spring. They lived precariously—their words for *cold* and *hunger* were soon known to the explorers— in a land that now supports ten million people, more than Sweden, Greece, or Austria. A British army officer paddling down

R. L. Hartt, *Atlantic Monthly* 84(November 1899):684.

the Ohio River in 1766 called it the most pleasant, healthy, and fertile country on the globe. It was, as many writers have declared, a land of promise. Its history might be flawed and blemished, but it could hardly fail to be a story of success. The flag-shaped state, like the American nation, is a realm of varied resources. Before history the great woods covered it like a rug, threaded with rivers and the tribal hunting trails. The forest sprang from a deep, rich soil, and underground lay beds of sand, clay, salt, coal, oil, gas, iron ore, and limestone—the materials of modern industry. The sites of vanished Indian camps are now mines, mills, potteries, foundries, refineries, and power plants.

The state has no ready images or symbols. When the *Ohio Guide* was compiled by the Federal Writers' Project in 1940, there was the question of a cover design. The buckeye was proposed and discarded; few Ohioans recognize a buckeye tree. Finally a design was made: a sheaf of wheat bending over an automobile tire. No folk feeling was gathered there, although Ohio once led the nation in grain harvest and now leads the world in manufacture of rubber products. But it also leads in soap, pottery, matches, Bibles, playing cards, golf balls, pumps, power shovels, cash registers, and coffins. Before mid-nineteenth century Scioto Valley farmers introduced shorthorn cattle, Butler County breeders developed Poland-China hogs, and Cincinnati foundries were casting steamboat boilers. There is no ready symbol because Ohio, half urban and half rural, is too varied for a single characterization. Like the American nation it is hugely productive in both agriculture and industry. It has broad farmlands, dwindling villages, busy towns, and cities of soaring beauty and sullen ugliness. Unlike the other states where population is centered in one or two major cities, Ohio has seven metropolitan centers: Cleveland, Columbus, Cincinnati, Toledo, Akron, Dayton, Youngstown.

Scattered across the state are London, Dublin, Berlin, Geneva, Moscow, Holland, Poland, Smyrna, Cadiz, Lisbon, Antwerp, Zaleski, New Paris, and New Vienna. The northern belt was once "New Connecticut"; the south central counties were originally the Virginia Military District—bounty lands for veterans of the Revolution. Land-loving Virginians made Ohio green and fruitful. The Yankees were merchants and manufacturers; they filled Ohio with the hum of trade and the throb of industry. With the emigrants from the original colonies came immigrants from northern Europe. In the summer of 1817 the English colonizer Morris Birkbeck stopped at a farmhouse outside St. Clairsville, Ohio, across the river from Wheeling, and talked to an Irish settler.

He came to this place fourteen years ago, before an ax had been lifted, except to make a blaze road, a track across the wilderness, marked by the hatchet on the trees, which passed over the spot where the town now stands. A free and independent American, and a warm politician, he now discusses the interests of the state as one concerned in its prosperity; and so he is, for he owns one hundred and eighteen acres of excellent land, and has twenty descendants. . . . He still inhabits a cabin, but it is not an *Irish* cabin.[1]

In Ohio Northerners ceased to be primarily northern, Southerners became less southern, Old World people were no longer European. They all became American—"the first of the Americans"[2] Howells called them. The acute and caustic Mrs. Trollope sensed that new character in 1830; her book that pictures burgeoning Cincinnati and the Ohio valley she named *Domestic Manners of the Americans*.

These Americans were the first to make a defined wilderness domain into a sovereign state. They had a breathtaking opportunity and a back-breaking task. In place of a shared past they embraced a shared future. It made them purposeful, practical, and forward-looking.

The mingled strains gave the state a strong, bright life-force, capable of many pursuits, resourceful in various ways, invigo-

---

1. Morris Birkbeck, *Notes on a Journey in America* (London: Severn & Co., 1818), pp. 58–59.
2. William Dean Howells, *The Story of Ohio* (New York: American Book Company, 1897), p. 287.

rated by common aspirations. From the older colonies and the
Old Country, Ohio people came with high hopes and purposes.

> 'Tis I can delve and plough, love,
> And you can spin and sew;
> And we'll settle on the banks of
> The pleasant O-hi-o.[3]

As they gave themselves "to the land vaguely realizing westward," [4] their hopes persisted in the face of hardship and dif-
ficulty. After jolting over a log-ribbed road in northern Ohio in
1848, John Peyton, a young lawyer from Virginia, waited at
Sandusky harbor for a lake steamer. In that town he met a tall
young German, a native of Dresden, who was suffering from
chills and fever. After a fit of shaking, the immigrant told his
story. From a brief stay in Pennsylvania he had come on west to
Ohio, believing that was the true El Dorado. Now he had the
ague for his pains. But euphoria, as well as malaria, possessed
him; he had no thought of going back across the mountains. He
even praised the Black Swamp country, unhealthy as it was.
"You will not find precious stones or metals here," he told the
Virginia lawyer, "but innumerable dangers, discomforts, and
toil; but these are inseparable from a new country, and if surmounted by industry, any man can accumulate a fortune." [5]
Next spring his wife and children in Pennsylvania and a brother
from Saxony would join him at Sandusky.

   The first state in the Northwest Territory, Ohio entered the
Union in 1803 with the most democratic constitution yet
evolved. It limited the powers of the governor, vested the General Assembly with authority to appoint state officials and
judges, and gave the vote to all white male taxpayers. A simple
constitution, drawn up by thirty-five delegates in twenty-five
days, it expressed a people's drive for self-government. Here in
sprouting towns and wildwood counties sprang up the little re-

   3. *Edinburgh Review* 55(1832):480.
   4. From "The Gift Outright" in *The Poetry of Robert Frost,* edited by Edward Con-
nery Lathem (New York: Holt, Rinehart and Winston, 1923, 1960).
   5. John L. Peyton, *Over the Alleghanies and Across the Prairies* (London: Simpkin,
Marshall and Co., 1870), pp. 146–147.

publics that Jefferson had said must undergird the great republic.

The yeasty Ohio grew and developed—every year new clearings, new roads, new town sites; every decade larger cities, more production, a growing commerce. Towns and villages sprang up faster than people could think of names for them. In 1828 Timothy Flint from Massachusetts counted nineteen Jefferson townships in Ohio and twenty-four Washington townships. Some village names, he noted, were repeated four to ten times. Though awkward for mail delivery, this indicated the practical, matter-of-fact character of people "who can make fields, towns, mills, and legislators issue faster than the latter can task their invention for names." [6]

A guidebook for new settlers exclaimed:

Such an extent of forest has never before been cleared, such a vast field of prairies was never before subdued and cultivated by the hand of man in the same short period of time. Cities and towns and villages and counties and states never before rushed into existence and made such giant strides. [7]

Said the *Ohio Gazetteer:*

Without boasting we aver, and challenge the world to contradict the assertion, that this great and growing state possesses more of the essential ingredients of future greatness and more self-sustaining and self-creating principles than any other territory of equal size on the face of the globe. [8]

If this sounds like bluster, there was the word of a thoughtful young scholar from Paris. In Ohio Alexis de Tocqueville was stirred to romantic eloquence by the spectacle of "a people without precedents, without traditions, without habits, without dominating ideas even . . . cutting out its institutions, like its roads, in the midst of the forests, which it has come to inhabit

---

6. Timothy Flint, *History and Geography of the Mississippi Valley,* 2 vols. (Cincinnati: E. H. Flint and R. Lincoln, 1832), 1:419.

7. J. M. Peck, *New Guide for Immigrants to the West* (Boston: Gould, Kendall & Lincoln, 1837), p. vii.

8. Warren Jenkins, *The Ohio Gazetteer* (Columbus: Isaac N. Whiting, 1841), p. v.

and where it is sure to encounter neither limits nor obstacles." [9]
Success unlimited seemed destined there.

Cincinnati, midway along the great artery, gateway to the
rich Miami country, took the lead. In 1832 in the *Edinburgh
Review* a traveler from Scotland reported:

> Cincinnati on the Ohio: thirty years ago a forest crossed only by
> the red man; now a rising town, with 20,000 inhabitants, and
> increasing at the rate of 1400 houses a year. . . . Our
> astonishment has been speechless in finding that such a spot
> possessed in 1815 a Lancastrian school, a public library of 1400
> volumes, four printing-offices, and three weekly papers. During
> Mrs. Trollope's stay, Mr. [Timothy] Flint printed there his
> 'Western States' in two volumes 8vo; a work that would do
> honour to a London publisher. She speaks of two museums of
> natural history, a picture gallery, and an attempt by two artists at
> an academy of design. After this, what town in England, Scotland,
> or even Ireland, will turn up its nose at Cincinnati? The men can
> have little or no leisure. But what must be said of the spirit of the
> place! [10]

The spirit of the place was large, vigorous and buoyant.
"There are new lands, new thoughts, new men," [11] wrote
Emerson, as though looking westward from his study window
he saw in the great Ohio forest the ragged clearings and isolated
settlements with names like New Concord, Hopedale, Athens,
and Utopia. Ohio's legislators adopted a state seal in 1803, but
it was sixty years before they thought up a motto. In 1865 they
chose the classical *Imperium in Imperio*—An Empire Within an
Empire. Two years later that action was repealed; their slogan
was too scholastic and too pompous for the people. The state
went without a motto until 1959, when the matter was discussed
in Ohio schoolrooms. In Cincinnati a twelve-year-old boy of
Italian descent offered a phrase from the New Testament

9. George Wilson Pierson, *Tocqueville in America* (New York: Doubleday & Company, 1959), p. 363.

10. *Edinburgh Review* 55(1832):481–483.

11. Ralph Waldo Emerson, *Selected Writings* (New York: Modern Library, 1940), p. 3.

(Matthew 19:26) ''With God All Things Are Possible,'' which
was officially adopted.

In six words that schoolboy, James Mastranardo, read the
character of Ohio more clearly than all the historians have done.
The motto links religion with drive, the drive being more pronounced than the godliness. Presuming some kind Providence,
it says that success is expected in Ohio, success is natural there.
Put in the vernacular—Give It a Try—the maxim speaks for
Ohio's hopes and for its history. It calls up examples great and
small: Zane's Trace through the wilderness and young Harvey
Firestone making rubber rims for buggy wheels; Henry Tim-
ken's roller bearing and Armco's revolutionary rolling mill; a
Columbus man's locomotive cowcatcher, O. C. Barber's first
book matches, and John Leon Bennet's wire fly swatter; a
Reynoldsburg seed merchant's development of the edible to-
mato and Dr. Edwin Beeman's flavored chewing gum; Dan
Beard's Boy Scouts and A. B. Graham's 4-H Club; a pioneer
kindergarten in Columbus and college innovations at Oberlin,
Hiram, and Antioch; young Tom Edison watching the glimmer
of whale oil lanterns on Lake Erie schooners and the Wright
brothers flying a winged crate over a Dayton cow pasture.
''. . . all things are possible''—how assured that motto is.

Ohio's early history, charged with hazard and privation, is
marked by high spirits. In January 1786 there appeared in New
England newspapers an item headed ''Information.''

> The subscribers take this method to inform all officers and
> soldiers, who have served in the late war, and who are by an
> ordinance of the honorable Congress to receive certain tracts of
> land in the Ohio country, and also all other good citizens who
> wish to become adventurers in that delightful region, that . . .
> they are fully satisfied that the lands in that quarter are of much
> better quality than any other known to New England people.[12]

It was signed by Generals Rufus Putnam and Benjamin Tupper.
The two generals were of the same age, forty-eight years, but

12. Samuel P. Hildreth, *Pioneer History of the Ohio Valley* (Cincinnati: H. W.
Derby & Co., 1848), p. 193.

the West had made them young again. They were ready for adventure.

In the winter of 1788 the first forty-eight men of the Ohio Company, toiling from Massachusetts and Connecticut over the frozen Alleghenies, called themselves "adventurers." They were beginning something that colonial people had never envisioned, the conquest of a continent. Ahead of them were promise and danger, staggering problems and heroic prospects. No other people anywhere had consciously, deliberately embarked on such a venture. The Northwest Ordinance called for the responsibility of self-government and eventual partnership in the federal Union. These adventurers were founders of a new commonwealth.

In ice and snow on the Youghiogheny River in western Pennsylvania they built a floating shed and named it *Adventure Galley*. (Years later the history-conscious citizens of Marietta, Ohio, would call it *Mayflower*.) Floating down the Ohio with horses, wagons, baggage, and implements, they marked out a town site at the mouth of the Muskingum, while their hungry horses filled up with lush buffalo clover. Their first historian reported that all were delighted with the fertility of the soil, the healthful climate, and the beauty of the country. In three days that company of adventurers cleared four acres. They built a fortified square called Campus Martius and named their town Marietta in honor of Marie Antoinette. On July 4, 1788, they laid down their mattocks and axes for a celebration. Only the first forty-eight men were there, all Revolutionary officers and soldiers; their families would arrive six weeks later. Two newly appointed judges of the Territory made speeches under the trees, and from Fort Harmar across the Muskingum came a salvo of thirteen guns. The roar of cannon, echoing from the Virginia hills, startled some onlooking Indians, but they stayed for the feast of venison, turkey, roast pork, and a whole broiled pike, six feet long, that had been speared in the river. For drink there were pitchers of grog, punch, and wine. A cloudburst interrupted the dinner without dampening the spirit of celebration. When the sun came out, the men stood under dripping trees drinking toasts to Congress, General Washington, the King of

France, the Chief of the Delawares, all Patriots and Heroes, and the Northwest Territory. One of the celebrants wrote in his journal: "Pleased with the entertainment we kept it up until twelve at night, then went home and slept till daylight" [13]—when it was time to swing the ax again.

A few months later, in November 1788, a flatboat passed Marietta carrying twenty men, four women, and two boys, mostly from New Jersey, two hundred miles deeper into the wilderness. They landed at the mouth of the Little Miami River. While the winter wind rattled a bare pawpaw thicket, they raised a song of praise and a prayer of thanksgiving. Knocking apart their flatboat, they used the timber to build huts and cabins and chopped poplar logs to make a blockhouse. This was the first settlement of future Cincinnati. In midwinter their food gave out, but there were fish in the river and game in the woods. Next season they grew fabulous crops of corn, some lots producing a hundred bushels to the acre.

To the northern bank of the Ohio in 1790, forty miles below the mouth of the Scioto, came the Virginia surveyor Nathaniel Massie. He chose a town site, offering settlers a hundred acres of land. Twenty-five families built cabins inside a log stockade on the riverbank, and so began the first settlement in the Virginia Military District. Though Indian wars were imperiling the Miami valleys a hundred miles to the west, life was blithe at Massie's Station. The men cleared a willow island in the river and grew a crop of corn. The woods offered game, the river, fish, and on the spring current came flatboats with Monongahela whiskey. One of Massie's men described that social island in the wilderness. "The inhabitants were generally as playful as kittens and as happy in their way as the heart could wish. The men spent most of their time in hunting and fishing, and almost every evening the boys and girls footed merrily to the tune of the fiddle." [14] If they were making history, they made it lightly.

13. Henry Howe, *Historical Collections of Ohio,* 2 vols. (Centennial Edition, Published by the State of Ohio, 1900), 2:802.

14. John McDonald, *Biographical Sketches* (Cincinnati: E. Morgan and Son, 1838), p. 32.

The Connecticut charter, in 1630, assigned that colony land to the western ocean, which lay somewhere over the western horizon. In 1786, along with other colonies, Connecticut yielded to the federal government her western estate, save for a strip of land extending 120 miles beyond the western border of Pennsylvania—a reserve that was relinquished in the year 1800. On July 4, 1796, a party of fifty men led by huge and swarthy Moses Cleaveland, bound for Connecticut's Western Reserve, trekked the brushy shore of Lake Erie to Conneaut Creek, and found there the northwest cornerstone of Pennsylvania. After sixty-eight days of strenuous travel, the party had reached what Cleaveland called the good and promised land. That arrival, on the day of American Independence, called for celebration. Lined up on the sand beach the men fired a federal salute of fifteen rounds, followed by one for New Connecticut. After three cheers General Cleaveland named the place Port Independence. At that celebration grog gurgled from the jugs, and the exploring party drank to the President of the United States, the State of New Connecticut, the Connecticut Land Company, and the future of Port Independence. (Now it is Conneaut, Ohio, where long lake freighters bring huge cargoes of iron ore for an industry no one foresaw or comprehended in 1796.) After three more cheers, Cleaveland noted in his diary, the men downed several pails of grog, ate supper in the twilight, and retired in good order. So ended the first day of the first colonists to the Western Reserve where they staked out a prospective town that Cleaveland called Cuyahoga. His men gave the place their leader's name, misspelling it Cleveland.

Early Ohio was long on democracy but short of revenue—too short to build a statehouse. From 1803 to 1810 the legislature met in the old territorial capitol on Paint and Main streets in Chillicothe. Need for a more central location took the state government to Zanesville in 1810, where citizens had raised funds to erect a capitol. Known as Old 1809, that building housed the legislature from 1810 to 1812. The assembly's first action in the new setting was to resolve that the permanent capital should be within forty miles of the geographical center of Ohio. Zanesville did not qualify, and, as if to emphasize its temporary status, an earthquake during the first session sent the lawmakers scrambling out of the building. Old 1809 survived that tremor, serving the legislature until 1812 when it moved back to Chillicothe. Not yet paid for, the vacated building became the Muskingum County courthouse.

Still looking for a permanent home, the assembly was approached by four land merchants from Franklin County. If the state government would locate on the high bank of the Scioto River across from the new settlement of Franklinton, the land company would 1) lay out a town (Columbus) in the Scioto woods, 2) convey a ten-acre tract as a statehouse site and a similar tract for site of a penitentiary, 3) donate $50,000 toward the cost of these public buildings. The proposition was accepted; town lots were first auctioned on June 18, 1812, lots on High and Broad streets bringing between two hundred and five hundred dollars. The land merchants then gave a bonus of a half-acre for a public graveyard.

A roomy penitentiary was ready for inmates in 1813, and a cramped statehouse was completed three years later. The brick building had four chimneys on a peaked roof and a pump outside the front doorway. In 1815 the seven hundred settlers of Columbus subscribed two hundred dollars for removal of stumps from High Street. Ten years later a thousand people gathered for the ground-breaking of a branch canal to connect Columbus with the Ohio Canal (Grand Canal, they called it) at Circleville. The first earth was raised by the keeper of the penitentiary (his prisoners would dig most of that ditch) and wheeled away by the state auditor and the state treasurer. Then came a public dinner and the toasting of Ohio and its future.

In 1838 Caleb Atwater of Circleville published *A History of Ohio,* the first and most buoyant outline of the state. This Massachusetts Yankee, a failed businessman and lawyer with nine children to support, had soon caught the Ohio excitement. Remarking on Columbus as a seat of government, he stated:

> Its buildings are, many of them, large, commodious and handsome. The state house is not such a one as Ohio ought to have this day. . . . The penitentiary is a large, handsome building of stone, built mostly by the convicts who are confined in it. . . .

That we have prospered [despite hardships and dangers and sufferings] more than any other people did in the world, is most certain; but our exertions to improve our conditions are by no means to be relaxed—to make Ohio what it ought to be, the first state in the Union in numbers, knowledge, wealth, and political power. . . . Our position in the nation is peculiarly felicitous as to soil, climate, and productions, and it will be our own fault if we are not the happiest people in the Union.[15]

But troubles lay ahead. In that year, 1838, the first Ohio-born governor, Wilson Shannon of Belmont County, took office, and the assembly voted for an imposing new statehouse. The cornerstone ceremony on July 4, 1839, brought on a quarrel between Columbus citizens and the legislature. For six years the lawmakers passed the raw building site on the way to their old chambers. At daybreak on a Sunday morning in February 1852, the old statehouse burned down. Before the brick walls crumbled, the wooden belfry, burning like a torch, swayed in the flames, the bell tolling as it fell.

It was this old pile that Henry Howe from Connecticut had visited during his Ohio tour of 1846. He was depressed by the building but reassured by the Ohio spirit. He described the state capitol as a crude structure that scarce any Ohio village of the 1840s would erect for a schoolhouse. But with zeal and patriotism in the worn old halls the assemblymen had made wise and hopeful laws. "So young was the land," he wrote, "that in that year the very lawmakers, 84 out of 107, were born strangers." [16] He listed their nativities: they came from fourteen states and six countries of Europe.

Howe arrived there on the night of adjournment. The legislators had been away from their families for many months, undergoing the grind and monotony of long and strenuous sessions. What he saw was not a room full of tired, dejected men, but a scene of lively disorder. After months of harsh debate and disputation, he wrote, the members were "hilarious as so many frolicsome schoolboys, and to my astonished eyes from their

15. Caleb Atwater, *A History of Ohio* (Cincinnati: Glazer & Shepard, 1838), pp. 355–356.

16. Howe, *Historical Collections* 1: unpaged Introduction.

seats some of the more frolicsome were pelting each other with paperwads." [17]

In 1840 Herman Melville, back from far lands and waters of the world, made a trip to the American Northwest—by lake steamer to Mackinac and riverboat down the Mississippi and up the Ohio. What he saw and surmised of Ohio came out several years later. Writing his satiric allegory *Mardi* in 1847, he described a fabulous archipelago that embraced the Old World and the New. In that fable America became "Vivenza," a new-found land of unmeasurable promise. "Here," Melville's Polynesian spokesman exclaimed,

> lie plantations held in fee by stout hearts and arms; and boundless fields that may be had for seeing. Here your foes are forests, struck down with bloodless maces. . . . Ye who starve or beg; seventh sons who slave for earth's first-born—here is your home; predestined yours. Come over, Empire-founders! fathers of the wedded tribes to come! Abject now, illustrious evermore. Ho: Sinew, Brawn and Thigh! [18]

Arrived on the shores of this young and forward country, the travelers found an arch of welcome with a chiseled slogan: *In-this-republican-land-all-men-are-born-free-and-equal.* A closer look found a bottom-line hieroglyphic: *Except-the-tribe-of-Hamo.* Asking for this people's king, the visitors were told, "we are all kings here; royalty breathes the common air. But come on, come on. Let us show you our great Temple of Freedom." [19] Soon they were there—in the United States Senate—amid the spokesmen of Vivenza's thirty provinces. The loudest voice was that of Alanno, thundering against the king of Dominora (Britain). This character was Ohio Senator Allen, whose stentorian voice was known in Washington as the "Ohio gong," [20] originator of the Oregon boundary slogan "Fifty-four forty or fight!"

17. Howe, *Historical Collections* 1: unpaged Introduction.
18. Herman Melville, *Mardi,* 2 vols. (Boston: Small, Maynard & Company, 1922), 2:167.
19. Melville, *Mardi,* 2:167.
20. Howe, *Historical Collections,* 2:517.

In 1832, at age twenty-five, William Allen had been the youngest member of the Twenty-third Congress, but a leading orator. From the House he went to the Senate in 1837, serving till 1849, where he became one of the loudest proponents of Manifest Destiny. Alanno, Melville's *Mardi* spokesman explained,

> was from a distant western valley called Hio-Hio [even its name was an exclamation], one of the largest and most fertile in Vivenza, though but recently settled. Its inhabitants and those of the vales adjoining—a right sturdy set of fellows—were accounted the most dogmatically democratic and ultra of all the tribes in Vivenza: ever seeking to push on their brethren to the uttermost.[21]

They meant to give American destiny a wholehearted try.

21. Melville, *Mardi,* 2:173.

2

Wind in the Forest

IN 1846 when young Henry Howe came west with sketching pad and notebook, he found Ohio strewn with history. All one had to do, he said, was look around and pick it up. A scrap of history was picked up by some Marietta boys on a summer day in 1788. After swimming the Muskingum, they scrambled onto the riverbank. Halfway up the weedy slope they found a piece of metal jutting from eroded earth. With driftwood they pried it out—a flat, smooth tablet no larger than a schoolboy's slate but twice as heavy. Like a slate it was covered with writing, of a kind strange to them. At home they tried their knives on it, cutting off bits for rifle bullets. Lead was dear in frontier Ohio.

Before the boys had used it up, the tablet came to the notice of a Marietta lawyer who recognized the inscription as French. From what was decipherable—LAN 1749 . . . . ROY DE FRANCE . . . DE POSSESSION . . . RIVIERE OYO . . . PAR LES ARMES— he could guess that it was an assertion of French claim on the Ohio Valley.

The lead tablet had come from Quebec, seven hundred miles distant, and it had farther to go. To Circleville, Ohio, in 1815, came Caleb Atwater, ex-teacher and ex-clergyman from Massachusetts. In Circleville, with streets surrounding a round enclosure left by ancient mound builders, Atwater turned to geology and archaeology, and in 1820 he brought out a book on

17

"antiquities" in Ohio. The next year, 1821, he got hold of the lead plate from Marietta. He sent it to Governor DeWitt Clinton of New York, who later gave it to the Antiquarian Society of Massachusetts. This was one of six lead tablets, each bearing a proclamation of French possession of the Ohio River and lands on both sides of it—a claim unlimited. The tablets were planted in 1749 at the mouths of tributary rivers by a military company in charge of Captain Céloron de Bienville. The expedition, 250 men in twenty-three canoes, was a gesture in the grand French manner. It involved ceremonious meetings with Indian leaders, the smoking of peace pipes, the giving of presents, the fixing of the royal arms to a forest tree (like a No Trespassing sign) and the depositing of an engraved tablet. When the men chorused *"Vive le roi!"* their words came back from the brooding hills. In three months Céloron made a looping journey that roughly outlines the present state of Ohio. He lost just one man in his party, who drowned in a river. But he failed to win the Ohio Indians to the French side.

The Ohio country was first known to Europeans not for its unguessed wealth of oil, coal, clay, and salines, but for the profits of the fur trade. To grasp that richness came the great nations of Europe. History began in Ohio with France and England contending for a country described by the chief engineer of the British army's Western Department as "the most healthy, the most pleasant, the most commodious, and most fertile spot of earth known to European people." [1]

While the French, from their citadel at Quebec, dreamed of a commercial empire in North America and sent their merchants and missionaries deep into the interior, the British planted small colonies on the Atlantic seaboard and pushed slowly up the coastal river valleys. By 1750 Virginia hunters and Pennsylvania traders had crossed the Appalachians into the luring West. While Céloron was proclaiming French dominion on the Ohio, a group of Virginia gentlemen were planning settlement and occupation of the upper Ohio Valley. In 1750 they sent veteran

---

1. Clarence W. Alvord and C. E. Carter, eds., *The New Regime, 1765–1767* (Springfield: Illinois State Historical Library, 1916), p. 292.

surveyor Christopher Gist on an exploring tour. He was to record river courses, map the location of Indian camps and trading stations, and to note the tracts of land most suitable for settlement. Instead of an expedition, Gist had only a Negro servant and a change of horses, with which he scouted the very country claimed by Céloron a year earlier. He kept his compass ("big medicine") hidden from the Indians, who had been told by the French that the English coveted their lands. But he mapped rich river bottoms, good mill sites, and navigable waters.

In the rivalry of European nations for Indian lands, religion was employed along with rum and brandy, traps and rifles, threats and promises. At a Wyandot town where the Tuscarawas River joins the Muskingum (site of present Coshocton) Gist spent Christmas. He marked the day by reading some prayers that an interpreter repeated for him. This was all the formality that the camp-stained scout, smelling of smoke and bear grease, could offer. But any ceremony pleased the Indians. One of them showed him a calendar given them by the French; by moving a peg each morning they could know when it was time for Sunday devotions. The French had told them that Christ was born in France and crucified by Englishmen. Gist's Christmas prayers were the first Protestant pieties in that wild country.

Long before Ohio had a Cleveland, Cincinnati, or Columbus, its principal town was Pickawillany on the upper Miami River, where weedy cornfields encircled a huddle of sixty Indian cabins in a log stockade. As a trading post it was the focus of the British-French commercial rivalry. The Indians liked bright colors, and both flags fluttered above the trading house. French traders had come there by canoe from Lake Erie and the Maumee-Miami portage; English pack-horse trains came overland from Pennsylvania. The tribal chief, Unemakami, was known to the French as La Demoiselle, the French name for the darting dragonfly that his name signified in the Indian language; the English called him Old Britain. He was, indeed, on their side, for with shorter trade routes the British could be more generous with presents and trade goods.

At Pickawillany Gist was welcomed with fifteen minutes of musket fire. He gave token presents and promised more to come. Old Britain's warriors pulled down the French colors, leaving the Union Jack in place, and the chiefs put their mark on pledges of peace and alliance with the English. Some Indians gave Gist a tame parakeet to take back to Virginia. On the long way home Gist was cheered by the chirpy green-and-gold bird perched on his saddle horn. But at a rocky crossing his horse fell and the parakeet was crushed. The old woodsman minded that loss—"He was perfectly tame and had been very brisk all the way, and I still had corn enough to feed him" [2]—more than his own sore bruises.

A year later, keeping his promise to the Ohio tribes, Gist was back at Logstown, just below Pittsburgh, with four long canoes full of presents. While an interpreter relayed his words in several tongues, he declared that the French meant to exterminate the Indians but the English wanted to live peacefully with them. (This was a precise reversal of the facts.) On the Monongahela, homeward bound, he met an Indian "who desired to know where the Indian lands lay, [since] the French claimed all the land on one side of the River Ohio and the English, on the other side." In his journal Gist confessed: "I was at a loss to answer him." [3]

Around Pickawillany, deep in the wilderness, the green forest sighed and rustled in the summer air; the bare woods rocked in the winds of November. With winter came the snow, falling white and silent on cabins and cornfields, softening the trails and traces, blanketing the trampled salt licks, erasing the charred circles of council fires. It seemed a place removed from history.

But Pickawillany's trails came in from four directions, and water routes led to Lake Erie and the Ohio River. It was the key to the western trade. At times the English and French flags fluttered together over the head chief's cabin, while the Old World rivalry intensified. In 1752 French officials concluded that Pickawillany was expendable, and at Detroit they gathered a flotilla

2. *Christopher Gist's Journals,* edited by William M. Darlington (Pittsburgh: J. R. Weldin & Co., 1893), p. 62.
3. Gist, *Journals,* p. 78.

of 240 French and Indians. Soon the summer wind would carry whoops and cries, the drone of drums and the rattle of gunfire, and the smoke of a burning town.

On the morning of June 21, 1752, Pickawillany was a quiet place. The breakfast fires were sinking, and the Indian women were hoeing corn in fields on the northern fringe of the village. Some old men sat against the shady side of the lodges, but the warriors were away on a summer hunt. La Demoiselle—alias Old Britain, the Piankeshaw king—was there, smoking his clay pipe in a doorway. In their huts outside the stockade were eight English traders. From willow trees along the creek came the turtledoves' languid song.

Into that serenity came a burst of gunfire. Dogs and children scattered before a band of shooting, shouting raiders. Five English traders and twenty Indians got into the fort and closed the heavy gate. From behind huts and trees the invaders fired through the gaping stockade. After six hours of siege they had killed fourteen Indians, including Old Britain. In midafternoon the British flag came down.

Before leaving the place the raiders feasted; Old Britain was quartered, boiled, and eaten. They pillaged the fort, set fire to some lodges, and emptied the shelves and bins of the trading house. In canoes heaped with plunder they paddled back to Detroit.

That brief assault, far out in the Ohio forest, anticipated the French and Indian War. Its crucial actions, with Indians fighting on both sides, came at Niagara, Pittsburgh, Lake Champlain, and the French cities on the St. Lawrence. But the Ohio country was at stake. When Montreal was surrendered in 1759, the vast western wilderness passed into control of the English.

In 1763 Britain prohibited settlement beyond the crest of the Allegheny Mountains. But that Proclamation Line, so emphatic on the royal maps and surveys, was not there at all when men climbed the Allegheny ridges. Settlers pushed into new green valleys, and hunters, following the game trails, loaded pack ponies with hides and peltry. They sold buckskins for a dollar apiece (A dollar is still a "buck" in this country) and talked about the rich green land beyond the mountains.

George Washington went to the Ohio Valley in 1770 to look
at lands marked as military bounty for soldiers of the French
and Indian War. With Indian guides he paddled down the wild
Ohio to the mouth of the Kanawha. For himself he mapped
some thirty thousand acres of river frontage. His journal pictures fine meadows framed in wooded hills. The land abounded
in ducks, geese, turkeys, deer, and buffalo, and the river
teemed with fish. Walking across broad bottomland, he noted a
smoldering coal bank that the Indians said had burned forever.
He measured a sycamore trunk forty-five feet around. In that
wild country he glimpsed the future more clearly than any other
of his time. The great valley, he said, would soon attract a great
population; it would be settled and civilized more rapidly than
any similar domain in history. At the end of his tour, on November 18, 1770, he "agreed with two Delaware Indians to
carry up our canoe to Fort Pitt, for the doing of which I was to
pay six dollars and give them a quart tin can." [4] In his will,
years later, Washington listed forty-one thousand acres of Ohio
Valley land.

British authority withered in the American Revolution, and
with the Peace of Paris, 1783, possession of the territory extending to the Mississippi River came to the United States. The
ensuing rush of settlers into Indian lands impelled the government to deal with the border tribes. In councils at Fort Stanwix,
1784, and Fort McIntosh, 1785, some of the western chiefs sold
the tribal claim to parts of Ohio; other chiefs stayed away. It
would be thirty years and more before the last Indian titles were
surrendered.

Meanwhile, history would not wait. The new nation had a
magnificent birthright—a wilderness domain larger than the entire realm of the original colonies. To provide for occupation
and development of the Northwest Territory, Congress enacted
the Land Ordinance of 1785. This act called for purchase of
land from the Indian inhabitants, and for its survey and sale to
frontier settlers. It was followed by the Northwest Ordinance of

4. *The Writings of George Washington,* edited by W. C. Ford, 14 vols. (New York:
G. P. Putnam's Sons, 1889), 2:311.

1787, that prescribed laws to go with the land and outlined a provisional government of territory that should eventually become new states of the federal Union. Americans could now start westward under laws of hope and aspiration.

But the original Ohio people, the roving Indians, were in the way. Though confused and divided by the white man's treaties, the tribes made a stand in western Ohio. They threw back the army troops of General Harmar in 1790, and almost annihilated the expedition of General St. Clair a year later. In 1793 General Anthony Wayne, after careful preparations, moved deliberately into Indian country, building a chain of forts in western Ohio. In the Battle of Fallen Timbers, near Fort Defiance, he met the full force of Indian resistance and put the tribes to rout. With the ensuing Treaty of Greenville, the doors of Ohio were open to the future.

At Wayne's side in the great council with eleven hundred chiefs and warriors, was a white man who had lived with the Indians. At the age of twelve William Wells had been captured by a band of Miamis. He had fought on both sides during the border wars. Now, in 1795, he was chief translator at the Greenville Treaty.

Wells understood the difference between savage and civilized life—the inborn freedom of the Indian and the harrying ambition of the white man. He knew the wild country, the hunting and trading trails through the forest and the fording places on the rivers. He knew the Indian towns with their dust and dogs, their trophies of hunting and warfare, the charred logs of their council fires. He also knew the white man's barges on the big river, loaded with muskets and cannon, and his forts where the bugle shrilled and flags fluttered in the wind.

He knew the Indian's contempt for the tamed life of the white man, a life as pallid as his skin. The whites were fearful, covering themselves with clothing, enclosing themselves in roofs and walls, locking their doors, reading from the Bible and quoting distant presidents and kings. They were afraid of hunger and solitude. They wanted cattle in their pastures, corn in their stables, fences around their fields. They were rarely silent and never at ease. A weak and fearful people, they could not survive without their axes, guns, and horses. They were destroyers, leveling the forest, hacking out roads where the mossy deer trail ran, driving the game away. They were at war with the earth.

In the Ohio country were others like William Wells, men and women both, who had been taken in childhood and reared by Indian tribes. Few of them ever chose to return to their blood people. Indians were stoic, improvident, and proud; Americans were restless with ambition, anxious for the future, meaning to change the wilderness forever. Swarthy Captain Wells knew both sides in the struggle. In some ways Indians were the stronger people, but the whites had won.

3

The Witness Tree

*T*HE nation's dramatic expansion in its first century has sometimes been described as the westward march of America. It was, actually, a movement of greatly varied tempo, often plodding and laborious, again, quickened by an irresistible urgency and drive.

It took 170 years for colonial settlement to spread thinly from the Atlantic Coast to the Appalachian mountains. The Northwest Territory, as large as the entire thirteen colonies, was occupied in half a century. To that vast, inviting country came people of many kinds from many backgrounds. Thousands came from the seaboard states, others from lands across the stormy Atlantic. Some were sober and resolute, with a dream of independence and opportunity. Others were reckless and raffish, thoughtless of the future but allured by moving on.

The first to come into the Territory were a new breed, native to America and given a new American name. For centuries in England "to squat" meant merely to crouch down in posture, but here it took on a meaning that was debated in the Congress and incorporated into public laws. Squatters were intruders on the public land, ahead of survey and legal purchase. They had no maps or charts, no land warrants or certificates, and no specific destination. They simply made their way into wild country, looking for a southern hillside with a trickling spring or a green opening where deer paths crossed. They came lightly laden—a rifle, ax, plow, and a bag of seed corn, a dog and a horse, perhaps a few pigs and chickens.

Put venturesome people on the edge of a luring land and the laws of nature outweigh the laws of government. Legal settlement was orderly: land cession by the Indians, survey into townships and sections, sale in district land offices. Each of these steps took months or years, and the squatters wouldn't wait. On Indian lands north of the Ohio they chopped out clearings and dropped seed corn into ax-gashed ground. The Indians burned some cabins and ran a few intruders off, but more were coming. When the chiefs complained at Fort Pitt, the American commander sent sixty soldiers to drive squatters from the "Indian side" of the Ohio. The troops set fire to squatters' huts and plundered their garden fields. Next season more trespassers took up the same locations.

Meanwhile in the Confederation Congress two viewpoints were colliding. Alexander Hamilton, speaking for the Federalists, saw the public domain as a national resource to pay the crushing war debt. Thomas Jefferson, whose Monticello mansion faced the luring Blue Ridge, saw public lands as an opportunity for poor people to find freedom and independence. Small landholders, he said, are the most precious part of the nation, and he justified their trespass on the public territory. "Whenever there is in any country uncultivated lands and unemployed poor, it is clear that the laws of property have been so far extended as to violate natural right." [1] Asserting that needy settlers should not be made to pay the war debt, he predicted: "They will settle the lands in spite of everybody."

In 1785 Fort Harmar was built at the junction of the Muskingum River with the Ohio. A small log pentagon with a blockhouse overlooking the two rivers, it was there to keep squatters from the Indian lands—the only fort ever raised to curb unlawful settlement. But when surveyors went into the woods, the troops were sent to protect them from Indian attack. The soldiers found few Indians but plenty of trespassing whites. They destroyed a few isolated cabins—which the squatters soon re-

1. Paul Wallace Gates, *History of Public Land Law Development* (Washington: U.S. Government Printing Office, 1968), p. 62.

built. On hearing the eviction orders, one stubborn squatter "declared they never came from Congress, neither did he care from whom they came, for he was determined to hold possession, and if [the troops] destroyed his home he would build six more within a week." [2] At settlements of a dozen or more families, the soldiers, outnumbered, posted eviction notices on the trees but allowed the trespassers to save their crops before leaving. To the squatters saving the crop meant feeding their cattle there the next winter and planting again in the spring. They meant to stay.

While Eastern editors and congressmen branded frontier trespassers as outlaws, those few squatters who bothered to justify themselves claimed both natural and ideological rights. Sir William Blackstone in powdered wig and poplin gown had first read his lectures on the common law to the students of Oxford University in 1753, voicing principles that would be applied in times and places beyond his ken. "Occupancy is the true ground and foundation of property, or of holding those things in severalty, which, by the law of nature, unqualified by that of society, were common to all mankind." [3] Now that proposition supported Ohio squatters in their disdain of legal process. For mutual support they formed claims associations, a germ of revolution in a revolutionary land. One group in the Muskingum Valley found a spokesman who, echoing Jefferson's conviction, appealed to an older and higher law than that of the Confederation Congress. He declared:

I do certify that all mankind agreeable to every constitution formed in America, have an undoubted right to pass into every vacant country, and there to form their constitution, and that from the confederation of the whole United States, Congress is not empowered to forbid them, neither is Congress empowered from that confederation to make any sale of the uninhabited lands to pay the public debt. [4]

2. A. B. Hulbert, *Ohio in the Time of Confederation* (Marietta: Marietta College, 1918), p. 107.
3. William Blackstone, *Commentaries on the Laws of England*, 4 vols. (London: Sweet, Pheney, Maxwell, and Stevens & Sons, 1829), 2:258.
4. R. L. Downes, "Ohio's Squatter Governor," *Ohio State Archaeological and Historical Quarterly* 43(1943):277.

Most of the intruders didn't bother with a manifesto; they merely made hatchet marks at the corners of their "claim." They came on season after season, pushing into new country, the Hocking Valley, the Scioto, the Little Miami, and the Great Miami. In 1796 Governor St. Clair ordered intruders out of the public lands; six months later he found the district west of the Miami dotted with the huts of trespassers. Here was a pioneering democracy at work in spite of public laws. These people claimed "squatters' rights." On their side they had the right of discovery, of occupation, of cultivation and improvement.

Legal entry was orderly and deliberate. It waited on Indian cession, survey, and the eventual creation of a district land office where selection and purchase were made. But after legal purchase the owner might find his land already occupied. Here, out of countless cases, are two examples, twenty years and two hundred miles apart:

When federal land went on sale at the Cincinnati land office in April 1801, two newly arrived Welshmen were among the first in line. Ezekiel Hughes had bought two sections in Hamilton County, and Edward Bebb was the first purchaser in Morgan Township, near the southwest corner of Ohio. When Bebb pushed through the deer brush on Dry Fork, he found smoke sifting up from a chimney and a farmer standing in a cabin door. His name was Aaron Cherry, and he had raised two crops of corn. When Bebb offered to pay him for clearing and breaking the land, Cherry shrugged his shoulders; this was the thirteenth time he had squatted, but the first time any pay was offered for his improvements. He moved cheerfully on to a fourteenth location, where his sons became notorious horse thieves. Bebb, having secured his claim and put seed into the ground, walked back to Ebensburg, Pennsylvania, married a young Welsh widow there, and brought her to his Ohio homestead. Their son William Bebb, born in 1802, became governor of Ohio forty-four years later.

A young army officer in the War of 1812 took a liking to a pleasant campsite in Sandusky County. While breaking camp, he drove a stake into the ground, meaning to return there when the war was past and to build a home that would become the nucleus of a future town. Eight years later he came back, searched the woods for his weathered stake, and saw smoke lazing up from a squatter's cabin. With a barrel of whiskey he bought off the intruder and took possession. In eight more years a settlement began and the town of Clyde was plotted. In 1919 Sherwood Anderson made it famous as "Winesburg, Ohio."

Within half a century there evolved in Ohio a land policy that moved westward with national expansion. The original land law of 1796 was meant to raise federal revenue. Minimum purchase was a full section, 640 acres, at two dollars an acre; half the price to be paid in thirty days, the rest within a year. It was an undemocratic and unrealistic measure. Very few frontier farmers had that much money, though speculators did. They bought land, gave terms to settlers, foreclosed when payment lapsed, and sold the land again. Until 1800 the law was a bargain to land merchants but a barrier to ambitious farmers.

At the Treaty of Greenville in the summer of 1795, the tribes had ceded two thirds of present Ohio. Beside General Wayne in the council house stood his aide-de-camp young William Henry Harrison, sweating in the slow smoke of the ceremonial fire and the long treaty speeches. As he caught the Indian words for hills, woods, plains, waters, and heard the names Pickawillany, Chillicothe, Scioto, Tuscarawas, Wapatomica, his mind filled with pictures of the Ohio country: the meeting of the rivers at Fort Pitt, the dense green of the Big Hocking forest, the great trees arching over White Woman Creek, the flint ridges of the Tuscarawas where the Waldhoning flowed down from the dark woods of the north, the Indian town on the Pickaway Plains with trails fanning off toward the Ohio River and the great northern lake. Now it was all public domain, a part of the nation—but who would possess it? The soldiers passing outside the council house, stripped to the waist in the August sun, had land sense. They had marched through wilderness, seeing farms of the future. They talked about sloughs, bogs, bottoms, about clay, loam, and marl. They could judge soil even in dense woods: white oak, walnut, hickory, beech, and sugar maple signify good ground; but never blaze your corners on locust, swamp oak, or sycamore. Men like these would clear the forest and plow the fields—if the land merchants didn't get there first.

Three years later, in 1798, President John Adams named Harrison, age twenty-five, secretary of the Northwest Territory. In a log office near the Cincinnati landing he recorded ferry licenses, county boundaries, and land disputes between speculators, claim holders and squatters, while congressmen in Philadelphia were debating the federal land policy. In 1800 Harrison was elected congressional delegate from the Northwest Territory and assigned to the Committee on Public Lands. To veteran legislators the lean young Westerner declared that the public domain must offer opportunity not to profiteering landlords but to ambitious settlers. On May 10, 1800, spring planting time, his proposed Land Act became law.

The Harrison Land Act allowed sale of half-sections, 320 acres, to be paid for in installments over four years. In 1804, additional legislation reduced the minimum purchase to 160 acres; it offered smaller tracts on easier terms and assured the claimant of a clear title. Back to Ohio Harrison sent word:

This law promises to be the foundation of a great increase of population and wealth to our country, for although the minimum price of land is still fixed at two dollars per acre, the time for making payments has been so extended as to put it in the power of every industrious man to comply with them.[5]

These steps were the beginning of a policy of public land for the public, a policy that was liberalized in the Old Northwest and then enlarged in territories beyond the Mississippi. Under the 1796 law less than fifty thousand acres had been sold by 1800. In the first three years of the Harrison law land sales surpassed a million acres.

Under the new Land Act, frontier population swelled, the survey was extended, new land districts were formed. By 1820 there were fourteen land offices north of the Ohio. From them came the expression "a land-office business," an Americanism that has outlasted the frontier. Now a New Orleans journalist

5. Charles S. Todd, *The Civil and Military Services of William Henry Harrison* (Cincinnati: J. A. and U. P. James, 1847), p. 20.

reports: "A practical printer . . . could do a land-office business here," a magazine writer tells of a Cape Cod man "doing
a land-office business in homemade clam chowder," [6] and the
biographer of William McKinley remarks that Canton's hotels,
restaurants, and saloons did a land-office business. In early
Ohio the businesses were bigger than these, and the rewards
seemed certain. Success was in the air. To the land offices came
shrewd speculators, eager young settlers, and veteran squatters
who had accumulated enough cash to make a down payment on
locations they had occupied.

Installment buying was a cheerful system but unrealistic.
Ohio people were by nature hopeful, always expecting a better
season and a bigger crop. The West attracted young men who
had not learned caution; they took up more land than they could
farm or pay for. By 1820 the government had sold $44 million
worth of land and had collected $22 million.

In Congress the argument went on, Eastern men insisting that
public land should produce federal revenue, Westerners urging
cheaper land in smaller tracts to encourage settlement. Eastern
congressmen feared that cheap land would drain population
from the older states; Westerners wanted to remove all barriers
from the "public patrimony." Both sides saw the evils of the
credit system.

In 1820 a new law was enacted. This, too, was accomplished
by an Ohio man. Senator Jeremiah Morrow, chairman of the
Committee on Public Lands, had led the movement to sell
eighty-acre tracts at $1.25 an acre, cash.

Jeremiah Morrow, pioneer settler in Warren County, was a
citizen-farmer small in stature but large in the annals of Ohio.
When the young German aristocrat Bernard Karl, Duke of Saxe-
Weimar-Eisenach, was touring Ohio in 1825, he took a carriage
from Cincinnati to call on the governor in Columbus. On the
way he was told that the governor was more likely to be on his
farm in Warren County. There the visitor found several men
rolling logs in a rough, charred clearing. Accosting a worker in
red-flannel shirt and homespun trousers, his face besmudged

6. Mitford M. Mathews, *A Dictionary of Americanisms.* 2 vols. (Chicago: University
of Chicago Press, 1951), 1:954.

with charcoal, the Duke asked: "Where is your master?" "Master!" exclaimed the man, "I own no master—no master but Him above." Stiffly the duke explained, "It is the governor of the state, Governor Morrow, I am inquiring for." "Well," said the man, "I am Jeremiah Morrow." [7] When he had finished cutting a wagon pole, he invited the duke into his plain frame house on a hillside above the Little Miami—where the duke spent a homely, hospitable night.

Hospitality—the latchstring out—was expected in Ohio. It was even included in the earliest list of laws. At Marietta, that first nick in the vast Ohio forest, the forty-eight original settlers had arrived on the rainy morning of April 7, 1788. Two days later they approved a chart of laws posted on a tree trunk. Of thirteen ordinances—calling for creation of a judicial and executive council, four days a year of military duty, observance of the Sabbath, and the eventual establishing of common schools—ordinance number seven required that "all members must entertain emigrants, visit the sick, clothe the naked, feed the hungry, attend funerals, cabin-raisings, logrollings, huskings; have their latchstrings always out." [8] It didn't occur to these confident people that they could not legislate morality and humanity.

After the Land Act of 1820 a settler could buy a small farm instead of going into debt for a large one. If he prospered, he could buy another eighty acres, owning it outright. Speculators could still bid on choice locations, hoping to sell them at a profit. But when $100 would buy clear title to eighty acres, the speculators had new competition from the federal land agents. No longer must a poor farmer go to a land merchant for a small tract; he could get it at government price in a district land office. In some Ohio counties pioneer farmers paid for their claims in wolf bounty—$4.25 for scalps of grown wolves, $2.50 for cubs.

Still, intruders found the way into new districts ahead of legal entry, not waiting for the slow processes of law. Indian cession involved a summoning of chiefs and sachems, the ritualistic presentation of gifts, a deliberating council; it was a drawn-out

7. Howe, *Historical Collections*, 2:756.
8. Howe, *Historical Collections*, 2:803.

business. Survey was even slower. The surveyor sighted the line with his transit. Axmen cleared the path, blazing trees along the line; a chain man measured distance. At the end of forty chains they set the quarter-section stakes and notched two witness trees. The township corner was witnessed by four trees with blazes facing the corner stake. Chain men had to measure all the country—ponds and marshes, rocky gorges and dense hillsides, as well as rich bottomland and meadow openings.

Meanwhile squatters found the way to choice locations. They were the first ragged wave of settlement, scarring their witness trees, building huts and clearing fields miles ahead of the law rather than outside it. Many of them expected to buy at the government price, with no land jobber in the way. They demanded squatters' rights.

A few years earlier that phrase would have sounded like right of trespass. But now the squatters were too many to be evicted and too useful to be denied. They improved wild country— opening roads, building bridges, locating fords and traces. The new republic was a country of laws, but the people shaped the law more than the law shaped them. In 1807 Congress had passed an Intrusion Act, dispossessing squatters on the public lands. But the law could not catch up with successive waves of people overrunning the surveyed boundaries. In 1830, more aware of realities in the West, the legislators approved a pre-emption law that made intrusion legal; settlers who had invaded public land could buy as much as 160 acres at the $1.25 price. Enacted as a temporary measure, it was renewed throughout the boom-and-bust years of the 1830s. Then came the Pre-emption Act of 1841, permanently sanctioning settlement before purchase; squatters could settle anywhere on unsold land and buy it later in the land office. In 1854 the Graduation Act reduced the price of unsold land, in relation to the time it had gone unsold, to as low as 12½ cents an acre. Finally in 1862 the Homestead Act offered free land to any settler who would live there and improve it. After seventy-five years the practice begun on the first Seven Ranges in Ohio had completed its evolution.

The early land laws sought revenue for the government, but increasing numbers of Western people saw the public domain as public opportunity. As the spread of settlement grew more urgent than the funding of federal debt, the squatter moved from opprobrium to approval; he changed from an outlaw to a pioneer. Wild land, the nation agreed, was not for the private speculator or the public treasury. It was for the people who would tame it and bring it to harvest.

4

The Shining Road

*L*OOK at the unborn nation in colonial times—a strip of coastal settlement, hard won, arduously extended from the seaboard to the Appalachian highlands. Beyond that wall of mountains lay a vast interior wilderness thinly peopled by primitive tribes. It was a magnetic horizon. Even before the American Revolution venturesome people were trekking over the mountain ridges toward the luring West. If wishes were horses, beggars would ride. The wish was fulfilled by a generous gift of geography. A broad, free avenue led through the wilderness, a highway of water. It would have been a gift even with an adverse current; a great gift if it were still water. But it was more than that. Flowing west in line with American destiny, it was a magic carpet into the heart of the continent. At its junction with the Mississippi, the rain that fell in Appalachian valleys mingled with snow water from the glaciers of Montana. The map and the history of America required the westward-flowing Ohio.

In early times the river was the road of exploration, migration, and frontier commerce. Its first vessel was the Indian canoe, hollowed out of a poplar log, propelled by willow poles and paddles of light pawpaw wood. This craft carried LaSalle on his vague exploration in 1669–1670 as far west as present Louisville. A hundred years later, while the valley was still unbroken wilderness, it brought young George Rogers Clark into the Old Northwest, which he would make an American territory. During the Revolution and the Indian wars the Ohio was a military road, freighting men and material for the winning of the West. By then it was carrying pioneer settlers and a crude frontier commerce.

Many voices have sounded on the Ohio. The first were wind and water, older and more lasting than the voices of men. History began with the murmured Angelus of the missionary-explorers, French priests petitioning in Latin: *May the divine assistance always remain with us / And may the souls of the faithful departed through the mercy of God rest in peace.* Then came other voices—the steersman's cry, the oaths of the oarsmen, the halloo of travelers in lonely country. Through morning mist echoed the boatman's bugle, the haunting call of the keelboats "All the way to Shawneetown, long time ago." [1] Steam came to the rivers, and above the splash of paddle wheels rose the high, clear music of the pilot's bell. From the size of a water pail the bells grew to a hundred, five hundred, a thousand pounds. To enrich their melody quarts of silver dollars were melted in the metal. By 1840 bells rang up and down the Ohio, the staccato landing bell rousing the roustabouts on the levee, the departure bell fading in the rush and rumble of the paddle wheel.

Steamboats had a short life—they averaged four and a half years on the Ohio—but the bells lived on. They were removed from sunken wrecks and salvaged from old hulks on the riverbank. Many of them went into other steamers; some became church bells and school bells in river settlements. Today a rich-toned bell rings from a storied passenger boat on the Ohio. First cast for the side-wheeler *City of St. Louis* in 1883, the bell went onto the stately *Queen City* in 1897. After forty-three years on that charmed packet, it passed to the towboat *John W. Hubbard.* In 1948 it was mounted on the hurricane roof of the *Delta Queen,* where it rings arrivals at Pittsburgh, Cincinnati, Louisville, and many other landings.

In the 1840s, with traffic heavy on the Ohio, steamboat bells

---

1. Walter Blair and Franklin J. Meine, *Mike Fink* (New York: Henry Holt and Company, 1933), p. 45.

signaled for passing in the channel. But wind often carried the sound away, or a drumming rain drowned it. Regulations then required the use of a steam whistle. The first whistle shrilled from the chimney of the steamer *Revenue,* built by Captain William Fulton at Pittsburgh in the early 1840s. Captain Fulton had heard a steam whistle on the roof of a factory in Philadelphia. When he tried it on his packet, a new voice reached the rivers. The steamers came with windy shouts of arrival. They left with restless toots and sent back baleful calls, fading with distance. Like steamboat bells, the whistles grew larger and more mellow, each with its own pitch and resonance. Rivermen knew boats by their whistles, and boys at the landings could name approaching packets before they came into view. The third *Kate Adams* had a deep bass voice like a thousand bullfrogs. Bass and treble blended in the organ voice of the *Eclipse.* From the chime whistle of the *St. Lawrence* came plangent chords and melodious diphthongs. There was no sound in the world so filled with mystery and longing as a riverboat at midnight blowing for a landing.

The Campus Martius Museum at Marietta contains a trove of river lore. Among hundreds of photographs and scores of name boards, steering wheels, and steamboat bells, is a collection of steam whistles, some small as a dinner pail and some as big as a barrel. The River Room is a silent place in the museum basement—silent until you imagine that great bass-and-treble medley. On May 7, 1966, all those whistles were taken to the big Union Carbide plant at Long Reach (Mile 146), where they were connected to steam lines for a "whistle blow." With jetting plumes, the old whistles coughed and wheezed and found their forgotten voices. After years of silence they soloed, then blended one with another in varied pitch and key. Finally, all shouting together, a great steam chorus filled the valley, echoing and re-echoing from the river hills.

A century and a half ago Thomas Hart Benton and William Clark talked of the inland rivers, tracing them on the map and foreseeing a vast network of navigation. As Senator Benton recalled:

Governor Clark and myself undertook to calculate the extent of boatable water in the valley of the Mississippi; we made it about fifty thousand miles! Of course we counted all the infant streams on which a flat, a keel, or a bateau could be floated, and justly; for every tributary of the humblest boatable character helps to swell not only the volume of the central waters but its commerce upon them.[2]

Of that fifty thousand miles of navigable water, the most important part was the 981 miles of the Ohio, a natural highway for the immigrants to new country and for the commerce they created.

To Pittsburgh in the early years came families worn and weary from a punishing journey across the mountains. Some had jolted over the rocky road in cart or wagon. Some had left the wagon broken at a fording place and come on, trundling a few goods in a wheelbarrow. Many had measured, step by step, the Allegheny ridges; years later a Marietta woman remembered her mother leading a reluctant cow, leaning on the creature during the long way up and over Laurel Mountain. For all, it was the dream of a river flowing west that kept them going. At Pittsburgh, at last, they saw the Monongahela and the Allegheny join to form the dreamed Ohio. After the looming barrier ridges, after the dark trace hemmed in forest, after mud and mire, rocks, roots, and tree stumps, there lay the river, the beckoning, sunlit river winding westward between the wild green shores. This was the main channel of the westward rush, the current that carried the greatest tide of settlement and expansion the world has known. All their lives the immigrants would remember that shining road, like a gift, like a promise, like God's providence in an unfeeling world.

At the Pittsburgh boatyards thirty-five dollars would buy an oblong flat-bottomed craft with a shedlike shelter for its people and a railed deck for horses and cattle. Commonly called a "broadhorn," it had a pair of long steering oars set in timber crotches on the shed roof. Like a floating barnyard it moved down the shining road, horses munching at a pile of hay and

2. J. Thomas Scharf, *History of St. Louis City and County,* 2 vols. (Philadelphia: L. H. Everts & Co., 1883), 2:1037.

chickens scratching at their feet. On the roof a woman rocked a cradle and a man leaned on the steering oar while the tireless river carried them toward the future. By a great gift of geography the promised land of Ohio had a moving, gleaming highway to bring its people home.

At Wheeling a flatboat family could put in for stores—salt pork, hominy, dried apples, cornmeal, and molasses. Then on the way again, past great headlands, little creek mouths, long, curved willow islands, and shelves of green bottomland under the lifting hills. While the changing shores slid past, emigrant families talked of lands they would claim, houses they would build, harvests they would gather. The flatboat was a one-way craft. At journey's end it was broken up and put together again as a one-room dwelling.

After the Indian wars, in the 1790s, a trip down the Ohio must have been the cheapest and most pleasant travel anywhere. In 1818 Thomas Hulme of Lancaster, England, voyaged downriver in an ark with eight assorted travelers. At Steubenville they were joined by two young men, a carpenter and a saddler, who had come from Pittsburgh in a skiff. Hitching on to the ark, they stood their turns at steering and often took their rifles ashore to shoot squirrels and pigeons. These two traveled seven hundred miles on the Ohio at an expense of seven dollars each, including the cost of their skiff. Hulme left the ark at Cincinnati, having come five hundred miles at a total cost of fourteen dollars—for food, shelter, and transportation.

More durable than the flatboat was the keelboat, used for military transport and for early commerce throughout the Ohio Valley. Up to eighty feet long and twelve feet wide, it had a sharp keel, a shaped hull, rounded bow and stern, and a roofed cargo hold and crew's cabin. It was commonly fitted with mast and sail. The keelboat voyaged downstream and up, an easy trip followed by a hard one.

The first two decades of the nineteenth century saw the peak of keelboat commerce. Flour, salt, iron, bricks, and barrel staves went west and south on the rivers. Molasses, sugar, coffee, lead, and hides came back upstream. A standard keelboat carried three hundred barrels of freight, a formidable load to propel against the river current. From runways at each side of the boat, a line of sweating men pushed the boat upstream, lifting and setting their poles to the cry of the steersman. In swift water the boat hugged the riverbank while the men pulled on willow branches. Where it was too deep for this "bushwhacking," boatmen swam ashore with a towline. Scrambling through mud and thickets a dozen men hauled fifty tons through deep water. Then they resumed the treadmill toil with their poles. It was a rugged way to earn eighty cents a day—if that. Said an Irish immigrant who was working his passage in a keelboat: "Faith, if it wasn't for the name of riding, I'd sooner walk." [3]

By 1815 there were some three thousand boatmen in three hundred keelboats on the rivers. When two boats met, the men shouted information, banter, and curses till the rival craft was past. Hung on a peg beside the tiller of each boat was a signal horn of varying pitch and volume. After 1820 keelboats continued to serve the side rivers while steamboats carried a growing commerce on the mainstream. The boatman's horn gave way to the steamer's bell, and setting poles were replaced by churning paddle wheels. But the keelboat men lived on in river lore.

The boatman was not a settler but a riverman; he belonged to the river as a seaman belongs to the sea. While frontier farmers took root, the boatman was a rover. Working the steering oar while the forest drifted by, he sang in jubilation:

> The boatman is a lucky man,
> No one can do as the boatman can.
> The boatmen dance and the boatmen sing,
> The boatman is up to everything.
>   Hi-o, away we go,
>   Floating down the river
>   On the O-hi-o!
> When the boatman goes ashore
> He spends his money and works for more;
> I never saw a girl in all my life
> But what she'd be a boatman's wife.

3. B. H. Botkin, ed., *A Treasury of Mississippi River Folklore* (New York: Crown Publishers, 1955), p. 488.

Hi-o, away we go,
Floating down the river
On the O-hi-o! [4]

The boatman's song was carried onto steamboats when the keelboat age was past.

In 1790 a young woodsman named Mike Fink wandered into
Pittsburgh and saw the river landings thick with skiffs, rafts,
arks, flatboats, and keelboats. When he heard the long, wild
music of the boatman's horn—a perforated bullock's horn that
produced mellow minor notes—the river spell was on him. For
the rest of his life he was a keelboat man. A natural riverman
with a love of roving, he had great strength, great gusto, and
great skill. "Hell's a-snortin'," said Mike Fink, wading onto a
mudbank or into a tavern brawl. Soon he was known the length
of the Ohio. Bold and reckless, ready for riot or rampage, he
was called the Snag and the Snapping Turtle. When steamboats
came to the Ohio and the Mississippi, he went with keelboats up
the wild Missouri. In 1823 at a trading post on the Yellowstone
he was killed in a fight over an Indian woman.

That was the end of a robust life and the beginning of a
legend. In 1829 a Cincinnati writer pictured Mike Fink as the
loudest bragger and the fiercest fighter, a Hercules with a long
oar and a setting pole. The legend spread, in sketches, stories,
stage plays, and eventually in television. In 1933, more than a
century after his death, the illiterate Mike Fink was featured in
the *London Times Literary Supplement*.

When a flatboat left the landing, it would not be seen again.
It carried emigrants away. But the keelboat linked people
together. It traveled downstream with passengers and produce—
chiefly pork, flour, and baled peltry—all the way to New Orleans. Months later it came back, bringing barrels of sugar and
bags of coffee, bales of cotton, crates of crockery, kegs of iron
nails. The sound of its horn, often heard in fog or darkness, became the subject of a poem that circulated, like the Mike Fink
legend, through the Ohio Valley.

---

4. *Minstrel Songs, Old and New* (Boston: Oliver Ditson & Co., 1882), pp. 146–147.

> O boatman, wind that horn again,
> For never did the listening air
> Upon its ambient bosom bear
> So wild, so soft, so sweet a strain.[5]

To autumn fogs was added the smoke of a thousand valley farmers in their clearings. For days the river was shrouded in a pungent haze. Through that vague stillness came the wild, weird, mellow music—more like a reaching through loneliness than a navigating signal. Many boats passed unseen while those melancholy notes faded into silence.

> What though thy notes be sad and few,
> Yet, boatman, wind thy horn again!
> Tho' much of sorrow mark its strain,
> Yet are its notes to sorrow dear;
> Yet is each pulse to nature true
> And melody in every tone.[6]

This was the other side of the Mike Fink mythology. The boatman's horn belonged to moonlight and the misty morning. It was a half-imagined music, felt as much as heard. In it were the mystery and melancholy of the wilderness, the questing of a people, and their loneliness and yearning in a savage land.

On this river of destiny the steamboat appeared at the very time when multitudes of people were migrating to new lands. Within three years after Robert Fulton's navigation of the Hudson, a steamboat took shape on the riverbank at Pittsburgh. Named for its destination, the *New Orleans* was 138 feet long, twenty-six feet wide, with a main deck cabin surmounted by a boxy pilot house. It had a tall chimney, two masts with schooner sails, and a pair of big side wheels. Late in 1811 it headed westward. After waiting at Louisville for rising water to run the falls, it reached New Orleans in January 1812. This pioneer ves-

5. "The Boatman's Horn" by General William O. Butler, who traveled the rivers as an army officer during and after the War of 1812. Quoted in William Cooper Howells, *Recollections of Life in Ohio* (Cincinnati: The Robert Clarke Company, 1895), p. 84.

6. W. C. Howells, *Recollections*, p. 84.

sel did not return to the Ohio. It remained on the lower Mississippi, running between New Orleans and Natchez until it was snagged near Baton Rouge one summer night in 1814.

Other steamboats followed. In 1815 the *Enterprise* and the *Aetna* ran profitably between Louisville and New Orleans. In 1816 at Brownsville on the Monongahela, Henry M. Shreve launched the historic *Washington*. This four-hundred-ton, two-decked stern-wheel steamer had a shallow, flat-bottomed hull to ride the river currents and rub over the shoals. Its main deck housed a two-cylinder, high-pressure, horizontal engine. Above it was a cabin deck with a pilot house framed by two tall chimneys. This shallow-draft vessel set the pattern for all future steamboats on the western rivers.

The *Washington* voyaged down to New Orleans in 1816. Next spring it made a historic run upstream, reaching Louisville from New Orleans in twenty-five days. This trip proved that steam could master the willful rivers, and immediately the boatyards of Cincinnati and Pittsburgh clamored with building. By 1820 sixty steamboats were churning the Ohio and the Mississippi. The number reached 740 by 1850, the peak year of steamboat commerce.

In the 1840s two million people traveled the Ohio every year, and in 1846 ninety new packets were launched from Ohio River shipyards. Every valley newspaper ran long columns of *River Commerce*. At the landings teamsters cursed and shouted, wagons clattered on the stones, bells and whistles called above the chanting of the stevedores. All humanity traveled on the river: natives and foreigners, parlormen and backwoodsmen, ladies in silk slippers and moccasined squaws, drab Quakers and brass-buttoned army men, gamblers and missionaries, speculators and journalists, scientists and philosophers. In those years a steamboat was a microcosm of the human species.

Steamboat travel was both glamorous and squalid. The stately four-deckers, white as a wedding cake, had floral carpets, inlaid woodwork, and oil paintings on the stateroom doors. They provided a nursery, a barbershop, gaming rooms, and a gleaming bar. Their cabin passengers sat down to five-course dinners with orchestra music. But most of the travelers never saw the splendors of the grand saloon. Immigrants, woodsmen, and frontier farmers were crowded among cargo and livestock on the lower deck, cooking porridge on the boiler flues and drinking river water. They slept on bales and boxes. Living close to the engines and the waterline, they were the first victims of collision and explosion. The one inducement to deck passage was economy. For a dollar a decker could travel five hundred miles—one-fifth the fare for cabin passengers.

On the Cincinnati riverfront in the spring of 1848 a new bookkeeper began work in a shipping office. His name was Stephen Collins Foster. In his big ledger each page was a packet: *Fairmont, Messenger, Oswego, Bolivar, Ohio Belle, Gladiator, Hibernia*. Outside his window, carts rumbled on the pavement, passengers thronged the wharf boat, and a parade of big white steamers lined the levee. In the chill wind, tatters of smoke blew from the tall chimneys. But the river led to the languid, fragrant Southland.

Stephen Foster had melodies in his mind. Forgetting bills of lading, he began to write:

> I come from Alabama
> Wid my banjo on my knee.
> I'm gwan to Louisiana
> My true love for to see.
> Oh! Susanna, do not cry for me,
> I come from Alabama,
> Wid my banjo on my knee.

From the river a whistle sounded, and he saw the handsome new stern-wheeler *Telegraph* backing off from the landing. The young clerk dipped his quill again.

> I jumped aboard de *Telegraph*
> And trabbled down de ribber— [7]

7. Stephen C. Foster, *Oh! Susanna* (Louisville: W. C. Peters & Co., 1848). Although some evidence suggests that this song was composed in Pittsburgh, Foster's biographers think it more likely that Cincinnati was the place of its composition. The song was spread, and altered, by many pirated editions. Its California versions are said to have given the gold fever to thousands who otherwise would have stayed at home.

In the spring of 1849, hundreds of gold-seekers took passage down the Ohio and up the Missouri. At Independence they joined the wagon trains trekking westward, singing their own version of "Susanna."

> Ho! California, that's the land for me.
> I'm bound for Sacramento
> With my washbowl on my knee.[8]

The song crossed the plains and mountains. It rounded Cape Horn in square-riggers and climbed the mountains of Panama on muleback. It livened the streets of San Francisco, the road to Hangtown, and the trail to Grizzly Flats.

After six years the steamer *Telegraph* was beached and broken, but it went on voyaging in Stephen Foster's song. In 1853 in Delhi, India, an American traveler heard British officers sing of jumping on the *Telegraph* and heading down the river. A century and a quarter later, in October 1975, when the worst typhoon in a decade lashed Hong Kong harbor, tearing big ships from their anchorage and blowing small craft like autumn leaves into the typhoon shelters, I watched from a hotel window. As great seas slammed the harbor wall, blown spray and sheets of rain whipped through deserted streets, and signal number 10, the hurricane alarm, was torn off its mooring on the weather station. Then I heard a calming, reassuring music. Over the hotel's stereo came a familiar medley: " 'Way down upon the Swanee River . . , Oh! Susanna, do not cry for me . . . My Old Kentucky Home, Good night! . . .'' Long after Stephen Foster said Good-night, his river songs were traveling around the world.

During the Civil War riverboats, hastily armed and armored, carried both troops and military cargoes. When the war was over, there came a revival of steamboat building. A new queen of the river was the handsome *Ruth,* launched in 1865. A stately four-decker, she carried 2,500 tons of freight and 1,600 passengers. Soon this splendid steamer was surpassed by the *Great Republic,* built in 1867; when she first steamed down the Ohio,

---

8. Quoted in Octavius T. Howe, *Argonauts of '49* (Cambridge: Harvard University Press, 1923), p. 78.

crowds cheered from every landing. The *Great Republic* had calendar dimensions: 365 feet long for the days of the year, 52 feet wide for the weeks, 12 feet deep for the months, and 7 decks high for the days of the week. Her reported cost was $365,000, a thousand dollars a foot. Invisible was the $100,000 mortgage she dragged up and down the river. After two years her owners were bankrupt.

Of the hundreds of side-wheelers that came from Ohio River shipyards, the finest was built in 1878, when river trade was ebbing. At her launching a reporter described the vessel as a magic palace, built by Aladdin overnight, and given a name as shining as her snowy paint work. From her oak keel to her 2,880-pound roof bell, her five-toned whistle, and her eighty-foot chimneys, the *J. M. White* was incomparable. In the great saloon all her dinnerware showed her own handsome picture. Her Irish linen was monogrammed JMW; her twin-stacked silhouette was engraved on her silver. For fruit and nuts alone this steamer's bill was one hundred dollars a week. Her pilots, turning the spokes of her eleven-foot wheel, were lordly men until a December day in 1886 at a Louisiana landing when the vessel caught fire. As flames licked over a cargo of gunpowder in the hold, she went up with a bang heard fifty miles away. Slowly the river silt buried her under the cottonwoods.

The *White* never carried her full capacity of freight or passengers, though her roustabouts had a ten-tier cotton song: after loading cotton ten bales high, they bragged of stoking the furnace till smoke put out the stars, and racing up the river to beat the railroad cars. But they couldn't beat the cars. Speed always wins the transportation business, and the railroads had it. When locomotives were whistling from Pittsburgh to Cairo, the packets left the landings with decks half empty. Then Ohio shipyards built steamboats for the Nile, the Congo, the Amazon, and the Orinoco. To jungle towns in Brazil and Africa went the deep-toned whistles, full of distance and longing, while grass grew over the Ohio levees.

A river is always the same and always changing. At Cincinnati in September of 1881 boys waded across to Kentucky; in mid-channel the river was twenty-three inches deep. Two years later the Ohio rose to sixty feet, and steamboats steered down Water Street. After the dry summer of 1887 the Ohio shrank to thirty-two inches and a coral reef made an island in midstream. In 1890 that reef lay under fifty-five feet of swirling river. As far back as 1824 the U.S. Army Corps of Engineers was given custody of the Ohio River. The engineers pulled up snags and stumps, blasted some rock ledges, and dredged out sandbars. But those measures did not alter seasonal changes—the river brimming in the spring and baring its bones in midsummer. There was water enough, if it flowed evenly through the year, to carry the largest steamboats in all seasons. That was the aim of the engineers' project that has taken ninety years and a billion dollars to accomplish.

The first movable (collapsible) dam was built a few miles below Pittsburgh in 1885, when coal was the major river cargo. For the coal fleet that first dam created a deep-water staging basin at the head of the river. The engineers then projected a system of sixty-eight dams that would maintain a six-foot channel from Pittsburgh to Cairo. But in the rush of railroad building the river project was shelved.

During World War I the railroads were overwhelmed with traffic, and in that crisis the War Department rediscovered the Ohio River. One towboat could do the work of ten locomotives; one train of barges could carry the freight of several hundred railroad cars. Recalling old pilots from retirement, building new towboats and barges, the government formed the Federal Barge Lines to carry the commerce of war. In 1924, with revived river traffic, engineering plans were revised, and Congress began appropriations for canalizing the Ohio. By 1929 the project was completed—forty-six collapsible dams maintaining a nine-foot channel and locks accommodating tows six hundred feet long.

The controlled river then seemed adequate for all the future, but traffic, even in the depression 1930s, outgrew it. In World War II and the postwar years the river trade surpassed all expectations. Petroleum came up the river in enormous volume. In hundreds of industrial plants new technology produced aluminum, asphalt, plastics, steel, fertilizers, and chemicals. Mountains of coal moved downstream to huge new power plants.

Back in 1885, when the first dam was built, thousands of tons of Pittsburgh iron went into horseshoes. Sixty years later it went into alloy steel for airplane engines. Every season larger towboats pushed longer tows up and down the river. That new commerce required a new waterway, and a new river project took shape on the engineers' drawing boards. In place of 46 dams, it showed 19 high-lift dams creating long pools of slack water with a minimum depth of 12 feet. Beside each dam stretched a huge main lock, 1200 feet long and 110 feet wide, and an auxiliary lock 600 by 110 feet.

A century and a quarter ago big white steamboats carried the people and the produce of the newly developed valley. Today diesel-powered towboats push acres of oil, coal, grain, steel, aluminum, chemicals, and other bulk cargo. The tonnage of a single tow exceeds that of fifty of the vanished steamers. The new river commerce dwarfs the old—except for the passenger traffic. For years there was just one overnight passenger boat left on the river, the steamer *Delta Queen*. But on an April day in 1975 a new boat, built in the historic Howard shipyards across from Louisville, was christened *Mississippi Queen*, and a Bicentennial flag was presented to the five-decked, four-hundred-passenger vessel. It has passenger elevators, stem-to-stern air conditioning, a swimming pool, and a cinema theater— amenities that were unheard of in the romantic packets of the past. But its steam whistle and calliope echo the old-time river music.

In the spring of 1848 when Stephen Foster wrote the lilting lines of "Oh! Susanna," Samuel A. Hudson announced the exhibit of his "Great National Painting of the Ohio and Mississippi Rivers Executed on over Twenty Thousand Feet of Canvas, Showing Nine Different States and Delineating an Extent of over 1400 miles of River Scenery." [9] Ten years earlier, a young man of twenty-five, Hudson had left a tailoring shop in Boston to see the Ohio Valley. Four times he journeyed up and

9. Joseph Earl Arrington, "Samuel A. Hudson's Panorama," *Ohio History* 66(1957):353.

down the river, traveling in flatboat, keelboat, ark, and steamer, sketching hill shores, bottomlands and wooded islands, seeing the river's solitude and its busy commerce. At last, working from sketchbooks and memory in a river warehouse, he began painting on reels of canvas ten feet high. His finished panorama was three-quarters of a mile long. When it was unrolled, spectators made a vicarious journey from the Monongahela hills to the marshlands of the Mississippi River. On the way they saw ancient Indian mounds and modern kilns and potteries, moonlight on Blennerhassett Island and sunrise over the old French town of Gallipolis. From Hanging Rock, a lofty shelf of sandstone, they saw the smoke and gleam of iron furnaces beside the river. Above harbor traffic rose the seven hills of Cincinnati, and on the height of North Bend stood the grave of William Henry Harrison, Old Tippecanoe, who, as an eighteen-year-old ensign, had come down the river on a flatboat with eighty raw recruits for Anthony Wayne's army.

Hudson's kaleidoscopic painting was shown to crowded halls in Cincinnati and Pittsburgh, then in Baltimore and New York. In New England it was so popular that a copy was made for showing in Boston while the original was in Providence, drawing a thousand viewers daily. The copying was fortuitous; soon afterward the original canvas, showing in Troy, New York, was consumed by fire. By that time half a million Americans had seen the panorama.

In 1849 it was taken to Europe. For an entire year it toured in Germany, where the Ohio Valley was as well known as the Old Testament land of promise. To the gray cities of Bavaria, Saxony, and Württemberg, Hudson's canvas brought the shining river in a new green world. *"Wunderbar! Ganz Wunderbar!"* cried the audience as the Ohio's shores unrolled.

The Ohio extends from the coal hills to the corn belt, and at its juncture with the Mississippi it seems reluctant to mingle with those other waters. For miles the two currents flow side by side, a clear gray river beside a muddy brown one. The gray river is crowded with memories—George Rogers Clark in a dugout canoe, Major Long setting out to explore the far Missouri,

Lewis and Clark on their way to Oregon, Audubon seeking the birds of the wilderness, Robert Owen bringing Utopia to the Wabash, Andrew Jackson, Henry Clay, William Henry Harrison, Zachary Taylor, Abraham Lincoln, journeying to the nation's Congress and its White House. Add to these men of destiny the anonymous people of the great migration. Writing in the Rhineland a century and a half ago, Victor Hugo pictured one family beginning its long journey from the Old World to the New:

> A few moments before crossing the far-famed battlefield of Montmirail, I met a cart rather strangely laden; it was drawn by a horse and an ass, and contained pans, kettles, old trunks, straw-bottomed chairs, with a heap of old furniture. In front, in a sort of basket, were three children, almost in a state of nudity; behind, in another, were several hens. The driver wore a blouse, was walking, and carried a child on his back. A few steps from him was a woman. They were all hastening toward Montmirail, as if the great battle of 1814 were on the eve of being fought. . . .
>
> I was informed, however, that this was not a removal; it was an expatriation. It was not to Montmirail they were going—it was to America. They were not flying to the sound of the trumpet of war—they were hurrying from misery and starvation. In a word, it was a family of poor Alsatian peasants who were emigrating. They could not obtain a living in their native land, but had been promised one in Ohio.[10]

10. Victor Hugo, *The Rhine*, 2 vols. (Boston: Dana Estes & Company, n.d.), 1:9–10.

5

A for Ax

The ballads of the people are the bulwarks of the State.

—Eugene Fitch Ware

*O*N the Miami University campus in Oxford, Ohio, stands a neat white house that in 1960 was designated a Historic Landmark. This was the home of William Holmes McGuffey, built in 1833 across the street from the old college grounds. Behind the house was a woodshed where the early-rising professor spent an hour before his seven-o'clock classes. A good man with saw and hammer, he was making an octagonal desk with swivel top; its eight pie-shaped drawers were for sorting pages and papers. In them grew the materials for his readers, for which a firm of Cincinnati publishers had agreed to pay him a total of one thousand dollars.

Fifteen sets of school readers were published in America between 1820 and 1841, but the McGuffey series ran away from all the others. For more than half a century it rode the wave of national expansion. McGuffey books went west in Santa Fe wagons and emigrant caravans; traders freighted them into Indian reservations; they were used in sod schoolrooms on the prairie, in cow towns on the plains, in mining camps in the Rockies and the Sierras. By 1860 the publishers were printing

Eugene Fitch Ware, *Some Rhymes of Ironquill* (Chicago: A. C. McClurg and Company, 1892), p. 152.

two million copies a year. When Cincinnati presses could not fill the orders, printers in New York, Philadelphia, Nashville, and Chicago were licensed to produce the texts. They became standard school texts in thirty-seven states. Except for New England, where they never took hold, McGuffey's Eclectic Readers blanketed the nation. In the 1890s the texts were translated into Spanish; American imperialism took them to thatch-roofed schools in Puerto Rico and the Philippines. By the early 1900s they had sold an estimated 122 million copies, a phenomenon unmatched in the long history of education.

There were widely used textbooks before McGuffey. Five million children in many generations learned the alphabet from the famous old New England Primer. It began with A for Adam, in a somber couplet: In Adam's fall / We sinnéd all. The letter T was a negation: Time cuts down all / Both great and small. Then came a gloomy lesson about the warrior king of ancient Persia: Xerxes the Great did die / And so must you and I.

After the alphabet came a graveyard poem:

> Our days begin with trouble here,
> Our life is but a span,
> And cruel death is always near,
> So frail a thing is man.[1]

The New England book was burdened with submission and death.

McGuffey's Primer began with *A Ax,* the picture showing a child not as tall as the ax-helve beside a stump. At that time the ax was clearing roads and fields; it was building barns, dwellings, churches, schoolhouses; it was clearing the Ohio country. On the frontier everything was done by individuals, nothing by organized society. The ax was a one-man implement. It could never be used in an assembly line or on a welfare board. Whitman called it the homely weapon of democracy.

After A in the McGuffey alphabet came Box, Dog, Hen, Jug, Lark, Ox, Tub, Vine, Yoke—all homely and familiar things from the child's everyday world, the rough-hewn, hopeful, equalitarian frontier West. Instead of looking at the graveyard,

1. *The New England Primer* (New York: M. Day, 1815), p. 22.

McGuffey saw the brightness of an Ohio morning. Home from school came a first-grader with a poem on the sunrise:

> The lark is up to greet the sun,
> The bee is on the wing;
> The ant its labors has begun,
> The woods with music ring.

Here was the spirit of a new nation, not weighted with death but lifted with life and eager to build a future.

> Shall birds and ants and bees be wise
> While I my moments waste?
> O let me with the morning rise
> And to my duty haste.[2]

After a few short seasons of schooling, most of these children would swing the ax, hollow out the wooden tub, and yoke up the oxen. Those who kept on to the Fifth Reader and Sixth Reader were introduced to Hawthorne, Irving, Lamb, Goldsmith, Dickens, Milton, Shakespeare. These books were read at the family fireside, at church socials and grange suppers, as well as in the schoolroom. To a largely bookless people they brought glimpses of the world of history and literature. In the Fourth Reader an essay by Daniel Drake, scientist and civic leader in Cincinnati, voiced the western people's need to know and share their own beliefs, hopes, and aspirations, a need the McGuffey texts were fulfilling. The Readers tirelessly repeated the theme of democratic opportunity, though they said nothing about equality of ability. Tocqueville had already observed that Americans, much given to extolling individual freedom, actually valued liberty less than equality.

In the endless woods of Ohio *A for Ax* was a lesson soon learned by strenuous experience. Democracy there was not a theory or even a creed; it was a circumstance. Frontier people, as James Truslow Adams has said, did not have to chop off the head of a king but to chop down a forest. The trees were their adversary. Even at church pioneer settlers thought less of their contest with the devil than of their war with the woods. In later,

2. *McGuffey's Eclectic Primer* (Cincinnati: Wilson, Hinkle & Co., 1849), p. 54.

easier times people could make a sentiment of "Trees," but in sparsely settled Darke County the enlightened sinner saw the power of God not in creating but in getting rid of a tree. In 1823 in the village of Versailles, the Hardshell Baptists built the second church of the county. For membership they required that an applicant have faith in God. A man named Stoner, who lived by himself up the creek, wanted to join the congregation, and was ready for the test. He rose and said, "I got up this mornin', greased my shoes, combed my head, and started to meetin'. As I was comin' along I saw a tree; I says to myself, Kin one man pull that ar tree up? No! Kin two men pull that ar tree up? No! Kin three men pull that ar tree up? No! Kin ten men pull that ar tree up? No! Kin twenty men pull that ar tree up? No! Kin God Almighty pull that tree up? Yes! I feel like suthin' is going to happen." He sat down. The preacher rose and said, "Brethren, extend the right hand of fellowship to Brother Stoner, for this is the true blatin' of the lamb." [3]

The ax is an ancient implement, as old as stone-age man with a jagged flint or bone lashed onto a club handle. To the New World, Europeans brought a wedged metal blade fitted onto a straight round handle that lacked the reach and balance for a steady, biting stroke. Its three-pound bitt could not attack a forest wilderness. The American ax was a native product. Many craftsmen contributed to its evolution, which was completed in time for the Ohio settlers; although some Ohio smiths, having a way with iron, claimed to make the best axes ever.

From a crossroads forge came a ringing clangor and a fiery glow that showed a bare arm pounding a mass of plate iron. Sparks leapt from the anvil, showering the smith's leather apron. With tongs he plunged the white-hot iron, hissing and steaming, into a tub of water. It came out a purple clod, ready for shaping. The anvil clanged again as the cooling blade was fitted to the lean, curved handle.

The shag-barked hickory, long-trunked, straight and tall, was more than a sign of good soil. Its wood was both tough and re-

3. Howe, *Historical Collections,* 1:539.

silient. Its twigs were relished by rabbits and deer; its ripe nuts split their hulls into four neat quarters, and their meat was sweet to the taste of both domestic and wild creatures. Its outer wood peeled readily into slender wythes, to make a broom for sweeping or to bind in hoops a bucket or barrel. In the chimney mouth hickory gave a long, steady, glowing heat, and it made the best of all charcoal. But its most satisfying and indispensable use was in the ax-helve. A well seated hickory handle would last as long as the wrought iron it carried.

Of the two components, blade and helve, some axmen gave most care to the helve. It was that way with the French-Canadian Baptiste in Frost's poem, who kept a bundle of them he had made from second-growth hickory—"tough, tough." He showed that the true lines of a helve were there, in the grain, not laid on by lathe or knife. When he stood it on its horse's hoof, curved, slender and erect, his ax was poised and living: "See how she's cock her head!" [4] The same pride marked the crossroads craftsman who fused black plate iron with Ohio hickory of subtle balance and resilient strength. Weighing five or six pounds, this ax sold for from three to five dollars, and a settler would make a three-day journey to get it. In shops and taverns axes were discussed as earnestly as politics and land laws.

Alive and limber and so lightly balanced that the wielder's arm flowed through it, the ax became an extension of the man. There was the free sweep of the upward arc, the two hands joining in the accelerated swing, and at the end of the blow the slight twist that sent white chips flying. The woods were dark and mighty, lofty branches roped with vines and massive trunks that dwarfed everything around them. But with that ax a six-foot man could bring down a sixty-foot tree with barely rest or pause. Tock . . . tock . . . tock. The ax made a nick, then a white-wedged notch, finally a mortal cut that sent a tremor to the topmost leaves. At another stroke the big dark column began to go. With a tearing sound came a gathering whoosh and the cushioned thump, breaking lesser trees in its fall. There was the sweet-sour smell of sapwood and the ticking of torn fibers as the axman moved on to another tree.

4. From "The Ax-Helve" in *The Poetry of Robert Frost*.

The settler needed a cleared place for his cabin. At first it was a tangle of trunks and broken branches, but the ax trimmed them into logs for building. Then the settler girdled surrounding trees, chopping through the sapwood to make a deadening over his first few acres. Deep gashes were needed to kill oak, ash, and sycamore. For hickory and willow it was enough to girdle the bark. Small growth was grubbed out by the roots, saplings were cut off and saved for roof and fence poles. Then the ax was used for planting. Into gashed ground went seed corn and quartered potatoes already soaked and sprouting. Planted in June, these would make a crop by the end of summer.

While he shaped logs and poles for his cabin, the settler saw sunlight shafting through the deadened trees. Up in the green canopy leaves had withered, and twigs, bark, and vines began to fall. In two months his cabin stood in a dead forest, and his crops grew green around the great tree trunks. That fall he heaped limbs and brush over the fallen trunks, charring them off with smoldering fires. The singed segments were rolled together, oxen leaning into their yokes and the log chain jingling. More brush was added and soft columns of smoke rose in the autumn air. Whole counties were pungent with that burning. Gradually the forest wilderness went into ashes that mellowed the earth.

The first fields, gashed and trampled, lay like charred islands in the forest. In time they would be clear and clean and many-colored, a patchwork quilt on the Ohio land. But in the first years it was a hard-won battleground. William Cobbett, remembering the neat fields and hedgerows of Hampshire and Sussex, remarked that American farmers knew nothing about banking and hedging.

> They have no idea of the use of a billhook. . . . An ax is their tool, and with that tool at *cutting down* trees or *cutting them up,* they will do ten times as much in a day as any other men that I ever saw. Set one of these men upon a wood of timber trees, and his slaughter will astonish you.[5]

5. William Cobbett, *A Year's Residence in the United States of America* (Fontwell, Sussex: Centaur Press Limited, 1964), p. 179.

When the Ohio constitution was framed in 1803, its prohibition of slavery signaled a surge of migration from New England. In that year James Kilbourne (sometimes called Colonel and sometimes Reverend; he was both) led a hundred movers from Connecticut and Massachusetts to a new home in Franklin County, Ohio. Their first cabin served as a schoolhouse and a church. That summer the community celebrated July 4 with axes rather than firearms. Seventeen tall trees, for the seventeen states, were deeply notched, so that another blow or two would fell them. At sunrise on the Fourth seventeen axmen timed their strokes so that the trees fell, one after another, with seventeen crashing thumps. With that national salute another Ohio field lay open to the sun.

Those formidable labors became a lingering folklore after the land was cleared. A story told in Ohio, years later, described two boys, nine and eleven years old, left all winter in the woods of the Western Reserve while their father took his ailing wife to her kinfolk in the East. Keeping a fire smoldering in a drafty cabin, the two boys lived on rabbits caught in hollow logs and the remains of deer that the wolves had left. Once a month they tramped fifteen miles down the old Indian trail for a bag of cornmeal. They didn't have a gun, but they had one ax between them. When their father returned in the spring, he found the boys had made a two-acre clearing.

The first fences, needed to keep livestock *out* of the fields, were merely piled brush and logs enclosing a patch of garden. Pole fences were small logs laid in the crotches of live saplings. For the eventual rail fence, zigzagging around a field or garden, the best woods were ash, oak, walnut, chestnut, and poplar. The rail-splitter used wedges, of iron and wood, driven into the grain of an eight-foot log. The log was halved, quartered, often double-quartered, and finally the heartwood was split off for an extra rail. A hundred rails a day was a common stint; an expert and tireless rail-splitter would do twice that. Not the blade but the butt end of the ax head drove in the wedges, until the farmer made for himself a maul of twisted hickory root ringed in iron to keep *it* from splitting.

Cobbett heard of frontier youths "born with an ax in one

hand and a gun in the other.'' [6] The farmer shot for protection of his livestock as much as for meat on his table. To combat natural predators the settlers sometimes joined together. From frontier years in the Western Reserve the Great Hinckley Hunt has been remembered.

In heavily wooded Medina County farmers had lost hundreds of cattle and sheep to marauding wolves and bears. Their hen coops were raided by foxes and their cornfields riddled by deer, raccoons, and squirrels. To combat the predators, settlers organized a systematic hunt, enlisting men from the entire township. Before daylight on December 24, 1818, six hundred settlers took assigned places on the four sides of Hinckley township. With that twenty-four-mile border they made a loose battle line, which closed as the men drew toward the center. They advanced noisily, boys shrilling and shouting, men whooping and blowing horns, dogs barking and baying—driving the game before them. An occasional gunshot felled or crippled a predator that was soon dispatched with axes, hay forks, and butcher knives lashed to poles. Gunfire heated up as the circle tightened, and smoke blew through the leafless woods. By good fortune just one hunter was slightly singed with buckshot.

Toward sundown the game was brought together, and in one account of it the hunters barbecued and feasted, washing the hot meat down with cold whiskey. When the jugs were empty, the hunters made high jinks, greasing themselves with bear fat, whooping and dancing till the dogs slunk off, fearing they might be next. Before parting, the hunters divided the harvest—unnumbered squirrels, rabbits, foxes, and raccoons, along with seventeen wolves, twenty-one bears, and more than three hundred deer. Most Medina County families had venison for Christmas dinner.

Except for the sigh and whisper of summer air and the rush of autumn rains, the great woods were silent. There were no songbirds in the forest. Through spring skies streamed rivers of passenger pigeons. For a few days they settled in vast roosts, thou-

6. Cobbett, *A Year's Residence,* p. 56.

sands of trees bending with their weight and the evening filled with the murmur of wings and throaty voices. By bonfire light farmers harvested the birds, felling them with hoes and pitch-forks, flailing the bent branches with poles. Amid rustling and fluttering came the thump of feathered bodies. Daybreak found thousands of gray-blue birds scratching out seed corn, beech-nuts, and winged maple seed. After more slaughter farmers raked up and loaded the dead birds into their wagons; the hogs would fatten on them.

Along the streams flocked the chattering, fearless Carolina parakeets. Red and green and yellow, they were as pretty as spring flowers, but in half a day a flock could scratch up a wheatfield and ruin a new orchard. Farmers killed the friendly birds with reluctance. As settlement grew, wild turkeys re-treated into the deep woods; farmers seldom saw or heard them. Turkey was tasty, and pigeons, once they were plucked, were edible, but the parakeet had a stringy, bitter flesh that even hogs avoided. People believed that the heart of the pretty green bird was deadly poison—the same frontier folklore that said bears sucked their paws in their winter sleep, and all jays went to hell on Friday so you never saw one then.

Now in Ohio the cardinal nests by the kitchen door. Fence-rows harbor meadowlarks and red-winged blackbirds. Vireos, bluebirds, grosbeaks, finches, flickers, the gray, melodious cat-bird and the silent, jeweled hummingbird enliven gardens, parks, and barnyards. Bobwhites whistle from the thickets, the rain crow reads the weather. Chickadees, titmice, woodpeckers, juncos, and creepers winter, like the handsome redbird, in Ohio woodlots. They all came with the clearings. Cultivation brought them—the seeds, berries, grubs, worms, and insects of the fields.

"Yes," thought Sayward Wheeler in Conrad Richter's recre-ation of frontier Ohio, "the country around here was taming up a little, with the woods partly cut down. It didn't seem like the Ohio wilderness any more on a soft day like today. . . . Little birds were here, flushing out of the winter wheat and feeding along the cleared ground." [7]

7. Conrad Richter, *The Fields* (New York: Alfred A. Knopf, 1946), pp. 251–252.

Along came her neighbor, that spring morning, old Billy Harbison in his fur cap and buckskin hunting frock. The birds, he said, were coming in.

> I seed a bee bird last summer . . . feeds and hums like a honey bee. Quail, pa'tridges comin' in, too. Redbreast robins and bluebirds! . . . The game's moved out and they're a-movin' in. I reckon the woods is done for. It's farmin' country through here now.[8]

Like the songbirds, law followed the ax in Ohio counties. At the end of Marietta's first summer, while the Indians were still friendly, the community gathered, 232 people, for the first court session in the Northwest Territory. They marched through newly cleared acres, past their first small fields of corn, potatoes, pumpkin, squash, and cabbage, to the commons along the Muskingum. There the Reverend Manasseh Cutler invoked a blessing, and huge Colonel Ebenezer Sprout, just elected high sheriff, declared that court was convened for the administration of justice in the light of law and without respect of persons. While some Indians who had come down the river to make a treaty looked on with wondering curiosity, Sprout read the commission of the judges, the clerk, and the sheriff. Then, there being no cases on the docket, the court adjourned. In that brief ceremony the first legal settlers of Ohio reminded themselves that they were bringers of civilization. Law had come to the wild land. At their next court session, in March 1790, there was a case on the docket. "A grand jury was impaneled and found a bill against Ezra Lunt for stealing a hogg." [9] The first jail was a snug cabin on the shady bank of the Muskingum.

At the mouth of the Little Miami, where Benjamin Stites's company had cleared the site of the first settlement of Cincinnati, the problem of justice arose when a stolen barrel of flour was found under a settler's bed. When an impromptu court of thirteen men found the culprit guilty, each juror laid three lashes on the thief's bare back. In neighboring Losantiville the settlers,

8. Richter, *Fields*, pp. 255–256.

9. Joseph Barker, *Recollections of the First Settlement of Ohio* (Marietta: Marietta College, 1958), p. 55.

gathered under a spreading tree, listed a code of laws and penalties. When Patrick Grimes was found guilty of stealing cucumbers, he was given twenty-nine lashes, one for each cucumber. Up the Little Miami River an early settlement was Xenia, the seat of Greene County, laid out in the woods in 1803. The first courthouse was a log hut, and the jury deliberated under a huge sugar maple. That tree served as a whipping post when the first crime was punished in 1806; a man who had stolen part of a cowhide to mend his shoes was tied to the tree and given one stripe across his shoulders.

Into the Ohio woods came plain and common people, the kind that make a nation. One of them, looking back in 1846, was astonished at his own memories. In 1802 young Amos Dunham from Connecticut, without purse or prospect, claimed sixty acres of the Ohio Company's wild land, on credit, and built himself a half-faced camp—three low log walls with a fire in front. On a half-cleared acre he scattered small grains broadcast (how far that earthy word has gone since then) amid stumps and deadenings. After a solitary season, he brought to that place a young wife and built a log house twenty feet square. When a child was born, he walked ten miles to Marietta to get some calico, but without cash or credit he came back empty-handed. His wife then suggested that he might spare a worn pair of pantaloons. From those thin pants she made a frock to dress the child in. When land payment was due, Dunham bartered for some neighbors' cattle and drove them over the mountains to Romney on the Potomac, where he sold them. He tramped on to Litchfield, Connecticut, and paid for his claim in the land office. With a dollar and a half in his knapsack he began the six-hundred-mile journey homeward. For a dollar he bought a box of hair combs, which he traded for food and lodging on the way. To the family fireside he brought back fifty cents.

In Washington County the settler's ax had prepared for corn and wheat, and also for the state's first library. On the Ohio River, six miles from Amos Dunham's clearing lay the village of Belpre, whose settlers had collected a shelf of books for circulation. All winter Dunham kept a book-borrower's path worn through the woods. "I had no candles," he recalled, "but

the woods afforded plenty of pine knots—with these I made
torches by which I could read. . . . Many a night have I passed
in this manner till twelve or one o'clock, reading to my wife
while she was hatchelling, carding, or spinning." [10]

In the first settlement of Athens County one farmer irregularly
received the *United States Gazette* and shared it with his neighbors. Then, at a public meeting in the fall of 1804, Josiah True
proposed that the settlers of Dover, Sunday Creek, and Amesville collect coonskins to procure some books—and so began
the historic Coonskin Library.

Money was scarce in the Ohio Valley, and every transaction
involved some kind of barter—a bushel of salt, a barrel of flour,
a sack of wool. Wanting books and lacking money, the men of
Amesville that winter ran traplines for the benefit of a future
library. Next spring Samuel Brown of Sunday Creek loaded a
wagon with bearskins, wolf hides, and raccoon skins and drove
six hundred miles to Boston. He traded his mixed peltry for
$73.50 worth of books, fifty-one volumes altogether. They were
brought to Amesville on a packhorse. Young Thomas Ewing
was there when the sack was opened and the "treasure" was
poured out. It included Harris's Encyclopedia, the works of
Goldsmith, Robertson's *North America,* Butler's *Analogy,* and a
few volumes of sermons, along with such lighter reading as
Fanny Burney's *Evalina* and George Lillo's *The London Merchant.* This library was the means of Ewing's education; he became a United States senator, secretary of the Treasury, and the
first secretary of the Interior. Another alumnus of that bookshelf
was Edward Ames, who founded a college in Illinois and became a frontier bishop of the Methodist Church. Back in Amesville the Coonskin Library was enlarged. By 1812 the settlers
had added Locke's *Essays,* Shakespeare's dramas, the early
novels of Sir Walter Scott, and the early poems of Byron. One
young farmer who had contributed a pack of skins to the book
fund took *Childe Harold* to the field to read during lunchtime.
In London, when Lord Byron heard that his book was in the
Coonskin Library in the Ohio wilderness, he wrote in his diary:

10. Howe, *Historical Collections,* 2:214.

"These are the first tidings that have ever sounded like *Fame* to my ears—to be read on the banks of the Ohio!" [11]

In those years the first steamboat was splashing down the Ohio River, big Conestoga wagons were rumbling over Zane's Trace, sawmills were cutting timber to build the first towns in the backwoods. Now the steamboats are vanished, the freight wagons are gone, the sawmills have passed with the great forest. But the Coonskin Library is still intact—four shelves of books in the old vellum and buckram, displayed in the Ohio Historical Center at Columbus.

The dominant figure in Conrad Richter's story of Ohio pioneering is not a man with an ax but a woman, weathered and worn and lasting as leather, who cleared wild land and brought it to harvest. Her husband was from Massachusetts, a lawyer with a gift of words and a head full of dreams for the town he named Americus. Portius Wheeler was learned, withdrawn, intemperate, sardonic, skeptical, and visionary, reciting Greek and Latin poets in a crude log hut while his wife fought roots and brambles and raised a brood of children. Sayward Wheeler could not read her husband's books, but she dimly shared his dream. To her first child, born in 1803 while his father was in Chillicothe helping to frame the Ohio constitution, she gave a resolute name. When the circuit preacher splashed creek water on the infant's head—"I baptize thee Resolve Wheeler, in the name of the Father and of the Son, and of the Holy Ghost" [12]—the words were like the first light of an opening through the forest gloom.

Yet, ten years later, after a winter of chopping at the big butts beyond the barn and plowing up new ground, the woods were still dense, dark, and dismaying. They swallowed up her little farm. Sayward felt a longing—the woods sickness she supposed it was—to be in some other place where she could step outside her door to look at green fields and sunny meadows and a traveled road leading to a town. Then, one morning, a stranger rode in, tied his horse to a fence rail, and took some papers from his

---

11. The Works of Lord Byron, 13 vols. (London: John Murray, 1898), 9:360.
12. Richter, *Fields*, p. 33.

saddlebag. He wanted to trade her hard-won clearing for a town lot with a house on it and a street in front, near a church, a school, and a store. Strangely then, while her husband and the land merchant waited, Sayward shook her head. No, she couldn't live off there. She couldn't live that way, not while there was all this unfinished business with the trees.

She went out, alone, to walk the limits of her land, land she had chosen, for they were the first people in this district. All the trees were in full leaf, making a breathless twilight where she went. Crossing the trace that led to a distant neighbor's, she came to the big buttonwood tree on the riverbank. This was her witness tree; its hollow shell could hold almost as many people as the meeting house. From here the river was her boundary until it reached the riffles and turned west into the gloom of the swamp, more gloomy after the brightness of the water. On higher, dryer ground she looked up at the great ash trunks rising clean and straight to their lofty branches. At the old Indian mound she turned north and came back to the line where she had started. In a few more paces she saw her fields in the blaze of sunlight. There were some acres of wheat, a patch of potatoes, then a field of flax, fading now from its springtime blue, and her meadow pasture with the sheep somewhere out of sight at the far end where the woods closed in.

Resting on a stump at the edge of the wheat, her mind wandered and wondered. "You would hardly believe that field had barrels of flour in it, a-hanging on the stalk . . . a field of life, that's what it was." [13] Then that poignant thought came again: going through the dark woods and coming out to the bright fields, she didn't see how she could give up this place she had made. There was more work to do, as always, but she was ready to do it. She had unwittingly made a commitment, or a commitment had been made for her.

Ohio in the making is portrayed in that morning walk around a forest claim: the dark forces of the earth, the sternness of the contest, the richness of the prize. Sayward Wheeler's nine children were born in the wilderness. They would come to maturity

13. Richter, *Fields,* p. 187.

in a land of fields and fences, roads and bridges, mills and shops, canals and railroads, schools and libraries, churches and colleges, towns and cities. That astonishing accomplishment, in less than a lifetime, had begun with an ax thudding in the forest dark.

6

Horn of Plenty

*O*HIO has some somber-sounding names—Skull Forks, Widowville, One Leg River, Pandora, Lost Run, Devil's Hole. But the map is gladdened by Amity, Arcadia, Edenburg, Eldorado, Fairhope, Felicity, Prospect, Rising Sun, West Unity. Look twice at Xenia, Greek for hospitality, and at Bucyrus, named for the founder of an ancient empire with a prefix meaning "beautiful"—

> I'll tell you how Bucyrus, now
> Just rising like the star of morn
> Surrounded stands by fertile lands
> On clear Sandusky's rural bourn.[1]

Look at little Brimfield, named when Portage County was a cornucopia overflowing with wheat, corn, oats, hay, potatoes, apples, peaches, and wool. Every year its canalboats took to market a million pounds of butter and two million pounds of cheese. "Cheesedom" they called it, when Cincinnati was "Porkopolis."

When the first Ohio legislators convened at Chillicothe, they adopted a State seal—a sunrise scene with day breaking over a tumbled range of mountains. The radiant sun illumined a sheaf of wheat in an endless grain field. In all that landscape there

---

1. Howe, *Historical Collections*, 1:485.

was not a tree. This in 1803 when Ohio was nine-tenths forest, its people warring with the dark and ancient woods. Those legislators were mostly farmers, their hands calloused by the ax and grubbing hoe. But they had a sturdy, stubborn dream of another country. They lost the dark present in the bright future. Time justified them. By 1840 Ohio led the nation in production of wheat, with a harvest of sixteen million bushels. Ten years later it approached thirty million, or seventeen bushels for each inhabitant of the state. John H. Klippart, secretary of the Ohio Board of Agriculture, then made a mistaken prophecy, declaring that Ohio would remain the foremost wheat state and that the Maumee River was the limit of America's wheat lands.

Besides its lead in wheat, Ohio in 1850 ranked first in production of corn and wool. Belmont County, population 34,000, had four times as many sheep as people. In the corn-rich southwestern counties drovers herded thousands of hogs over the roads to market. The Miami Valley hog, begetter of the Poland-China breed, was making Cincinnati the largest pork-packing and soap-producing center in the world. In 1846 geologist Sir Charles Lyell, journeying up the Ohio in the fine new steamer *Sultana,* fell into conversation with a traveler from Cincinnati. Talking of the pork business the man abruptly asked: "How many hogs do you think I killed last season?" Lyell guessed three hundred. "Eighteen thousand," was the answer, "and all of them dispatched in thirty-five days." [2] When half a million hogs were slaughtered in 1848, calculation showed they would make a double string of sausages long enough to encircle the globe.

While rubber tires, cash registers, plate glass, and machine tools were yet unknown, Ohio was a cornucopia of agriculture. At Akron, Newark, Lancaster, and a score of other canal towns long lines of farm wagons waited to unload Ohio grain. Canal barges carried wheat to the Ohio River and Lake Erie.

At the mouth of Cold Creek on Sandusky Bay the village of Venice was settled soon after the War of 1812, and the creek was diverted into a millrace. Mills erected there brought a cash

2. Charles Lyell, *A Second Visit to the United States of America,* 2 vols. (New York: Harper & Brothers, 1850), 2:207.

market for Erie County wheat. The first exported flour, a cargo of one hundred barrels, went by way of the Erie Canal to New York, where hundreds of people watched the unloading of the foodstuff from the distant fields of Ohio. More shipments followed, though some of the Venice flour went west, by lake schooner, to the struggling village of Chicago. In the fall of 1836 Oliver Newberry bought five hundred barrels at eight dollars a barrel, selling it in Chicago at twenty dollars a barrel. In a public meeting Chicago settlers thanked him for not asking fifty dollars. The Venice flour got them through a hungry winter. Within a decade Newberry and Dole, Chicago commission merchants, were shipping Illinois grain to Buffalo and the East.

From Lake Erie the Huron River winds inland to the quiet town of Milan. First an Indian settlement under a Moravian missionary pastor, it became a town of Connecticut Yankees in the early 1800s. In 1832 gangs of Irish laborers, newly arrived from the Old Country, began digging a three-mile ditch that bypassed some loops of the serpentine stream. A dam across the dwindling river formed a summit pond to feed the canal basin. Cut through ancient mounds and earthwork, the canal was completed in 1839. On July 4, with banners and band music, the townspeople welcomed the 150-ton schooner *Kewaunee,* and Milan's shipping business began.

Over the roads came thousands of four- and six-horse wagons, trace chains jangling, wheels creaking under mounded loads of wheat. Fourteen warehouses lined the canal basin at the foot of Milan hill. The main wheat road ran up through Ashland, Richland, and Huron counties. At the Oleana crossroads the tavern keeper sometimes kept a hundred teamsters overnight; for fifty cents he gave supper and breakfast to a man and a four-horse team. At the peak of the season 365 wagons waited their turn on the Milan wharves. There the grain went into tall-masted schooners for shipment, via the Erie Canal, to the Eastern states and via the St. Lawrence to Atlantic coastal cities and seaports of Europe. In 1843 a total of 239 vessels loaded at Milan during the navigation season. In 1847 the town's shipment of wheat surpassed 900,000 bushels. In 1855 Ohio shippers boasted that only Odessa on the Black Sea outranked Milan as a world freshwater grain port.

For Milan the wheat bonanza lasted only to the mid-1850s, when the Lake Shore Railroad was laid through Erie County. It took the grain trade east while the Milan wharves decayed and the canal grew green with brush and brambles. No wheat goes out of Milan now, though town planners dream of a restored canal basin beneath the bluff where a white brick cottage stands behind a trim white picket fence. All year long streams of visitors come to see that cottage, where Thomas Alva Edison was born on a snowy February morning in 1847.

The most lasting memory from Edison's boyhood was of playing with friends in a wheat warehouse, where he once fell into a bin on the weighing platform. It was a soft landing, but the boy kept sinking—sinking deeper as he fought against it. His playmates' cries brought a warehouseman who held the boy's head above the surface until help came to dig him out. Years afterward Edison liked to recall the pale glimmer of whale-oil lights in the canal basin and the schooners bound for distant places.

In getting his ground plowed and planted, a man worked alone, but harvest brought neighbors together. For some years the wheat farmers of Champaign County held "cradling bees." Gathered in a ripe field they marched through the golden grain, swinging their scythes in time to a leader's song. The cradle, a kind of basket frame attached to the scythe blade, caught and held the severed grain before laying it in swaths on the stubble. At the end of a round, under a tree, a bucket of water or a jug of whiskey refreshed the reapers. A hazard of harvest was the copperhead, coiled under the swaths of grain or even in the bound sheaves. Hogs, the natural enemy of all snakes, followed the harvest, devouring copperheads with relish. When a porker found a snake, he soon had one end in his mouth and the other under a forefoot. According to William Cooper Howells, the father of Ohio's foremost writer, hogs were active, enterprising, and self-reliant. All they asked was a free range of fields and woods.

The threshing of grain waited until winter, when work had ended in the fields. In a day's work a good man with a flail could beat out ten bushels of wheat on the hard clay floor of his barn. It took all winter to thresh the grain of a ten-acre field, but the work was shortened when horses were used. A team of horses, tramping circles on the barn floor, could thresh 25 bushels in a day. The next step was to farm machines, which came into widespread use in mid-nineteenth-century Ohio.

According to Greek legend, when Hephaestus, the god of forging, wished to make an offering to Demeter, goddess of harvests, he employed the hammer to shape a sickle. After three thousand years it was still a sickle that the Ohio settler used in his hard-won fields. By 1825 the cradle scythe, supplanting the sickle, was increasing a farmer's cut from one acre a day to three or four acres. But it was a hard day's work—as none knew better than Obed Hussey.

Born in Maine of a Quaker family, restless Obed Hussey went to sea as a youth, sailing out of Nantucket. After a few years on salt water he came ashore, wanting to try his hand at farming in the promised land of Ohio. When his farm near Cincinnati produced more grain than he could harvest, while his horses grazed in the pasture, he thought that horsepower should be put to work. All through the winter of 1833 he tinkered with a machine that combined a sawtooth cutting blade with a shelf to catch the severed grain. His neighbors scoffed at the contraption, but Hussey kept right on. At harvest time in 1833 he gave a demonstration for the Hamilton County Agricultural Society. Behind a team of horses his rackety cutting blade went to work. Every hour or so the machine broke down and had to be repaired. Even so, the Agricultural Society gave it a certificate of merit. It was evident that one man on a mower could cut as much grain as ten or twelve field hands with scythe and cradle. Hussey secured a patent on the last day of that year.

When Hussey began manufacture of his machine, Ohio farmers were ready to give it a try, along with the more elaborate McCormick reaper, fitted with wooden reel and raking shelf. In Virginia, Cyrus Hall McCormick had been working with the same conception as that of Obed Hussey; his reaper was patented six months after Hussey's patent. Unknown then to each other the two men were beginning an agricultural revolution that eventually brought all the harvest processes into one mechanical operation. The chattering little mower was the first step on the way to the big combine pouring out a golden stream of grain.

Both Hussey's and McCormick's machines won awards at the London Exposition of 1851. At that time Ohio farm workers protested the mechanical reaper—the first such resistance in the state that would take a lead in farm technology. Actually, the reaper as Hussey developed it required a squad of men—a driver, a raker, several binders, and a final pair to shock the sheaves. These men and six horses could harvest three hundred bushels in a day. As steam engines came into use in the 1850s efficiency and volume increased.

During the Civil War mechanical reapers and threshers made possible a harvest largely done by women and children. In 1863 fifteen thousand mower-reapers were manufactured in Ohio. This figure, prodigious then, was but a beginning. In the next forty years agricultural implements from many Ohio cities went into every state and many nations. By the end of the century, Ohio farm machines were gathering harvests around the world.

This looks like another Ohio success story, but Obed Hussey turned out to be a loser. Though his machine was superior as a mower, other men devised new features for the reaper, improvements that McCormick promptly acquired. Stubborn Obed Hussey would not incorporate new ideas, and he also failed to build a business organization. While the McCormick works expanded in Cincinnati and then in Chicago, Hussey's fortunes declined. In 1858 he sold out and turned to other ventures. He died in a train accident in 1860 while working on a steam plow. By that time McCormick had laid the foundations of the International Harvester Company and of a family dynasty. Success had beckoned in Ohio's golden farmlands, but Obed Hussey missed it.

During their first two years the pioneer people of the Ohio Company pounded corn by hand, as the Indians did. Then an ingenious man, seeing the slack river on the inside of a bend and the strong current on the outside, thought up a floating gristmill and gave it a try. Near Blennerhassett Island he anchored two boats eight feet apart, connecting them by broad beams and a slanted roof. In that mill house he installed a waterwheel and two grindstones, and set the gears in motion. In seasons of brisk current his mill ground fifty bushels of grain a day. He had no tax for ground rent or mill dam, and the river was his millrace. Soon other floating mills were built at Cincinnati and on the Hocking and Scioto rivers.

In the wild territory, mill sites, where high-banked narrow creeks held a stable current, were noted by surveyors and sought by early settlers. The first mill for the Marietta settlement was built in 1790, with millstones bigger than a wagon wheel brought by flatboat from Pittsburgh. The buhrs, too heavy to handle, were levered into the river where a dam had been built near the mouth of Wolf Creek and hauled up by six yoked oxen. By 1850 there were two thousand gristmills in Ohio, and one of them was neatly pictured in McGuffey's newest Primer. "Here is a mill. Do you see the wheel? It is on the side of the mill. The wa-ter falls on the wheel and makes it turn. In the mill they grind grain and make flour for our bread." [3]

The gristmill kept several wooden parts working in unison: the waterwheel, the change gears, the buhrstones, the conveyor, and the screening apparatus. At work it sounded like a heavy wagon creaking and rumbling up a hill. "Observe the motion of the stone by the noise of the damsel," [4] counseled an old miller—the damsel being the spout beneath the hopper. As the buhrs revolved in their opposite directions, the miller on his dusty bench pulled the string of his plumbline, feeding the stream of whole grain from the hopper to the grindstones. The veteran continued:

> All things being set right, the miller's duty is very easy—he has only to see to the machinery, the grinding, and bolting, once an hour; he has therefore plenty of time to amuse himself by reading, or otherwise, rather than going to sleep, which is not safe. [5]

The mood of an old mill was patient and industrious: the steady flowing of the water, the creaking and spilling of the big wheel, the change gears rumbling into cadence. *Going-to-work,*

3. *McGuffey's Eclectic Primer,* p. 41.
4. Oliver Evans, *The Young Millwright and Miller's Guide* (Philadelphia: Carey, Lea and Blanchard, 1836), p. 258.
5. Evans, *Young Millwright,* p. 273.

going-to-work, going-to-work, they repeated—a solid, sober rhythm while the air grew hazed with dust. About 1810 the Welsh settlers at Paddy's Run in Butler County began a circulating library, keeping the books in the gristmill on Dry Fork. It was a convenient place. People came from all directions, and they took home a book or two—Plutarch's *Lives,* Rollins's *Ancient History,* Blair's *Lectures,* Butler's *Analogy*—a fare as wholesome and nourishing as their bag of fresh-ground meal.

As a young man in Rome township in Athens County, John Welch worked in a gristmill, studying law books while the stones were grinding. Once a week he brushed the flour dust from his clothes and walked fourteen miles to recite lessons to a professor at Ohio University. Admitted to the bar, Welch became county attorney, member of the Ohio legislature, United States congressman, judge of common pleas, and finally a justice of Ohio's supreme court. Another miller was Governor Jeremiah Morrow. When he was elected in 1822, a Warren County committee, coming to inform and congratulate him, found the governor-elect waist-deep in his millrace, clearing driftwood from the waterwheel.

One-man mills grew obsolete after the Civil War, when the flouring industry went into huge steam-powered roller mills, in which the grain passed through as many as twenty grindings and two hundred siftings and separations. Then the weathered old mill stood empty and silent, a relic of the simple and seemingly idyllic past. Young Tell Taylor grew up in Hancock County near the old Mesamore Mill on Blanchard Creek. The millstream flowed through his father's farm. Orange jewelweed along the millrace attracted bees and hummingbirds, bobolinks and catbirds sang above the quiet millpond; the little river chuckled to itself on summer evenings. For his own pleasure Taylor wrote the words and music of "Down By the Old Mill Stream." [6] His song, published in 1910, has sold five million copies. Tell Taylor's success was fabulous, and unsought.

The first flatboat cargo loaded in Cincinnati was some barrels of flour destined for New Orleans. By 1860 the city had twenty

6. D. W. Garber, *Waterwheels and Millstones* (Columbus: Ohio Historical Society, c1970), p. 129.

flouring mills, pouring out white wheat flour, farina, steam-dried cornmeal, oil-cake meal, and horse feed. Flour from Ohio mills was then deemed the best in the nation. So enviable was the Ohio name that shipments from the great mills of Minneapolis were labeled "Muskingum Mills, Troy, Ohio."

In the 1870s the proudest ornament of Cincinnati was the Music Hall and Exposition Building. A block-long structure facing the Miami and Erie Canal and Washington Park, it was an edifice of spires and cornices, columned doorways, arched windows, and fretted rooflines. This was the home of the Cincinnati Industrial Exposition of Manufactures, Products, and the Arts. The combining of art and industry was an innovation, but they were already together in Cincinnati, and they could be joined in a public display. Or so the sponsors believed, and they got the city to give it a try.

The first exhibition, filling seven acres of floor space, ran for a month in the fall of 1870. It drew 300,000 visitors and became an annual affair. In 1876, with the national Centennial Exposition in Philadelphia, Cincinnati skipped its show; the director of the Cincinnati enterprise had been named director-general of the Philadelphia celebration. But in that year in Cincinnati an army of workmen was erecting Music Hall as the central structure in the Exposition block. Flanking the great Music Pavilion were twin exhibition buildings, their upper stories connected with the amphitheater by inside bridges. Now the central hall of the enlarged construction had a cathedral look, with twin tapered towers framing a rose window above three tall, arched casements. The Grand Music Hall held 4,600 people, and accommodated 120 orchestra members and a thousand singers on the stage. Five hundred gas jets illuminated the hall, which contained the world's largest organ, with 6,237 pipes, 32 bells, 4 keyboards, and 42 pedal movements. Music swelled in Cincinnati along with the meat-packing business, the brewing industry, and the world's largest printing house, where the presses poured out millions of McGuffey Readers.

In 1880 Cincinnati made news at home and abroad with the Millers' International Exhibition. Europe had tried and failed to organize such an exposition, but Cincinnati succeeded. A huge

Power Hall, decked with the flags of all nations and the mul-
ticolored flour sacks of a hundred companies, was filled with
mills and machines. These made a historical display of milling,
from the rustic mill beside the rural stream to huge roller machines rising to the roof. The exhibit spanned time and countries: buhr millstones from Liverpool, silk bolting cloth from
Zurich, porcelain rollers from London, a disk mill from Germany, grain dryer from Cincinnati, bags and sacks from St.
Louis, machine parts from Dayton, wheat grinders from Indianapolis, piston packing from Glasgow, steam pumps from Cincinnati, elevator buckets from Chicago, on and on and on.

At the close of opening ceremonies on the afternoon of May
31, steam was sent into the massive engines, and thousands of
people watched field wheat become baking flour. In a cool
grotto water poured from a mossy wheel in a thatch-roofed mill,
while the great room throbbed with six two-hundred-horsepower
steam engines. From the Music Hall adjoining came a concert
of the ninety-piece Cincinnati Orchestra. In the Bakers' Hall
visitors devoured biscuits, rolls, and cakes, while prizes were
presented for the best Vienna bread, rye bread, rusks, and pret-
zels. When Washburn's Superlative Flour from Minnesota won
the gold medal a week later, it became Gold Medal Flour for
keeps.

During the Exposition weeks visitors from twenty countries
flocked to Cincinnati's celebrated restaurants. On the brink of
Clifton Heights stood Bellevue House, offering food, drink, and
music, and a sweeping view of the city. Lookout House, at the
head of Main Street on Mount Auburn, had Swiss yodelers and
an eighty-six-piece band tirelessly repeating German waltzes.
On Mount Adams the lavish Highland House accommodated
eight thousand in its dining rooms, beer gardens, and pavilions;
while Theodore Thomas conducted orchestral concerts, people
strolled on promenades above the curving river.

What they saw was a booming, bustling confusion, full of
energy and venture, bursting into song; a restless young society
where men would put new tools and knowledge to work for
private profit or the public good. Below handsome Highland
House lay the dark alleys of Rat Row and Sausage Row, and

squalid Bucktown huddled in the Culvert. Cincinnati was a place of contrasts—hilltop resorts and basin slums, white packet boats and grimy coal barges, concert halls and barrooms, the dark dens of Gamblers' Row and the plashing waters of Fountain Square. Through the city snaked the tawny canal with its commerce of sand boats, pork boats, ice boats from Lake Erie, lumber boats, whiskey and beer boats, boats bringing hay and corn and carrying away famous Cincinnati hams and bacon. Beyond the canal was "Over the Rhine," rich with the smells of German cooking and hearty with the rhythm of German bands. The big friendly Coliseum at Twelfth and Vine offered a German chorus between acrobatic acts and demonstrations of trick shooting, while people washed down hasenpfeffer, sauerbraten, and wienerschnitzel with mugs of malty beer.

The basin streets—Plum, Elm, Vine, Race (originally Millrace), Walnut, Sycamore—had once been forest paths. Now they were cobbled roads with hogs and dogs eating refuse in the gutters. In Church Alley, behind the county jail, were a whipping post and a pillory. At night the long, sad notes of signal horns came up from the landing. There were oaths and cries when police brought brawling rivermen and drunken vagabonds for flogging.

From the Mt. Adams promenade the sun set in a golden haze over the city. Cincinnati was full of music and gaiety, of prosperity and success. A rich Gemütlichkeit filled the air—until the night wind brought a stench of tenements, tanneries, and slaughterhouses. If the visiting merchants and millers wondered about the vaunted democracy of fortunate Ohio, they did not say so. The only criticism came from Herr J. J. Von den Wyngaert, president of the German Millers' Association. He complained of the flat ground flour used by Cincinnati bakers and the limp, tasteless loaves that came from their ovens.

7

To Market, to Market

I N less than a lifetime Ohio was changed from a silent wilderness to a busy state in a fast-growing nation. Its own growth was phenomenal. Between 1800 and 1820 the population multiplied seven times. In hundreds of places the forest became fields, and the fields became a town. Between 1820 and 1845 the population doubled, then doubled again. By 1850 Ohio was the third most populous state in the nation.

Beginning as a land of promise Ohio had, in that short time, become a land of fulfillment. It was a great garden, a huge workshop, a vast storehouse. As the wilderness was tamed, Ohio poured out farm harvests and factory products far beyond the needs of its own multiplying people. That bounty was made possible by a combination, unmatched in any other state or country, of natural resources, human energy and talent, and the great good fortune of being in the mainstream of national expansion.

The frontier state of 1803 became, in half a century, a state in the middle. From the middle it reached outward—to market, to market—with its lake and river transport, its roads, canals, and railroads. Nature gave to Ohio a great lake and a broad river, but men built the vessels that carried goods and people. Geography offered natural corridors for commerce, but men dug the canals and laid the railways.

Having cleared the forest, Ohioans turned to what they called "internal improvements"—a dull name for the excitement of canal and railroad building. In the 1830s and 1840s Ohio burned with canal fever, and when that subsided, a railroad fever began. This urge and excitement was essential to Ohio's coming of age. We can see it at work in one family that left a lasting mark on their adopted state.

In the long June days of 1810 three horsemen rode into Ohio along the Lake Erie shore. Joshua Stow had come west with Moses Cleaveland's exploring party fifteen years before. Now he was guiding two young men who would shape Ohio's future. One was a lanky medical student from Connecticut. Ahead of him in Ohio was a varied career as a pioneer doctor, a renowned naturalist, director of the first Ohio Geological Survey, and founder of an Academy of Science and of the Cleveland Medical College. His name was Jared Kirtland, and his writings on conchology made it known in many lands. The other was Joshua Stow's nephew, a short, compact, determined youth of 20, with a set of law books in his saddlebag. His name was Alfred Kelley. During the next fifty years he would be a dominant figure in the political, financial, and commercial life of the new state.

Throughout their boyhood Alfred Kelley and his brothers had heard their uncle's stories of the Western Reserve. In General Cleaveland's expedition Joshua Stow served as commissary. He doubled as flagman for the surveying crew, a job that took him ahead of the others through the lake shore brush and thickets. Every day he killed several large yellow rattlesnakes and slung them over his shoulder. At suppertime he dressed and cooked them, to the relish of some members of the party. This was recalled years later for the Early Settlers' Association, with the comment that although Joshua Stow "had a positive liking for snake meat . . . Moses Cleaveland was disgusted with snakes, living or cooked, and with those who cooked them." [1] Still, the general held on to his commissary, who kept the men fed when rations ran low.

By 1810 there were schooners on Lake Erie and a traveled

1. *Annals of the Early Settlers Association of Cuyahoga County,* No. 4 (Cleveland: 1883), p. 75.

road along the shore. The settlement of Cleveland had three frame houses and nine log cabins facing the wooded common that would become the public square. Here Alfred Kelley opened Cleveland's first law office, and sent beckoning reports back East. Soon his parents and five brothers joined him in the frontier settlement.

In January 1815, the Kelley brothers opened a general store on stump-filled Superior Avenue. That year Cleveland was incorporated as a village. At the first election twelve votes were cast, four of them by Kelleys, and Alfred Kelley became the village president. He was also elected to the state legislature, its youngest member. (When he retired in 1857 he was its patriarch.) In 1816 the Kelley brothers formed the Commercial Bank of Lake Erie, Alfred Kelley, president, and organized the Cleveland Pier Company. When Irad Kelley became postmaster, the U.S. mail was handled, along with salt, gunpowder, crockery, tea, and lime juice, in the Kelley brothers' emporium—the first brick building in Cleveland.

At that time the ten-acre common was enclosed by a picket fence. Refusing to go around, the direct Kelley brothers climbed the fence and cut across. Time bore them out; in 1867 Cleveland's city square was quartered by intersecting streets. Now its four quadrants are crammed with statues, monuments, a fountain, an information booth, a free-speech rostrum, and a bus station. In old Connecticut the common would have been kept intact, but Ohio people took the shortest way.

While sailing a sloop with merchandise for Detroit, Irad Kelley (his name, from the Old Testament, means "seeker") stopped for shelter at Island Number Six of the Connecticut Land Company's survey. When the back-East owners offered it for sale, Irad and his brother Datus bought the three thousand acres of limestone ledge and cedar forest, naming it Kelleys Island. Eventually the island stone went into buildings and breakwaters at Buffalo and Cleveland and into canal locks at Sault Ste. Marie. The island cedar furnished cross-arms for the first telegraph line to Chicago.

Year after year, traveling between Cleveland and Columbus for legislative sessions, Alfred Kelley saw both bounty and want. On fertile lands people lived in poverty while their harvests went to waste. The newly cleared farms produced more than they could consume, and there was no way to market. A state canal system would make all the difference. Along with Governor Ethan Allen Brown, 1818–1822, and Governor Jeremiah Morrow, 1822–1826, Alfred Kelley shouldered that cause—surveying possible canal routes and weighing the needs, potentials, petitions, and importunings of eastern and western sections of the state. On November 27, 1824, he wrote to his wife:

> I am now very busy in making out maps and plans of our canal lines—constant confinement leaning over a table gives me a little of the headache—but I think this will wear off as I become accustomed to it. . . . None of the other canal commissioners have yet arrived. I think we shall hardly be able to report by the 15th Dec[r]—but we may be." [2]

Two months later the legislature created a Board of Canal Commissioners with power to locate the route and begin construction of two principal canals—one from the Ohio River at Portsmouth to Cleveland on Lake Erie, through the Scioto and Cuyahoga valleys; the other through the Miami Valley from Cincinnati to Dayton, with eventual extension to Toledo on Lake Erie. Alfred Kelley then turned from his profitable law business to become canal commissioner at three dollars a day.

In 1825 Ohio's entire revenue was less than $200,000. The land was rich, but the state was poor. Wheat brought 25 cents a bushel, corn 12½ cents, oats 14 cents, potatoes 18½ cents, pork 2 cents a pound, beef 3 cents, butter 6 cents, eggs 4 cents a dozen, chickens 5 cents each—all to be exchanged in barter. To replace poverty with prosperity required only some means of conveyance. A canal system would irradiate Ohio like a summer sunrise.

On July 4, 1825, after three days of rain, the sun came out in Licking County. Over muddy roads the settlers followed a marching militia company and a troop of cavalry to a field three

2. Abbot Lowell Cummings, *The Alfred Kelley House* (Columbus: Franklin County Historical Society, 1953), p. 42.

miles southeast of Newark. Already gathered there was a restless throng of people, more than that half-wild county seemed to contain. "The commencement of any great public work," Timothy Flint had observed, "causes a rush from the woods and the forests which, like the tenanted trees of the poets in the olden time, seem to have given birth for the occasion to crowds of men, women, and children pouring toward the point of attraction." [3] On that same day a Fourth of July celebration in Van Wert drew seventy-five people to a forest picnic and a speech by the county surveyor, although the entire population of Van Wert County was but forty-nine. [4]

While the crowd at Newark cheered, out of a muddy carriage stepped Governor DeWitt Clinton of New York and Governor Jeremiah Morrow of Ohio. Later that year a cask of Lake Erie water would be taken by way of "Clinton's Ditch" to the Hudson River and ceremoniously emptied into New York harbor. Now burly Governor Clinton dug the first earth for a canal to link the Ohio River with Lake Erie. In prospect was a waterway that would connect the Atlantic seaboard and the huge interior valley. After that first bite of earth Clinton handed the spade to stubby Governor Morrow, who sank it deep—digging ground was more natural to him than running a state. Other officials dug in, filling a wheelbarrow. To the shouts of thousands the first load of earth was trundled up a plank platform to the future canal bank.

Onto that platform stepped strapping Tom Ewing of Lancaster. Already, at thirty-five, Ewing was a man of commanding voice and figure. But on this steamy afternoon his eloquence was wasted. To shield the speakers from the crowd, cavalrymen surrounded the platform, and with them were all the horseflies of Licking County. The stamp and swish of horses outdid Ewing's vision of the Future of the West. Afterward, over mugs of beer in the Newark and Lancaster taverns, reporters passed out copies of Ewing's speech while people reviewed the day's events. Growled Caleb Atwater, whose town of Circleville lay

3. Flint, *History and Geography*, 1:392.
4. Howe, *Historical Collections*, 2:728–730.

on the canal route: "I suppose it was all right to have the horses in front of the speakers' stand, for they cannot read and we can." [5] That ground-breaking had a national press, being reported as far away as Baltimore and Philadelphia. Chaplain for the ceremony was Episcopal Bishop Philander Chase, who after a brief, brisk prayer helped trundle a load of sticky earth. A year later he built a sawmill in the woods of Knox County to cut lumber for the first building of Kenyon College. All over Ohio the future was sprouting.

Two weeks after the Newark ceremony, another gala brought crowds to Middletown, on the Great Miami River. Ohio, giving a double try, was undertaking two canals at once. Construction of the Miami Canal was begun halfway between Cincinnati and Dayton, and again the New York governor was there. On July 21, Clinton's carriage led a procession to a field a mile south of straggling Middletown. On a flag-draped platform he stood between Governor Morrow and General William Henry Harrison. After speeches each man "raised a sod" where the canal would carry the region's commerce. In a jubilant rush Butler County settlers scrambled for that symbolic earth, carrying it home in hats and blouses to their huts and cabins.

Farm land worth five dollars an acre in 1825 brought twenty dollars a few years later, when canal barges—*Governor Morrow* and *General Harrison* among them—loaded Miami Valley wheat, pork, flour, and whiskey. Across the state, land prices climbed like corn in August. Industry, too, was advanced by the canal. Beside the towpath sprang up forges, foundries, lumberyards, salt works, malt works, breweries. In a few years the value of canal front leapt from $15 to $200 an acre. Manifests of the canal trade in the 1840s list an extensive range of products: anvils, ashes, axes . . . bacon, barley, beans, beef, blood, bristles, brooms . . . manure, marble, millstones, molasses . . . starch, staves, stone, straw . . . tallow, tar, tobacco, tombstones.

Behind them the Fourth of July crowd at Newark left trampled fields and a line of stakes half swallowed in brush and

5. Howe, *Historical Collections*, 2:72.

thicket and soon lost in the dense woods. To commissioners, engineers, and contractors that was the line of battle. It marked an avenue over hill and valley, through field and forest, swamp and meadow—a sixty-foot swath to be cleared, a forty-foot ditch to be dug and lined with towpath, 146 locks to lift and lower canal boats, fourteen aqueducts to carry the canal over ravines and rivers.

As an assemblyman Alfred Kelley had pushed canal bills through the legislature. As a canal commissioner he studied surveys, signed contracts, kept accounts, records, and rosters. Now as superintendent of construction, he followed the line, 333 miles from Lake Erie to the Ohio River, through rock and clay, mud and mosquitoes, ice and snow. Where the ditch was dug he prowled the canalbank, poking an iron rod at soft places in the towpath or the fill. He slept in shantytowns, ate with mule drivers and wheelbarrow men, watched over foremen on the job, and guarded the canal fund in Columbus. It was said that no canal in America or Europe was constructed at so low a cost per mile. The strain and exposure broke his health, but the Ohio Canal was built within budget and on schedule.

To build the Roaring Canal, as the work gangs called it, came Irish laborers from Clinton's Ditch. Alongside them worked Ohio farmers and farm boys, glad to be paid for digging their own way to market. On a canal, they were told, one horse could haul as much as thirty horses on a turnpike. They were lodged in movable shanties, fed at long mess tables, rationed a gill of whiskey five times a day against chills and fever. They toiled from dawn to dark for thirty cents a day.

On July 4, 1827, after two years of construction, the first segment of the canal was open. At Akron (the "high place") a line of barges was led by the *State of Ohio,* decked in flags and bunting. On the blunt bow Captain Job Harrington, shading his eyes ship-fashion, blew a horn as the mules leaned into their collars and the towropes came up dripping. The procession passed from Akron to Cleveland, people cheering all the way. At Cleveland crowds lined the riverbank and trailed officials to the public square. That night a canal banquet was followed by toasts to canals, roads, commerce, and progress. After some high-flown speeches came a realistic toast to "The People of the State of Ohio for their accomplishments despite their youth, poverty, diversity, and sectional jealousies." [6] That was Alfred Kelley speaking. He knew the friction and contention, the greed and grasping that underlay the project; he had cut through those obstacles while the engineers dug through swamps and ridges. The canal bypassed more towns than it connected, and Kelley made more enemies than friends. Henry Clay had said of him, "He has too much cast iron in his composition to be popular." [7]

When the canal was completed in 1833, lines of boats waited at every lock. Through morning mist sounded the blaring barge horns, shouts of teamsters, cries of "Lo-o-ow Bridge! Lo-o-ow Bridge!" and the jangle of trace chains on the towpath. From Lake Erie and the East came cloth, shoes, coffee, tea, chocolate, rum, gypsum, paint, and tinware; while other barges loaded Ohio wheat, corn, flour, beef, butter, cheese, tobacco, and whiskey for Eastern markets. To inland towns the canal brought a rash of peddlers. "Like squirrels at moving time," they flocked in, hawking everything from chimney clocks to cure-all medicines and palming off "counterfeit basswood nutmegs when everyone knows the genuine are made from sassafras." [8] With clatter of hammer and saw the canal towns threw up flour mills, woolen mills, packing plants, tanneries, distilleries, foundries, tile and brick yards. Wheat that had gone for twenty-five cents a bushel, in barter, brought seventy-five cents cash on the canal. A large landowner in Pickaway County had let potatoes rot in the ground; now at Circleville he sold them at forty cents a bushel, the first known cash ever received for Buckeye spuds.

In Wayne County, with some of the richest lands in the nation, farmers lived poorly despite their bumper harvests. Said a pioneer settler: "Wooster was the nearest point of trade, but it was a poor place to sell products of any kind. Wheat and flour

6. James C. Bates, *Alfred Kelley: His Life and Work* (Cincinnati: 1888), p. 210.

7. Bates, *Alfred Kelley,* p. 210.

8. Nelson E. Jones, *The Squirrel Hunters of Ohio* (Cincinnati: The R. Clarke Co., 1898), p. 299.

were often hauled to Cleveland, and hogs were driven there, as the nearest market." [9] Into Wooster came a shoeless farmer with a heaped load of wheat; at last he found an interested merchant—who offered two bits a bushel for enough to fill the mudhole in front of his store. But in 1833 Eastern agents were buying wheat, corn, pork, lard, and cheese for shipment to Buffalo, Boston, and New York. On the canalbank the little feet of the big mules bit deeper into the towpath. In a year they moved two million bushels of wheat, 600,000 barrels of pork, 300,000 bushels of corn, 100,000 barrels of salt, 12,000 barrels of whiskey.

Over the inland counties prosperity blew like a warm spring wind. In 1826 the lands of Ohio were valued at $16 million, in 1835 at $75 million, in 1841 at more than $100 million. Then a new version of the state seal showed a canal barge moving past a field of shocked wheat. A picture of Success.

Canal passengers could cross the state, from river to lake, in eighty hours of travel. From the cabin roof they saw a restless country—field pushing back forest, villages stretching into towns, settlements growing at the locks, lines of laden wagons on the roads. In 1834 one of those travelers was Alexander Philip Maximilian, Prince of Wied-Nuwied, returning from a safari on the upper Missouri. Toothless, bearded, bareheaded, his stocky legs encased in greasy trousers, the prince was attended by a burly manservant named Dreidoppel and the young German artist Karl Bodmer. At Portsmouth on June 21 they lugged their baggage onto a canalboat for Cleveland. The luggage included two young grizzly bears in poplar cages; Prince Max and his servant had caught them as cubs in the Yellowstone country and were taking them home to his castle on the Rhine. At feeding time the canal passengers crowded round the cages. In his diary the prince noted that stones for the building of the National Road—from Maryland to the Mississippi—were barged on the canal: a waterway serving a roadway, and more routes to market. At Circleville the prince had time to admire the earthworks that ringed the courthouse and to

9. *History of Wayne County, Ohio*, 2 vols. (Indianapolis: B. F. Bowen & Company, 1910), 1:361.

deplore the destruction of other antiquities. The Ohio he saw was fixed on the future and blind to the past.

In Cincinnati a building lot on the canal basin was sold in 1829 for $18,000. It had been bought for $400 in 1821, and the previous owner had got it a few years earlier for a horse bridle. In Summit County an out-of-step farmer had cursed the canal builders for gouging the big ditch between his pasture and his barn. When the first barge came through, his wife, caught in the crowd at the lock gate, lost her hat in the water. It was a brand-new bonnet, moaned the farmer; he knew the canal would ruin him. A year later he sold the farm for ten times its former value.

One of the Cuyahoga County farmers who labored on the canal ditch for thirty cents a day was a man named Garfield. He died in 1833, leaving an infant son. Growing up on a thirty-acre farm, James Abram Garfield did a man's work between terms in a country schoolhouse. At seventeen he strode into Cleveland and took a job as mule driver on the canal. He made fourteen dollars a month, and according to later reminiscence he fell fourteen times into the canal, making fourteen miraculous escapes from drowning, as he could not swim a stroke. That venture ended after two months, when he went home shaking with malaria. Thirty-three years later he was inaugurated President of the United States. After six months in office an assassin's bullet made a martyr of him, and twelve Garfield biographies appeared within two years. The most popular one, *From the Towpath to the White House,* traded heavily on his brief role as a canal boy.

At Canal Fulton in Summit County, Canal Street was lined with stores that had rear loading platforms on the water. Barge captains bought provisions and mule feed there, frequently on credit. On the next trip the barge might be renamed, the *Sam Duley* becoming the *Rocket,* and the *Water Witch* the *Nightingale,* and so pass through unrecognized by creditors. Here on summer days town boys would drop off the overhead bridge onto southbound canalboats, riding to the lock a mile distant. As the return trip, on loaded barges, took twice as long, the boys generally walked back on the towpath. They could stop to swim and catch a few turtles and still beat the northbound boat to town.

The last part of Ohio to be settled was the northwest corner of the state, long labeled on the maps *Black Swamp*. An area the size of Connecticut, all dense, dark forest with miles of bog and marshland, it was lifeless until mid-nineteenth century. Canal building in the Maumee Valley drained some of it. Middle Europeans, brought in for canal labor, were the first settlers; when canal work ended, they meant to farm there. Surveyors said it was hopeless, but these people, unable to read survey reports, didn't know any better than to give it a try. Exchanging shovel and wheelbarrow for ax and mattock, they chopped their way in, and for the first time ever, sunlight warmed the rich black earth. Along their drainage ditches these people grew vast beds of onions, and canal boats took the crop to market. Settlements grew up around church and school. In one of those towns in the mid-twentieth century a speaker at the high school commencement handed diplomas to thirty-two graduates—eager, erect, and smiling—without an Anglo-Saxon name in the class. These were descendants of the illiterate laborers who had turned the Black Swamp into a fruitful homeland. Now the rural mailboxes are neatly lettered with inviting names: Fair Field, Willow Bend, Long Furrows, Meadow Brook, Sunrise Acres, Bobolink Dale, All's Well Farm.

In the summer of 1975 when the American Freedom Train with a collection of national artifacts began its Bicentennial tour, interest and response were spotty. In Boston an average day's attendance was not quite 11,000. But in Archbold, Ohio, a brisk and airy town of 3,200 people in the former swampland, 40,000 thronged the train during a two-day stop. Having made a dark morass into a sunlit garden, these people did not take America for granted.

At present Ohio has more miles of railroad track, in proportion to its area, than any other state. Some of those rails are idle and rusting, while trucks haul freight over the high-speed highways and jet planes carry passengers far above. But a big bulk commerce—in coal, grain, chemicals, and machinery—goes by rail to every corner of the state. The old steam locomotive, with clanging bell and wailing whistle, endures only in memory, while diesel-driven trains, up to 150 cars long, roll through heartland Ohio. Because of Ohio's strategic location and level terrain much of the nation's east-west transportation passes through the state.

The first railroads in Ohio were stub lines running north and south, connecting inland counties with the river and the lake. At Sandusky (disappointed in its bid for a canal terminus) on a September morning in 1835 a procession formed at the Steamboat Hotel, while cannon boomed over the harbor. Between ranks of the Sandusky Rifle Corps and some feathered chiefs of the Wyandot nation, marched officials of the projected Mad River and Lake Erie Railroad. At the East Battery, after prayer and oratory, Generals William Henry Harrison and Joseph Vance dug the first spades of earth on the roadbed that would eventually extend to Dayton and Cincinnati.

After that lively ceremony came the lagging business of construction. During six years of sporadic labor, track crews laid thirty-eight miles of railroad. Its pioneer locomotive, the *Sandusky,* arrived by lake steamer in 1842 and began a daily run between Sandusky and Tiffin. One of its first passengers was Charles Dickens, rounding out his American tour. He reported that the train was very slow—it took five hours to go thirty-eight miles. Even so, the iron horse did better than canal mules.

During the 1850s railroads excited Ohio people as canals had done a generation earlier. After thirty surging years Ohio farm and factory production had outstripped the capacity of mule teams and tow barges. The man who had fostered Ohio's canal system then became the state's foremost railroad builder.

In 1845 a company was organized to build a railroad from Columbus to Xenia. To get construction started the officials turned to Alfred Kelley, naming him president. For three years he divided his life between Ohio and the East, trying to give some attention to his wife and nine children while directing surveys and contracts, selling bonds, and raising capital. The road was built with cedar cross-ties and a heavy T rail, the first such rails used in the state. Traffic began in February 1850. In 1847 a railroad had been projected from Cleveland to Columbus, but subscriptions lagged. Again the promoters turned to Kelley.

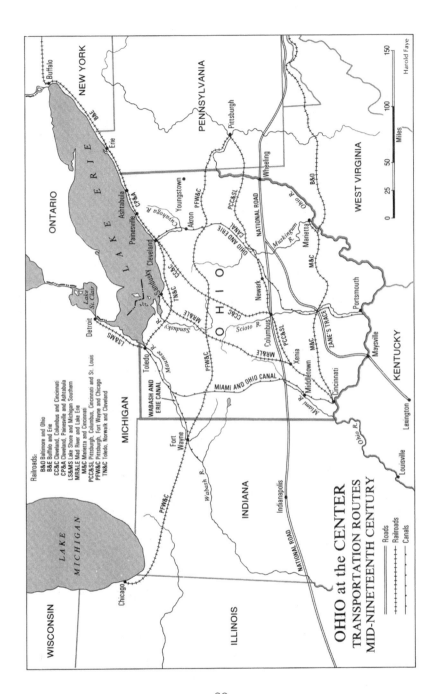

OHIO at the CENTER
TRANSPORTATION ROUTES
MID-NINETEENTH CENTURY

Railroads:

B&O Baltimore and Ohio
B&E Buffalo and Erie
CC&C Cleveland, Columbus and Cincinnati
CP&A Cleveland, Painesville and Ashtabula
LS&MS Lake Shore and Michigan Southern
MR&LE Mad River and Lake Erie
M&C Marietta and Cincinnati
PCC&SL Pittsburgh, Columbus, Cincinnati and St. Louis
PFW&C Pittsburgh, Fort Wayne and Chicago
TN&C Toledo, Norwalk and Cleveland

——— Roads
+++++++ Railroads
++++ Canals

Harold Faye

0   25   50   100   150
Miles

After declining the presidency, he reconsidered, judging that project vital to the state's continued progress. Promptly the line was located, 145 miles across northern Ohio, and construction was embraced in a single contract. While teamsters with scoop shovels graded the roadbed, Kelley was in Wales buying railroad iron. The first train ran, with whistle shrilling, on Washington's birthday, 1851.

Meanwhile the Cleveland, Painesville and Ashtabula Railroad Company was authorized to build to the Pennsylvania border. Alfred Kelley was made president. This was his most complex undertaking, as it involved problems with the city of Erie, Pennsylvania, and the state of New York. At a crisis Kelley bought, personally, five miles of disputed right-of-way and built that much of the road as sole proprietor. He then conveyed his segment to the corporation. In 1854 trains ran from Cincinnati to Cleveland, and from Cleveland to New York, and Kelley ended nine strenuous years of railroad building. When Alfred Kelley had become mayor of Cleveland village in 1814, wolves lurked in the streets and bears invaded gardens and barnyards. Now, at mid-century, it was a stretching young city. Like a gangly boy, its voice was changing; the canal horns and chanteys of the schoonermen were giving way to the steamer's chorded whistle, the engine's clanking, and the thump and thud of freight cars in the railroad yards.

Time winnows the successes from the failures. The losers are forgotten, while the winners endure. When Ohio was crisscrossed with railroads, many towns prospered but others withered on the backroads vine. Some settlements moved to the railroad, abandoning an old site and laying out a new one that straddled the track. But more railroads were outlined on paper than were laid on a right-of-way; there were more promises than fulfillments. Adams County, for example, between Cincinnati and Portsmouth, with good timberlands and productive soil, named its hopeful county seat West Union. Now the entire county contains but nineteen thousand people, and West Union has a bare nineteen hundred. It is recorded that in 1885 West Union boasted of being the only Ohio county seat without a railroad line. That wry boast was left from a long lament when Adams County people waited decade after decade to hear the train blow.

To south central Ohio the railroad fever brought sham, failure, and blind opportunism before the first train ran. The "Iron Railroad" was chartered in Jackson County in 1849. In this district, where Ohio's heavy industry began, the railroad was expected to bring in coal and carry out iron from the local furnaces. In 1851 outside promoters began selling stock to leading citizens, and the furnacemen stacked their pigs of iron along the proposed right-of-way. Business was waiting. As a civic example the county commissioners bought reams of stock in the phantom project. They never saw the railroad, but the certificates were worth twenty-five cents a bushel at a paper mill. Eventually the Ohio Southern Railway kept the promise broken by the phantom "Iron" line, and Jackson County had a route to market.

In "The Lost Farm" the Columbus poet John J. Piatt traced a familiar evolution: woods, field, village, town. Then came the greatest change.

> . . . and now behold,
> A wild strange rumor through the country roll'd.
> A railroad was projected East and West
> Which would not slight us, so the shrewd ones guess'd.
> Strange men with chain and compass came at last,
> Among the hills, across the valley pass'd.[10]

When surveyors were followed by construction crews, some farmers resisted, while others saw progress and improvement ahead. A few more years brought a second railroad, north and south, this time. The town's sawmill and gristmill were replaced by factories. Chimneys smudged the Ohio sky. Engines whistled over the old fording place in the stream. Then the idyllic lost farm lay underneath the city where the railroads crossed.

10. John J. Piatt, *Idyls and Lyrics of the Ohio Valley* (Boston: Houghton Mifflin and Company, 1888), p. 80.

When the locomotive, trailing smoke and steam, had outrun the plodding canal commerce, McGuffey's First Reader took notice. Lesson 13 of a new issue cautioned: "Take care, John; the train is coming." [11]

11. *McGuffey's Alternate First Reader* (Cincinnati: The American Book Company, 1887), p. 21.

8

State in the Middle

IVEN its place as a middle ground in the nation, Ohio had unmatched advantages for growth, progress, and prosperity. But the middle ground was not enviable in the years of crisis and conflict that tested the federal Union. Like the nation, Ohio in mid-nineteenth century was divided. It included some of America's most ardent unionists and most adamant states'-rights men. The northern counties, then predominantly of New England population, were imbued with abolition zeal; that part of Ohio felt far removed from the Southern states. But Ohio's southern counties shared a long border, 436 miles of river frontage, that faced the slave states of Virginia and Kentucky. From southeastern Ohio came Clement Vallandigham, leader of the Peace Democrats, who defended states' rights and opposed the Civil War. Cincinnati had strong ties with the South—commercial, cultural, even family ties. Yet—so torn was the middle state—Cincinnati was a center of the Underground Railroad and the home of Levi Coffin, its leading organizer. Oberlin College, a stronghold of antislavery influence, brought together abolition-minded scholars from both northern and southern Ohio. When protracted debates at Lane Seminary in Cincinnati provoked animosity there, a number of students and a faculty leader moved north to Oberlin, where in 1835 the doors were opened to black as well as white students.

In 1855, when "bleeding Kansas" became a testing place for

free- or slave-statehood, Ohio's John Brown, a Summit County
sheep farmer, felt called by God to join the antislavery settlers
in Kansas and to take a bloody part in their local civil war.
Back in Ohio, Brown gathered the small band that slipped into
Virginia and seized the federal arsenal at Harpers Ferry. That
fanatical action was applauded in the Western Reserve; when
Brown went on trial in Virginia, Cleveland lawyers conducted
his defense and great gatherings extolled him. Many Ohioans,
like millions in the Northern states, deplored Brown's violence,
while the abolitionists made him a martyr.

In the state contest of 1860 the election of a Republican governor showed that Ohio would uphold the federal authority.
When war began in the middle of April 1861, volunteers
streamed into Columbus, chanting "Union! Union! Union!"
That was the beginning of a massive war effort, which touched
almost every family in the state. More than 300,000 Ohio soldiers served on Civil War battlefields, the greatest number, in
proportion to population, in the Northern states. Inevitably there
were desertions and defections, thousands of them, but through
four wrenching years Union support prevailed in Ohio. In army
ranks and field headquarters, and in the federal administration in
Washington, Ohio men filled vital roles. Ohio women formed
the first soldiers'-aid societies (predecessor to the Red Cross),
carrying on relief work and helping to fit out a fleet of hospital
boats on the Ohio River. Those activities led to similar efforts in
other Northern states. Within Ohio three strong, courageous governors—William Dennison, David Tod, and John Brough—led
the state through years of turmoil and decision.

In 1835 William Neil began a 36-hour stage schedule between the Ohio capital (population 5,000) and Cincinnati. Neil
had come from Kentucky, with a knowledge of horses and
coaches, teamsters and taverns. In Ohio he developed stage lines
that crisscrossed the state. By 1840 his drivers were carrying
mail and passengers over 1,500 miles of road, with Columbus
as a center. Across High Street from the statehouse he built a
comfortable and friendly inn that became a favorite lodging
place for Ohio businessmen and legislators.

One of the Neil House lodgers was William Dennison, a tall and handsome young lawyer from Cincinnati, ready to try his fortunes in the capital city. His fortunes were good. He soon married Ann Neil, the proprietor's daughter, and began to rise in the city's commercial and political life. During a term as state senator, 1848–1850, he worked for reform of Ohio's "Black Laws" and for abolition of slavery in the District of Columbia. Resuming business, he became president of the Exchange Bank, a keystone in the state's financial structure, and succeeded Alfred Kelley as president of the Columbus and Xenia Railroad. While linking that line with the Little Miami Railway that had pushed up from Cincinnati, he organized the Hocking Valley Railroad to bring southern Ohio coal to the central and northern counties. By the mid-1850s Dennison's steam trains were putting his father-in-law's stage lines out of business.

In 1859 Dennison was named Republican candidate for governor of Ohio. After a campaign heightened by increasing national tensions, he was elected in a close vote. His inaugural address in January 1860 denounced secessionist movements and opposed extension of slavery into the western territories. That winter he met with legislators of Kentucky and Tennessee, defining the common interests of the border states and promising Ohio's co-operation. The promise was strained when Kentucky asked for the prosecution of people who aided fugitive slaves and Virginia demanded extradition of John Brown's raiders. The new governor did not comply.

At the Republican convention in Chicago that May, Ohio's delegates lined up behind three presidential candidates— William H. Seward of New York and ex-Governor Salmon P. Chase and Senator Benjamin Wade of their own state. On the fourth ballot Ohio swung to Lincoln, and bedlam erupted in the cavernous convention hall. Dennison returned to Columbus to work for Lincoln's election. In November Ohio gave Lincoln a plurality of 40,000.

In Ohio, however, as in the nation, there was a clash of feelings. The southern counties had cultural and economic ties with Kentucky and the slave South; the northern counties, imbued with New England tradition, were strongly antislavery. In some measure the National Road, through Zanesville, Columbus, and Springfield, was the state's Mason-Dixon Line. Yet abolitionism smoldered and flared along the Ohio River. Levi Coffin and Harriet Beecher Stowe lived for years within sight of the Kentucky hills, and the Underground Railroad, aiding the escape of fugitive slaves, made a network of lines from the river to Lake Erie. As tension grew in the early weeks of 1861, the first Ohioan, foreseeing mortal strife ahead, offered his services, in any capacity, to Governor Dennison. Not an impulsive youth but an able and accomplished man, the volunteer was Lorin Andrews, president of Kenyon College in the heart of Ohio. When war began, he organized a militia company in Knox County, was commissioned colonel, and led the Fourth Ohio Infantry into western Virginia and the first military combat of North and South. Fatigue and hardship broke Andrews's health. Invalided back to Gambier, Ohio, he died in September 1861, at the age of forty-two.

At the outbreak of war, without plans from Washington and the War Department, military authority and strategy had fallen into Governor Dennison's hands. He ordered militia troops, not yet mustered into United States service, into the western counties of Virginia to support the unionists there and push back Confederate troops over the mountains. "Ohio," he declared, "must lead throughout the war." [1] In three months the campaign succeeded, so that, as Whitelaw Reid wrote: "West Virginia was the gift of Ohio, through her State militia, to the Nation at the outset of war." [2]

Actually, the gift was not quite so freely given. During the campaign it was expected, both in Washington and in Columbus, that the War Department would federalize the Ohio troops. But when the camp-stained regiments returned, they found no paymasters and no muster-rolls. Nine thousand men went home unpaid, and the blame was heaped upon Ohio's governor. Eventually the troops were compensated.

1. Whitelaw Reid, *Ohio in the War*, 2 vols. (Columbus: Eclectic Publishing Company, 1893), 1:45.
2. Reid, *Ohio in the War*, 1:45.

For a decade Ohio men—Senator Benjamin Tappan and Congressman Joshua R. Giddings, both influential Free Soilers, Judge Benjamin F. Wade, vehement critic of the Fugitive Slave Law, and Senator Salmon P. Chase—had been political leaders in the antislavery movement. In 1852 a Boston publisher had brought out a book by a diminutive woman who said, "I hope it will make enough so that I may have a silk dress." [3] Ten years later she was greeted in the White House by a gravely smiling president: "So you're the little woman who wrote the book that made this great war." [4] Through the mail Harriet Beecher Stowe had received a pair of Negro ears from an anonymous reader who loathed her beliefs. In fact, during eighteen years in Cincinnati she had never joined the Abolition Society, objecting to its vehemence and violence, though she foresaw the nation's agonizing conflict. She had known Kentucky families that treated slaves with trust and kindness. But in her novel she pictured Eliza fleeing with her child across the ice-clogged river, and the patient, submissive Tom sold to a Red River plantation where he died of brutality. At this point the novelist cried out: "Farmers of rich and joyous Ohio, and ye of the wide prairie states, answer— Is this a thing for you to protect and countenance?" [5] The book concluded with a somber prophecy: "Not surer is the eternal law by which the millstone sinks in the ocean than the stronger law by which injustice and cruelty shall bring on nations the wrath of Almighty God!" [6]

On April 12, 1861, President Lincoln called for 75,000 volunteers, of which Ohio's quota was 13,000. In response 30,000 men streamed into Columbus. With fife and drum, militia companies choked the streets, and aimless men massed on the trampled statehouse grounds. Inside was the governor, overwhelmed

3. *Ohio Authors and their Books,* edited by William Coyle (Cleveland: The World Publishing Company, 1962), p. 605.

4. Carl Sandburg, *Abraham Lincoln: The War Years,* 4 vols. (New York: Harcourt, Brace and Company, 1939), 2:592.

5. Harriet Beecher Stowe, *Uncle Tom's Cabin or, Life Among the Lowly,* edited by Kenneth S. Lynn (Cambridge: Harvard University Press, 1962), p. 456.

6. Stowe, *Uncle Tom,* p. 460.

with problems. Where could the men be quartered? How could they be fed? What could be done with this inchoate army? The first answer was hotels, soon filled to overflowing. Then a sprawling camp was staked out in pasture and woodland beyond the railroad depot. There, at Camp Jackson, thousands of would-be soldiers stood in soup lines, slept in makeshift shelters, and waited for regimental organization and the issue of uniforms and weapons. While more men thronged in, Ohio newspapers urged that troops be sent at once to defend the national capital and crush the rebellion in a single battle.

Among the first volunteers was a young graduate of West Point who had just ended a tour as topographical engineer in a survey of the northern Great Lakes and taken up civilian life. Welcomed by Governor Dennison, Lieutenant Orlando M. Poe enrolled two regiments that, without uniforms and arms, entrained for Washington. After some quick survey of exposed points on the Ohio River, Poe joined General McClellan's staff, as topographical engineer, in the West Virginia campaign.

Born in Stark County, Ohio, Lieutenant Poe came from a notable pioneer family. His grandfather, Adam Poe, a farmer and tanner in Columbiana County, once took on five drunken Indians who were threatening his house. He sent his wife and children to the cornfield, saying: "There is a fight and more fun ahead," [7] then dropped the gun and grappled, bare-handed, with the intruders. In ten minutes he had felled all five of them, thrown them over the fence, and called his family back. As a small boy Orlando Poe heard from his grandfather many stories of the Indian wars. Now a larger war had come. Entering the regular service, he was assigned to engineering duty with the Army of the Cumberland. In 1864, declining command of a brigade, he became General Sherman's chief engineer in the Georgia campaign. After the war, as a general officer in the Corps of Engineers he built lighthouses on Lake Superior and canal locks at Sault Ste. Marie. Now, eighty years after his death, the great new Poe Lock, twelve hundred feet long and thirty-one feet deep, replaces the old lock that General Poe himself designed.

7. Howe, *Historical Collections*, 2:837.

On April 16, 1861, Governor Dennison had asked the Ohio legislators to appropriate funds for mobilization. Within three days the assembly authorized a war loan of one million dollars. The banks responded promptly, but Dennison encouraged private subscription so that the war effort would be broadly shared and supported. Further legislation empowered the governor to raise new troops, provide arms and equipment, reorganize the militia, and appoint general officers. On May 13 the assembly adjourned, leaving the governor with endless problems of mobilization.

Although Ohio would eventually give the Union its greatest generals, there was no military leadership in the state when war began. The governor's military staff, inherited from former administrations, had neither experience nor ability. Dennison asked the secretary of War to send him a West Point man, but the War Department had unfilled needs of its own. George B. McClellan, a West Point graduate of 1846, had resigned from the army in 1857 to become chief engineer of the Illinois Central Railroad. Three years later he was president of the Ohio and Mississippi Railroad, with headquarters in Cincinnati. To him Dennison turned, and on April 23, 1861, McClellan took command of all Ohio troops, both militia and volunteers. Another West Point graduate was William Rosecrans, of Delaware County, Ohio, who had left the army for a business career; in 1861 he had charge of an oil refinery in Cincinnati. He was made aide-de-camp to General McClellan, succeeding him, when McClellan was called to Washington, as commanding general of the Department of the Ohio. The two men were together in the West Virginia campaign.

Camp Jackson, the makeshift staging ground on the edge of Columbus, was soon returned to the farmers and their cattle. At the end of April a huge training camp was staked out along the Little Miami River a few miles northeast of Cincinnati. The first recruits trudged in during a downpour that made the place a swamp. Without cooks and adequate commissary the men put together their own crude meals, using well water from beside a slaughterhouse. Disease and misery filled this wretched Camp Dennison—so named by General McClellan. The governor got blamed for that, though he had no more authority there than did the irate editors across the state; Camp Dennison was a federal base under federal control. Its location was meant to provide protection for Cincinnati, under threat from across the river. Two years later the garrison was tested by Morgan's rebel cavalry on its dash through southern Ohio. At sunrise on a July morning the rebel horsemen skirted Camp Dennison and skirmished with its pickets. Racing on eastward, they left a rosy pillar of smoke from a burning corral of government wagons.

As a leader in the border states Dennison proposed uniting the troops of Ohio, Indiana, and Illinois, and so extending the Ohio Department from West Virginia to the Mississippi. In May 1861, he met with the other governors in Indianapolis. They were three strikingly impressive men—Dennison, tall, slender, distinguished, a man of courtly bearing; Oliver P. Morton of Indiana, big, broad, with bristling beard and a resounding voice; Richard Yates of Illinois, affable and impulsive, a stalwart man with confident smile and lighted eyes under a mane of curly hair. In years past they had been enrolled in the same Ohio college—Miami University—though of separate classes. At this meeting they proposed a western campaign that would keep the war from their borders and hearten the loyalists below the Ohio River. This recommendation, jointly signed, was sent to Washington. Months passed without decision there, but eventually the western troops were merged into the rugged Army of the Cumberland that fought decisive battles in Tennessee.

The first year of war, however, was a time of fumbling and frustration. Ohio had sent more than 100,000 men into the federal forces in 1861, but the next year recruiting lagged and war support faltered. In that disillusionment the Peace Democrats emerged as angry rivals to Ohio's Union Party, a coalition of Republicans and war-supporting Democrats. Leader of the Peace Democrats—Copperheads to their opponents—was a strong, brave, eloquent and dogmatic man, Clement L. Vallandigham, a congressman from the Dayton district. From the beginning of the war he had argued for peace by conciliation, urging all-out resistance to the Lincoln administration and its policies. Proud of his Virginia ancestry, Vallandigham predicted a Southern victory. To Union supporters he declared: "Defeat, debt, taxation, sepulchres, these are your trophies." [8]

In the chilly spring of 1863 Union military fortunes sagged, and the Copperhead movement was growing stronger. To silence its spokesman, General Ambrose Burnside, commanding at Cincinnati, issued Order 38, calling for the arrest of treasonous dissenters. Taken from his home in Dayton, Vallandigham was confined in Cincinnati's luxurious Burnet House—which he called a military bastille. President Lincoln, seeing that martyrdom would enlarge Vallandigham's following, ordered him released to the Confederacy—let the Rebels have their eloquent advocate.

Under Union Army escort, Vallandigham was put aboard a special train to Murfreesboro, Tenn., where armies of North and South were poised and preparing for battle. At midnight he was delivered to General Rosecrans and carried in a spring wagon past the sleeping camps of ten thousand Federal troops to General Braxton Bragg's headquarters. It was a bizarrely dramatic episode, as seen by the correspondent of the *Cincinnati Gazette:*

> Guard after guard, picket after picket, sentinel upon sentinel, was passed, the magic countersign opening the gates in the walls of living men which, circle behind circle, surrounded the town of Murfreesboro. The men on guard stood looking in silent wonder at the unwonted spectacle, little thinking that they were gazing on the great copperhead on his way through the lines. [9]

A few weeks later Vallandigham went to Bermuda on a Confederate blockade runner. From there he sailed to Canada, settling in Windsor, across the river from Detroit. In Columbus in 1864 a frenzied convention of Peace Democrats nominated him for governor. From Canada he conducted a correspondence campaign, and the outcome was watched by North and South alike. In army camps in Tennessee the Union and Rebel soldiers followed Ohio's elections, shouting news across their picket lines. The final word came with the rainy daybreak of October

---

8. *The American Heritage Picture History of the Civil War* (New York: American Heritage Publishing Company, 1960), p. 497.

9. Howe, *Historical Collections,* 1:443.

14, 1863—in a landslide vote Vallandigham was defeated by the rugged Republican John Brough—and cheering rose from every tent in the Union army camps. In Washington, Lincoln remained all night beside the telegraph, watching the Ohio returns. At five o'clock in the morning, Brough wired that his majority would exceed 100,000. Lincoln replied: "Glory to God in the Highest. Ohio has saved the Nation." [10]

In April 1864, Brough and three other western governors conferred with Lincoln in the White House. Grant, about to begin his massive move toward Richmond, was asking for support troops to follow. At Brough's prompting, the four governors proposed to send 100-day militiamen for patrol duty around Washington's forts and railroads, releasing army regiments for duty in the field. Lincoln directed Secretary Stanton to expedite this plan, under which Ohio sent 34,000 men for 100 days' service. By then, three out of every five Ohio men between 18 and 45 were serving in the Union forces.

John Brough was a big bull of a man with driving energy, but his strength had limits. In June 1864, after working all night in the governor's office, he stumbled in the statehouse yard, bruising his foot and spraining the ankle. Leaning his great weight on a cane caused inflammation, with gangrene gathering in both hand and foot. After prolonged suffering he died in August 1865. But he had seen the Union preserved.

While Vallandigham had voiced the strongest opposition to the Union, the sharpest rejoinder came from an Ohio editor in the town of Findlay. David Ross Locke was never a household name in the state or the nation, but "Petroleum Vesuvius Nasby" became known across the land. A grandson of a member of the Boston Tea Party and son of a soldier in the War of 1812, Locke had begun a printer's apprenticeship in upstate New York at the age of ten. At seventeen he set out as a journeyman printer. He ended up in Ohio, where in 1861 he began editing *The Jeffersonian* in Findlay, the small-town seat of Hancock County. For that obscure paper he wrote the famous Nasby

10. Daniel J. Ryan, "Lincoln and Ohio," *Ohio Archaeological and Historical Publications* 32(1923):212.

Letters, which became a powerful influence in supporting the Lincoln administration. Crude, ignorant, grasping, hypocritical, "Rev. Petroleum Vesuvius Nasby" damned the cause of the South by espousing it. Beginning with the comic secession of an Ohio village, the letters went on to a scathing satire of the Copperhead leaders and their movement. Widely reprinted, they quickly won a national audience. Lincoln read and re-read the Letters till he knew them by heart; his copy of *The Nasby Papers* (Indianapolis, 1864) is now in the Library of Congress.

In 1861 David Ross Locke had volunteered for army service, but Governor Dennison persuaded him to go on serving the Union as a journalist. After the war he became editor of the *Toledo Blade*. For a time he was a popular figure, along with Mark Twain and Josh Billings, on the lecture platform. But he is best remembered for his creation of the windy, illiterate, know-nothing Copperhead preacher. According to Locke, that scoundrelly character was modeled on a Findlay loafer who spent his time cadging drinks and slandering Negroes; his home, Wingert Corners, was an actual hamlet in Crawford County notorious for its antiabolitionism. In a speech at the end of the war Congressman George S. Boutwell of Massachusetts said the Union had been saved by three forces: the army, the navy, and the *Nasby Papers*.

Although the war had cut off Ohio's rich trade with the South, it spurred and broadened the state's industry. Shipyards launched new vessels and sheathed old ones with armor plating and artillery. Wagon works turned out ambulances, hospital beds, wheelchairs, and crutches. Factories poured out stoves, lanterns, mess kits, shoes, uniforms, knapsacks, tents, saddles, and harness. From packing plants came endless barrels of beef, pork, and lard for the army quartermasters. Farm implements plowed, planted, and harvested Ohio fields. Foundries produced caissons, gun carriages, and wheeled cannon. Always an energetic city, Cincinnati developed new drive and muscle with the demands of war. One contract called for eighty barges and 160 wagons within twenty days; they were delivered in a week and a half. At the Eagle Iron Works 60,000 muskets were modernized; a retooled weapon came off the line every fifty seconds. By the end of the war Cincinnati was spreading from the river basin onto its arc of hills.

Of the 320,000 Ohio soldiers who served on battlefields in every theater of the war, a few have been vividly remembered in Ohio folklore. From eastern Ohio came the Fighting Mc-Cooks, a Scotch-Irish family that gave seventeen men to the Union forces. Private Charles McCook was killed at Bull Run when he and the war were young. All the others served in many campaigns, with rank from chaplain and surgeon to major general. One was killed at Buffington Island in the battle with Morgan's raiders. One, lying wounded in an ambulance, was shot by guerrillas in Alabama. One died at the head of his brigade on Kenesaw Mountain. The surviving McCooks had eminent careers in the expanding nation: an acting governor of Dakota Territory, a two-term governor of Colorado Territory, a secretary of the U.S. Senate, an attorney general of Ohio, a theologian and entomologist, a professor of Modern Languages at Trinity College. Colonel George McCook, a law partner of Edwin M. Stanton and later the Democratic nominee for governor of Ohio, had been a schoolmate of Clement Vallandigham in Lisbon, Ohio, when baa-ing flocks of sheep passed through the peaceful town on the way to the river landing.

Along with its great generals Ohio has remembered its youngest and smallest soldier, the Drummer Boy of Shiloh. Now in the *Ohio Almanac* in the roster of "Great Ohioans of the Past" his name appears between Chief Justice Salmon P. Chase and Physicist Arthur H. Compton.[11]

In Newark, Ohio, Johnny Clem peddled his father's vegetables from door to door. In the spring of 1861 when all his customers were talking about the call for volunteers, Johnny was nine and small for his age. He made a drum out of an old keg and whittled a pair of drumsticks, but no one in Ohio seemed less likely to become a war hero than this undersized boy.

On a mid-May Sunday, a month after the attack on Fort Sum-

11. *Ohio Almanac* (Lorain, Ohio, 1970), pp. 22–23.

ter, Johnny announced at breakfast that he would like mighty well to be a drummer boy. His father reminded him that he was not yet ten, and his mother sent him off to Sunday School with his youngest sister and brother in tow. (Fifteen years later that brother, Lewis Clem, was massacred with Custer on the Little Big Horn.) Johnny left them at the church door, having taken a notion to go swimming in the canal. He did not return.

Instead of going swimming Johnny went to the railroad depot and worked a train conductor for a ride to Columbus, where he enlisted as a drummer. He was too young to be mustered in, but the men made a mascot of him.

During the next four years Johnny saw the fury of war. His first battles were Rich Mountain and Carrick's Ford. When spring came to the Tennessee Valley, two great armies clashed on Easter Sunday, and Johnny's drum was shattered by a shell-burst in Shiloh churchyard. After that, with a new drum, he was Johnny Shiloh. At war's end, wearing a Grand Army medal, he returned to Newark and went back to grammar school.

Johnny was a success story when success was sorely needed. This undersized child of Rhineland immigrants was said to be a favorite with Generals Grant, Rosecrans, and George H. Thomas, "the Rock of Chickamauga." After Johnny was nicked by a rifle bullet, Chief Justice Salmon P. Chase sent him an inscribed medallion. If there was more folklore than fact in the stories, that only enlarged his reputation. Folk-say travels faster and farther than army bulletins.

The drummer boy was easier to identify with than the War secretary and the commanding generals. To countless people Johnny Clem was an embodiment of their own unformulated patriotism. Something in them marched to that small drum—the sense of duty that New Englanders had brought over the eastern mountains, the nerve and mettle of the Irish immigrants, the love of liberty that led German settlers to Ohio, and, most of all, the widely shared belief of Ohio people in the future of a united nation.

To the World's Fair in Chicago in 1893 Ohio sent the monument—now on the State House grounds in Columbus—of seven leaders in the Civil War. On a granite pedestal stand the bronze figures of Ulysses S. Grant, William T. Sherman, Philip H. Sheridan, Edwin M. Stanton, Salmon P. Chase, James A. Garfield, and Rutherford B. Hayes. Two were generals who became presidents. Two were colleagues in Lincoln's cabinet. Three were Union generals who in the welter of war rose to greatness. All had grown up in Ohio.

On the pedestal they stand passive in rumpled army dress, but Sherman, Sheridan, and Grant were three men of action, wholly different from each other except in remorseless determination and a willingness to risk greatly for great ends.

Sherman, lean and wiry, hands clenched, eyes roving, with bristling red hair and stubble beard, had a lightning mind and volcanic emotions. In Georgia he broke all the rules of warfare. Without baggage and supply trains he marched through the heart of enemy country, cut off from reserves, nowhere to fall back to. Tacticians abroad said he was undertaking the most brilliant or the most foolish feat in modern conflict. Week after week, month after month, summer and autumn and winter, his great column swept on, over mountains and across rivers, through villages, towns, and cities, driving the enemy before him and thrusting it aside, leaving a swath of ruin all the way to Savannah and the sea.

Little Phil Sheridan, one of six children of an Irish immigrant, grew up in Perry County where stagecoaches and freight wagons rumbled over the National Road. One morning in 1847 while Henry Howe sketched the courthouse in Somerset, he saw across the road a pink-faced boy lugging goods into a general store. On Munster Day the Irish had a free fight, with that scrappy boy in the middle. Seventeen years later, commanding the Army of the Shenandoah, he pounded up and down the battle lines, cheered by men whose lives he was gambling. A fiery, forceful leader on his black horse Rienzi, he put strength into exhausted men, will into the lagging, heart into the hopeless. Now a bronze Sheridan on horseback dominates the courthouse yard in Somerset.

Grant had neither the build nor the bearing of a commander. But he had a stubborn mind and an unrelenting will. Stumpy, stocky, slouchy—only a horse could give him stature. His favorite mount was a big bay named Cincinnati; Grant had come from Brown County, just upriver from the Queen City. He never lost the look of a country man, even when he was spilling cigar ash in the White House and saluting to crowds in the great cities of Europe and Asia. The fiery Sheridan learned foresight from him and the voluble Sherman gave this closemouthed man his deepest devotion.

In 1893 when the monument was unveiled in the Court of Honor in Chicago, all seven of the bronze Ohio men were dead but not forgotten. The remarkable leadership that came from Ohio makes one wonder. What did these men have in common? In mind, character, and capabilities they were unlike each other. But they all, in a crucial time, seem to have believed in success. They believed in it enough to transmit that belief to others, and so to evoke from others the best that was in them. They make Herman Melville's brief characterization of Ohio look like something of a prophecy: the inhabitants of that large and fertile land, he said, were "a right sturdy set of fellows . . . ever seeking to push on their brethren to the uttermost." [12]

12. Melville, *Mardi*, 2:173.

9

M for Money

*The clocks in America—instead of moral lessons
inculcated by the dial in this country [England], such as
'Time flies' &c., teach one more suited to an American
feeling—'Time is money!'*

—Capt. Marryat

N McGuffey's First Reader the letter M was for Man.
The early editions pictured a man resting by the roadside,
his hat on the grass and hands leaning on an umbrella. At
mid-century the drawing was changed; it showed a man in an
easy chair with a newspaper at hand and a silk hat on the table
beside him. Implicit in that picture was Money.

Life in Ohio had changed. Growing more secure and more
comfortable, it became money-minded. War demands had stim-
ulated Ohio manufacturing, and in the decade following the war
the value of Ohio's industrial products surpassed the value of its
rich farm production. Essentially rural in 1850, Ohio, by 1880,
was steadily becoming industrialized. The fastest commercial
development came in northern Ohio, where the iron and steel
industry and the oil industry grew dramatically. As the river
served Ohio's lower cities, Lake Erie served the cities of the
north.

In 1832 a railroad began to reach inland from Sandusky. By

Frederick Marryat, *Diary in America* (Philadelphia: Carey & Hart, 1839), p. 7.

1846 it linked Lake Erie with the Ohio River. In 1850 it paid dividends of twelve percent. To gather custom from the lakes it operated two fine steamships, the *St. Lawrence* and the *Mississippi,* running direct from Buffalo to the railhead at Sandusky. Over the waters rode the fishing boats, each one manned by its owner. He baited his lines, hauled in his fish, unloaded the day's catch at Sandusky wharves, and went home with his earnings in his pocket. Then came a morning when two boats, alike green-hulled with a circled C on the bow, fished off Herring Shoals. A shrewd fisherman (we may call him Chance) had borrowed money from the Erie County Bank, employed some fellow fishermen, and organized a business. For a season he had two boats, then four, soon six. In five years he had a fleet. By that time Alec Chance was no longer a fisherman. He sat in a chair at a rolltop desk, keeping accounts in a Fisheries ledger. He bought an icehouse, stored his fish, and watched the market prices in Cleveland and Chicago. He was making money.

On Sandusky's lakefront the tang of timber mixed with the smell of fish. By 1880 the harbor was walled for half a mile with pine lumber and for another mile with fish houses. Fish came from the rich waters of western Lake Erie, lumber from the great woods of Michigan. Year by year the commerce grew, schooners beating in past Marblehead, where John Clemens, a kinsman of Mark Twain, was in the limestone business with tugboats and a fleet of barges. Now a new word was being used; men talked about the "biggest." Sandusky had the biggest wagon-wheel works in the world, and the biggest oar factory; it was called the greatest fish market on the globe. In 1880 a Sandusky man contracted to furnish cross-arms for a line of telegraph poles from Kansas to California.

Young Henry Flagler had come from New York state, sleeping on the deck of a canal barge and on a lake boat from Buffalo. In the village of Republic on the Sandusky River he took a job in a general store. He was paid five dollars a month and his board; he slept under a counter, covering himself with wrapping paper. But Henry Flagler was not content to measure muslin. He meant to make money. He became a dealer, buying wheat from the Republic farmers and selling it to millers in the town of Milan. His first profits were invested in a distillery owned by his wife's uncle Stephen Harkness. Having learned of an impending tax on whiskey, Harkness sent his nephew through the lake counties buying from other distillers. Harkness and Flagler sold ten thousand gallons when the price had risen. In his dealings Henry Flagler occasionally sold grain through a young commission merchant in Cleveland, a man named Rockefeller. Keeping his ledger by the light of a fish-oil lamp, Rockefeller pondered the discovery of petroleum at Oil Creek, Pennsylvania. To begin an oil business, Rockefeller needed capital, and Flagler persuaded his uncle to back a refinery for extracting kerosene. Soon the lamps of Cleveland burned with a brighter flame. Rockefeller organized a firm, confidently called the Standard Oil Company, with four thousand workers in fuming refineries and a cooperage factory that every day consumed twenty acres of oak forest to produce its daily ten thousand barrels that carried kerosene to every corner of the land.

With his Ohio profits Henry Flagler went to Florida, where he was entranced by the empty country's economic promise. He built the Florida East Coast Railway, extending it all the way to a clearing in the palm trees named Miami, on the edge of the Everglades. Then Flagler's Model Land Company began selling acreage in the vast tracts Flagler was given to bring his railroad there. When he died in 1912, the man who had slept under the counter in Ohio owned a chain of princely hotels from St. Augustine to Key West.

"Ten years in America," wrote Captain Frederick Marryat, "is almost equal to a century in the old continent." In a decade, he went on, the wilderness could be transformed into cities "with arts, manufactures, and machinery, all in full activity." [1] This rapidity of change appears most strikingly in the life of the man who became its greatest instrument. When John Davison Rockefeller was born, 1839, in the village of Richford, New York, a candle burned in the three-room cottage and farm wagons creaked to Hanford's mill where a waterwheel turned the buhrstones. These were the light, the power, and the trans-

1. Frederick Marryat, *Diary in America* (Philadelphia: Carey & Hart, 1839), p. 5.

portation of the time. In 1853 the family went west to Ohio, and John D. Rockefeller enrolled in Cleveland's Central High School. After a year there, and a bookkeeping course in a downtown business college, he began work in the office of a wholesale merchant on the harborside. At sixteen he was a tall, serious youth with qualities of steadiness, prudence, and thrift.

In 1859 a Cleveland merchant Thomas Hussey went to Venango County, Pennsylvania, where oil was bubbling out of laboriously drilled salt wells. He came home telling how petroleum was distilled into kerosene, which burned with a cleaner flame than unrefined coal oil. In 1860 Rockefeller went to Oil Creek, where he found a huddle of shacks in a forest of derricks and hundreds of wagons loading barreled petroleum. Some wagons made the long haul to Cleveland where several small refineries were extracting kerosene.

Five years later, at the age of 28, Rockefeller had his own pipe lines and tank cars bringing crude oil to his spreading refineries in Cleveland. Tank cars and tank ships carried kerosene to the Eastern cities and the seaports of Europe. Stifling and absorbing its competitors, the Standard Oil Company monopolized the industry. By 1880 Rockefeller was master of the oil business of the world.

Until the mid-nineteenth century the Cuyahoga was a clear stream winding through marsh grass and wildflowers, but in 1880 it was lined with sawmills, coal docks, blast furnaces, and overhung with smoke. Oil tanks rose like fortifications; a trestled maze of pipes laced the tanks to loading terminals where boiler-shaped cars crept under a forest of chimneys. At times a viscous oil glaze on the river caught fire and went smoking to the lake.

Almost as rapid as development of the oil business was the growth of Cleveland's iron and steel industry. Coal, limestone, and iron ore go into the making of steel. Geography put Lake Erie's cities in the path of these resources. Vast coal beds lay in Ohio's Hocking Valley, limestone quarries whitened the shores of Lake Huron, huge iron ranges ringed Lake Superior; and the lakes made a highway for transport of bulk cargoes. In 1855 a canal was built around St. Mary's Falls at the foot of Lake Superior, and a sailing vessel brought the first ore shipment, 132 tons, from upper Michigan to Cleveland. During the next century 200 million tons of iron ore were discharged at Cleveland docks. At first the heavy rock was handled by men with shovels and wheelbarrows, then by horse-drawn block and tackle, then in clamshell buckets powered by steam and later by electricity. Now the newest ore carriers are built with bottom hoppers, from which pelletized ore flows onto conveyor belts that discharge on the docks.

With 65,000 people in 1865, Cleveland had schooners and steamers crowding the river mouth, elevators, mills, and furnaces spreading in the smoky flats, a big new Union Station at the foot of Water Street, carriages rolling past the mansions on Euclid Avenue. On St. Clair and Water streets were offices of the iron merchants, dealing in Lake Superior ore. War had boomed the iron industry, which grew immensely in the postwar years. Two hundred thousand tons of ore came down the lakes in 1865; ten years later the annual cargoes exceeded half a million.

David Tod, who would be governor of Ohio, 1862-1864, grew up on Brier Hill farm, overlooking the village of Youngstown. The land was mostly sheep pasture, but it contained rich coal banks, easily worked, along the Mahoning River. That coal, the best in the valley, proved excellent for engine fuel and, eventually, for blast furnaces. About 1850 David Tod persuaded some Cleveland steamboat captains to try his coal in their boiler rooms. Within a decade coal supplanted wood as steamboat fuel. After the Civil War, Governor Tod turned to iron-making. On the Mahoning grew the Brier Hills Furnaces, with charcoal ovens, mill sheds, skip hoists, and big furnace stacks topped by smoking chimneys.

By 1880 Cleveland had reached deeply into mining, shipping, and manufacture. As small and scattered furnaces were bought by the new companies, great iron works replaced the local units and corporations supplanted family enterprise. So Youngstown grew into the biggest of the mill towns strung for thirty miles along the Mahoning River, where blast furnaces gushed white-hot iron and Bessemer converters flared in the murky sky.

Toledo, at the Maumee river mouth, was a trading town until after the Civil War. But when the Maumee Valley gas field offered cheap fuel for industry, population doubled and redoubled. By 1900 Toledo had miles of docks and acres of railroad yards. The new century brought new undertakings, the manufacture of glass, machinery, and motorcars. Heavy industry was spreading westward along a line just north of the forty-first parallel. Toledo lay in the path of this development, and the Toledo Furnace Company became the biggest producer of merchant pig iron in the country.

Meanwhile the coal trade had grown to huge volume, and new methods were at work. The old wheelbarrow gang was gone by 1880, and the bucket system went out when cardumpers were installed in 1895. These brawny machines picked up coal cars bodily, dumped them over with a dusty thunder, and set them on the track again. An hour later they were on the way back to the mines for a refill.

The leading family in Ohio's heavy industry was the Mathers, descendants of the Rev. Richard Mather of Toxteth Park, Lancashire, who came to Massachusetts in 1635. His youngest son, born in 1639, he named Increase—"because of the never-to-be-forgotten *Increase,* of every sort, wherewith GOD has favored the new country." [2] A century and a half later, following his grandfather's interest in the Connecticut Land Company's Western Reserve, Samuel Livingstone Mather came to Cleveland, in 1843, to sell the property. When he heard about discoveries of iron ore on Lake Superior, the family future swung in a new direction. In 1850 Samuel L. Mather helped to organize the Cleveland Mining Company. He made extended visits to the Marquette district in upper Michigan, and introduced his two sons to the iron business. One son founded Interlake Iron Company and the Interlake Steamship Company; the other became head of the Cleveland-Cliffs Iron Company.

While industry was darkening the Cuyahoga flats, the pride of Cleveland was Euclid Avenue, a regal street arched by great trees and lined with mansions and gardens of the millionaires.

2. Kenneth B. Murdock, *Increase Mather* (Cambridge: Harvard University Press, 1925), p. 34.

English manor houses, French chateaus, Italian villas and palazzos, graced the avenue. In them was a king's ransom of imported enamels, lacquers, ceramics, sculpture, Persian rugs, Oriental bronzes, and the paintings of European masters. A New York reporter wrote that Euclid Avenue was the finest in the West. Its opulence and ostentation dazzled everyone but Cleveland's tramp journalist Artemus Ward who reported that visitors, after carefully wiping their feet, were allowed to roam the elegant highway free of charge. "All the owners of Euclid Street homes," he explained, "employ hired girls and are patrons of the arts. A musical was held at one of these palatial homes the other day with singing. . . . The tenor had as fine a tenor voice as ever brought a bucket of water from a second-story window." [3]

Money bathed Euclid Avenue with a golden light, but in the river flats miles of narrow streets and alleys lay under a pall of smoke and cinders. Corporation profits were not published, but there are grim statistics on the working class. In a land of plenty, thousands of immigrant families—German, Irish, English, Italian, Russian, Hungarian—subsisted on a few dollars a week, a few steps ahead of starvation. Miners were paid $1.50 for a ten-hour day, skilled laborers the same; unskilled workers averaged less than $1.25. Women fared worst. As late as 1900 the average wage for women in Cleveland, Columbus, and Cincinnati was $4.83 for a fifty-seven-hour week. Some of them worked in flag factories, in dank, dark shops amid dangerous machines, turning out emblems of liberty and justice for all.

The most spectacular Ohio boom appeared in the unlikely locale of Hancock County, on the edge of the Black Swamp district. Long before the commercial discovery of oil, an itinerant preacher warned a neighborhood gathering that underneath them the fires of hell were raging. "Yes," cried a settler, "it's just under Shane's prairie, 'cause I dug a well last week and the water was so full of brimstone and sulphur . . . it turned every-

3. Quoted in W. G. Rose, *Cleveland: The Making of a City* (Cleveland: The World Publishing Company, 1950), p. 304.

thing black and caved in. . . . Hell's right under there." [4] A few years later a man on a farm clearing near the town of Findlay abandoned a kitchen well because of its sulphurous odor. He sank a wooden pipe into the pit and sometimes amused his neighbors by lighting the escaping gas. Another well digger, striking gas instead of water, piped the strange fluid to his chimney mouth for use in cooking. This, too, was a curiosity, and the neighbors went on burning their plentiful firewood.

After the Civil War the town of Findlay organized a company to install street lighting by artificial gas, produced from coal. In the early 1880s when new gas fields were developed in Pennsylvania, some Findlay men made a try of their own. Employing drillers from Pennsylvania, they struck a vein of gas at 314 feet, and others at deeper levels. Continued drilling tapped an extensive bed of gas at 1,648 feet. The well cost them $3,000; it produced 250,000 cubic feet a day. This was good enough to try some more. On January 30, 1886, after 24 days of drilling, the Karg well erupted with a roar heard across the county and a plume of fire 100 feet tall. While contractors figured the volume at eight million cubic feet a day, a standpipe was installed and the gas burned in the air. An observer wrote: "Gas from the Karg Well leaps and roars from its mouth night and day—a semi-volcanic pyramid of flame." [5] Before they brought it under control, the glare was visible for forty miles, and for half a mile around, the flame turned January into July. Grass grew green within a circle of snow, and crickets shrilled all night.

That summer throngs of people converged on Findlay for the Gas Jubilee. Bands paraded through arches of 30,000 flaming jets. In hotels, taverns, and on the never-dark street corners men talked about new glass factories in Toledo, the new process for converting iron to steel, the new pipeline from Hancock County to the mills of Cleveland. Some preachers in their pulpits foretold the end of the world, but it was just the ending of an era. A civilization resting on family, land, and community was giving way to the restless forces of industry and commerce. In that

4. Howe, *Historical Collections*, 2:725–726.
5. *History of Hancock County, Ohio* (Chicago: Warren, Beers & Co., 1886), p. 641.

change the old satisfactions were extinguished like starlight in the glare of a gas well's flame.

In Hancock County light and fuel became nearly as free as air and sunlight. A banner over Findlay's Main Street announced that household gas was delivered for $1.05 a year; another banner shouted "Fifty Million Feet of Gas Daily!" The Chamber of Commerce passed out broadsides: "Free Fuel! Free Lights! Free Sites! For the Manufacturer Who Will Locate in Findlay, Ohio." [6]

Findlay's gas was not, after all, inexhaustible. It ran low by 1890, but a new excitement had flared up as oil derricks spread like mushrooms through the woods and fields. A group of producers formed the Ohio Oil Company. They had more oil than they could market—even at fifteen cents a barrel. That problem brought the Rockefeller interests into the district with the Buckeye Pipe Line Company, and in 1899 Standard Oil bought out the Hancock County men. Several years before that time, the Standard Oil Trust had swallowed all its rivals and was dictating its own railroad rates. It was the biggest monopoly yet.

Ohio, the land in the middle, was not the only economic battleground, though it was the central one. Other business combinations in other states were controlling sugar, beef, lead, wool, and whiskey. But Ohio had a greater range of resources and, given its enviable location, the shortest routes to the materials it lacked and the markets it sought. No other state had such an endowment of coal, oil, gas, sand, clay, stone, and salines—the makings of many industries—and no other state had such ready transportation. With these advantages Ohio seemed destined for a leading role in commercial and industrial development.

In these years, however, the flag-shaped state, like the American nation, was an arena of contending movements and forces. Some of Ohio's best talent and energy was at work on the controlling of big business. Look at John Sherman, brother of the Civil War general, who served forty-three years in public life— first in the House of Representatives and then in the Senate, where he succeeded Salmon P. Chase, and in the cabinets of

6. William Humphrey, *Findlay, The Story of a Community* (Findlay, O.: The Findlay Printing and Supply Co., 1961), p. 107.

President Hayes and President McKinley. Sherman was sent to Congress from Mansfield, Ohio, just two counties away from oil-soaked Findlay. While industries mushroomed in his home state, he worked on problems of a national banking system, the government purchase of silver bullion, and the question of legal tender. In the 1880s he grappled with the growth of big business and the concentration of capital. Sherman did not oppose corporations but saw that they needed an umpire. In a country of laws the umpire must be not a czar but a system of laws and courts. Working with senators from New England, Sherman formulated an antitrust law that was enacted in 1890. That act made illegal any restraint of trade or commerce among the several states or with foreign nations. Out of the state that had harbored the biggest trusts came the author of an enduring antitrust statute. Again Ohio asserted its "middle ground" character.

In 1892 the Ohio supreme court judged Standard Oil guilty of violating the Sherman Act, though the trust was not dissolved until 1899. In 1911 Ohio Oil again became an independent producer. Under its later name, Marathon, it grew into an integrated company with production in many parts of the world and distribution concentrated in the midwestern states. Its base remained at its birthplace, the once boom-town of Findlay.

Writing in the *Atlantic Monthly* in 1899 an Easterner reported on the Ohio scene: "Oil abounds: whole counties are covered with derricks. . . . Coal, the logical premise of natural gas, covers enormous areas. . . . By combining coal and ore in a furnace and roasting them together, men transmute iron through steel into gold." [7] On this visitor Cleveland left a confused impression of ringing hammers, swinging cranes, the hot breath of furnaces and the gush of molten metal, and a skyline of smokestacks dimmed by their own outpouring. The Clevelanders, he said, endure it with a smile: "Smoke means business, business means money, and money is the principal thing." [8]

Add to the moneymakers in Ohio a man in Dayton who made a fortune from money itself. In the 1870s inventor John Ritty devised a "mechanical money drawer" that rang a bell and

7. Rollin L. Hartt, "The Ohioans," *Atlantic Monthly* 84(1899):681.
8. Hartt, "Ohioans," p. 681.

recorded figures whenever it was opened. It seemed a harmless plaything—until John Patterson came to Dayton in 1884. He bought Ritty's company for $6,500. On second thought Patterson regretted the purchase and tried to unload it on someone else. Finding no buyers, he gave the money box an all-out try. He built a glass-walled "daylight" factory, creating a new standard of working conditions and a new style of industrial architecture. With high wages he recruited skilled workmen. He named the money drawer a "cash register," and in its manufacture he combined precision craftsmanship with assembly-line production. Within a decade National Cash Registers were ringing all over America. By 1910 one third of the firm's production went to other lands, where the machines rang up shillings, marks, guilders, francs, lire, pesos, pesetas, kronen, cruzerios, milreis, rupees, and rubles. The "Cash," as Dayton people called it, could take and make money in any language. One of Patterson's salesmen, who learned about moneymaking, was Thomas J. Watson, founder of the prodigious International Business Machines Corporation.

One Ohioan who never climbed onto the business bandwagon was Sherwood Anderson. As a boy he belonged to rural Ohio, living first in the village of Camden in Preble County and later in Sandusky County, the location of his fictitious "Winesburg"; in his stories its horizons are dimmed by a smoky haze that suggests the overcoming of pastoral life by new industrial forces. As a man he made a tormented flight from the commercial Ohio that was spreading along the forty-first parallel. As a writer he brooded over the village poverty and the moneymaking mills, and the dilemma of people caught between them.

In a sardonic essay, "Ohio, I'll Say We've Done Well," Anderson found Ohio's cities as noisy, smoky, ugly, dirty, and mean in their civic spirit as any industrial cities anywhere. "We Ohio men," he wrote, "have taken as lovely a land as ever lay outdoors and . . . have, in our towns and cities, put the old stamp of ourselves on it for keeps." [9] Give the credit, he said,

9. Ernest Gruening, ed., *These United States* (New York: Boni and Liveright, 1923), p. 110.

to John D. Rockefeller, Mark Hanna, Harvey Firestone, John Willys and a lot of other Ohio men. They did so well that a workman could get up in the morning, go through a sooty street to a factory where all he had to do all day was drill holes in a metal frame—"make, say, twenty-three million holes in a piece of iron, all just alike, in a lifetime." [10] At night he could go home thanking God as he walked past the finest cinder piles and trash dumps anywhere.

Reading Anderson's diatribe, one may remember old Caleb Atwater's praise of Ohio in 1838, and his prompting: "It will be our own fault if we are not the happiest people in the Union." [11]

Of course the passion for money did not begin or end in Ohio. By its natural resources America offered many material opportunities, and its people grasped them. Ohio could not be a Vermont any more than Boston could be a Rockport or Old Sturbridge. Big business was inevitable for these people in this richly endowed land, and the trusts were not the only beneficiaries. An unparalleled variety of goods at low prices came from mass production. The drudgery of hand labor was lightened by machines. From great fortunes came public as well as private benefits: schools, hospitals, parks, museums, colleges, were fruits of Ohio's industrialization. Though it lagged far behind corporation profits, the standard of living was improving for all people—enough so that immigrant workers thronged the Old World seaports with their hopes fixed on America.

After saying that in Ohio money was the principal thing, the *Atlantic Monthly* writer in 1899 spoke of the higher culture developing there—"a notable development in literary taste, a devotion to great music, an enthusiasm for art, a novel admiration for good architecture, and an increasing desire to ennoble the surroundings of common life." [12] That must have been gratifying to read in Ohio's smoky cities, but if a higher culture was developing there, it had a long way to go.

10. Gruening, *United States,* p. 117.
11. Atwater, *History of Ohio,* p. 356.
12. Hartt, "Ohioans," p. 687.

10

At City Hall

MONG the prospectors swarming into the Findlay-Lima oil fields in 1885 was a big, weathered man who talked easily about derricks and drilling, pumps and pipelines, mules and machines. He had the hard, strong hands of a working man, but under his slouch hat was a pair of thoughtful, penetrating eyes. He could mix as easily with journalists and geologists as with work crews in the field.

This was Samuel Milton Jones, born in Carnarvonshire, Wales, and brought to America at four years old. In New York state, one of seven children in the immigrant family, he had a scant three years of schooling before going to work. At fourteen he was feeding logs into a sawmill, twelve hours a day. At twenty he was learning about rock, sand, clay, and petroleum on Oil Creek, Pennsylvania. By nature curious and inventive, he learned patience and persistence on the job. After trial and error and trial again, he perfected a "sucker rod" that brought up oil from deep underground. Having arrived at Titusville with fifteen cents in his pocket, he left there a wealthy man.

In the Findlay district Jones became a founder of the Ohio Oil Company, and his device brought in the first rich well in the Trenton field. When Standard Oil took over the Ohio Company, Jones moved to Toledo and organized the Acme Sucker Rod Company, manufacturing couplings, pull-rods, steel stirrups, and pumping jacks for the oil producers. It was an elementary fact that every driller needed a stockpile of sucker rods. Jones was on the scene of action, ready to reap more fortune.

That looks like a success story—the right man at the right place with the right goods at the right time. If money was all that mattered, Sam Jones had won the game already. The rest of his life could be a familiar American pattern in the Gilded Age—winter home in the south, summer home in the north, a private railroad car, perhaps a yacht on the Lakes, some token benefactions to hospitals and colleges.

But to Jones money mattered less than people. His ventures were just beginning. He meant to stay in Toledo and to fight some battles there. He was about to ask a basic question, basic for Ohio and for the changing nation.

The scene had changed. The essential Ohio now was not the forest clearing, or the crossroads settlement, or construction camps on the canal ditch and railway line. The vital scene was the city, the inchoate, restless, surging city, with its polyglot people reaching for a future. Jones would spend the rest of his life asking a momentous question. Can a city grow rich and powerful without becoming corrupt? Can its people become true citizens? Could civic virtue and social justice survive the headlong industrial revolution? With turbulence and agitation the American city was taking shape—hoofs ringing on cobble stones, wheels grinding the pavements, the clamor of many voices. Had righteousness a chance in that swarming life? Ohio had spawned a surprising number of cities. If the answer could be found in one of them, it would reverberate in others. Indeed, an Ohio example would be felt in distant places.

As an inventor Jones had brought curiosity, experiment, and innovation to the oil fields. Now, in Toledo, he began a social experiment with innovations in business and politics. In his rod factory on grimy Segur Avenue he posted a precept not from the rules of business but from the New Testament: "Therefore, whatsoever things you would that men should do to you, do you even so to them." [1] On his office wall he kept a motto: "The

1. Brand Whitlock, *Forty Years Of It* (New York: D. Appleton and Company, 1914), p. 115.

Business of this shop is to make Men.'' Ruling out child labor and overtime, he instituted an eight-hour working day, a week's paid vacation, and a year-end bonus for all his workers. A company dining room served a hearty lunch for fifteen cents. At the corner of Segur and Field streets he developed the Golden Rule Park and Playground, with a community meeting and recreation hall. To the meeting hall he brought Henry D. Lloyd, Jane Addams, the Rev. Washington Gladden, and other progressive spokesmen. He set up a co-operative insurance plan, managed by its members. After a few years he began a profit-sharing arrangement that gave employees a stake in the company.

Toledo at the turn of the century was the fastest-growing city in the nation. Numbering 81,000 in 1900, it had 150,000 population twelve years later. It had 750 manufacturing plants, 19 miles of docks, 13 railroads with 134 passenger trains daily. By railroad and lake steamer the people came, speaking a dozen languages and lining up for work as laborers at $1.50 for a ten-hour day. In spite of 87 churches it was a rowdy, roughneck city; hundreds of saloons, brothels, and gambling rooms lined the river streets. In 1897 there were more than fifty splintered labor unions, without leadership and direction. Jones marched with his workers in Labor Day parades. In radical unions that were anathema to other businessmen he saw nothing more fearful than a reaching for brotherhood. Like other Ohio cities Toledo had an ethnic mix that needed common ground of hope and purpose.

In 1897 Jones ran for mayor on the Republican ticket, contesting with entrenched city bosses of both parties. He campaigned on a platform of public ownership of city water, light, and power utilities and municipal control of street railways. When thousands of coins were streaming into hundreds of fare boxes, a streetcar franchise was richer than an oil well, and the operators fought reform. The Pastors Union—a ministerial association—rejected Jones because he did not intend to close saloons, theaters, playgrounds, and milk deliveries on Sunday. It was a close vote, but at midnight of April 15, 1897, Jones telegraphed to Washington Gladden in Columbus: "Am elected in spite of 600 saloons, the Traction Company, and the devil.'' ²

In his first term Mayor Jones showed less concern for the blue laws than for the monopolies that profiteered from city services. As civic leader he introduced ideas as new as his oil extractor. The man who had begun work after three years of schooling wanted to build new schools and a free kindergarten. He proposed replacing tenements with municipal housing and putting the police and fire departments under civil service. Rather than Sunday quiet he sought an improved social order. His salary as mayor he gave to the poor.

To the Toledo establishment Jones seemed a dangerous man with a head full of socialism. The press and the pulpit denounced him. As Brand Whitlock remembered, ''The most charitable thing they said was that he was crazy.'' ³ The Republican party dropped him before his term was up.

In 1899 Jones declared for re-election, and the issues were clear: reform vs. privilege, public benefit vs. private profit. Disavowed by his party, suspect by business, opposed by the press, rejected by the clergy, he looked like a sure loser. Even the saloon keepers, bossed by the party machines, deserted him. But Jones had attracted a band of zealous young lawyers, reporters, and social workers. As an Independent, without ward and precinct organization, he took his crusade to the people. His rangy figure and resounding voice and his directness and simplicity of speech were familiar in all parts of the city. In spite of chronic bronchial asthma he dominated undisciplined crowds. In a magazine story his young friend Brand Whitlock described this champion of the people's cause, addressing

   . . . immense audiences in halls, in tents, in the raw open air of that rude March weather, making his appeals to the heart of the great mass. . . . Long afterward [one] could hear those cheers and

---

2. Randolph C. Downes, ed., *Industrial Beginnings*. Lucas County Historical Series. (Toledo: The Historical Society of Northwestern Ohio, 1954), p. 119.
   3. Whitlock, *Forty Years*, p. 112.

see the faces of those working men aglow with the hope,
the passion, the fervent religion of democracy.[4]

Jones won the election with an overwhelming vote, carrying all but one precinct in the city. Elected again in 1901 and in 1903, he led Toledo into new measures of self-government. In city departments he established a civil-service system and an eight-hour day. He added a free kindergarten to the school system, and under the Complete Education League he developed a youth program of both cultural and vocational training. Giving public work to the unemployed, he cleaned the streets and removed overhead power lines. He enlarged the parks and joined them by boulevards. He visited the jails, talking with bums, gamblers, and prostitutes. When a Toledo minister urged him to drive out the streetwalkers, Jones asked "Where to?" and suggested that each clergyman might take in one of the homeless girls and give her a better life. In fact, Jones offered to join them in the venture. Instead of that, the Pastors Union refused to observe Golden Rule Day. Jones saw vice and crime as diseases of society rather than offenses of the culprit; he believed that social justice and brotherhood were the only cure.

Demands of business and politics drained the mayor's strength, and his bronchial trouble worsened. After a winter illness in 1904, he resumed work until asthma choked him again that summer. His heart gave out on July 12, and the next day the Toledo street-railway stock rose twenty-four points. Rapacity expected a reprise.

Fifty-five thousand people lined up on Ontario and Adams streets to file past the mayor's coffin in Memorial Hall. Then the casket was taken to the Jones house on Monroe Street where the doorstep was inscribed "A Wide House to Lodge a Friend." Inside, over the fireplace, was a Welsh proverb: "Y gwir yn erbyn y byd"—The Truth Against the World.

Newton D. Baker, then a young lawyer working for reform in Cleveland, came to Toledo for the funeral. He always remembered the summer afternoon when Brand Whitlock stood on the veranda and spoke about his departed friend and chief. "His au-

---

4. Brand Whitlock, "The Gold Brick," *American Magazine* 67(Nov. 1908):51.

dience consisted of acres of people who packed the lawn in front of the Jones home and overflowed onto the adjacent street. . . . The crowd was a family bereft of its father.'' [5] By that time "Golden Rule" Jones was known across the nation, and Ohio had a shining success story.

The mayor's death interrupted a struggle with the Toledo Railway and Light Company that controlled streetcar service. With Jones out of the way the company secured renewal of its franchise. But the young Independents rallied. Every Sunday Brand Whitlock spoke in crowded Golden Rule Hall or in the Golden Rule Park with streetcars grinding past and children shrilling on the swings and poles Jones had provided. After the 1905 election Whitlock, defeating the four candidates against him, moved into the mayor's office.

Brand Whitlock, son of a Methodist minister in western Ohio, went through high school in Toledo and in 1887 began work on the *Toledo Blade.* He never attended college, though he often spoke of a citizen who loves his city as an undergraduate loves his university; the city was Whitlock's alma mater. In 1890, at age twenty-one, he went to Chicago as a reporter on the *Herald,* and from there to Springfield, Illinois, as its political correspondent. A tall, slender, handsome young man with wide-ranging mind, Whitlock was drawn to homely, stubborn, stouthearted John Peter Altgeld, son of German immigrants to Ohio, who had become governor of Illinois. In Altgeld Whitlock found compassion for the poor and oppressed, and a hatred of the hypocrisy of privileged men who extolled democracy while exploiting the people. In Springfield Whitlock read law and was admitted to the bar, and there he began writing the political fiction that would be an important part of his career.

He returned to Toledo in 1897 and worked for Jones in the first campaign for reform. In the American embassy in Belgium, years after his own four terms in the mayor's office, Whitlock wrote: ''In Toledo something more than twenty languages and

5. *Letters and Journal of Brand Whitlock,* edited by Allan Nevins. 2 vols. (New York: D. Appleton-Century Company, 1936), 1:vii–viii.

dialects are spoken every day, and as the mayor is addressed, the chorus becomes a very babel, a confusion of tongues, all counseling him to his duty. The result is apt to be perplexing at times." [6] He remembered the voices of strikers and strike-breakers, of East Side and West Side, of owners and workers, of taxpayers and tax spenders, of the privileged and the oppressed.

The road to reform was long, but Whitlock made progress. Under his administration the streetcar monopoly was broken a second time, the Toledo police department became a model for other cities, labor unions found leadership and direction, and an Independent movement grew stronger than the corrupt party structure. Whitlock believed that the problems of democracy must and can be solved in the cities—though not easily or quickly.

After his years in office, he wrote a reflective essay deploring the literary tradition, ever since Theocritus and Virgil and the Psalms of David, that deplored the urban and extolled the rural community. "Not long ago," he wrote, "the men of a city church met one Sunday evening to study some of the problems of their city, and I recall with what amusement—and despair—I heard them open their exercises with the song 'No spot is so dear to my childhood/ As the little brown church in the vale.' " [7] He wished they had begun with some such chorus as *Ein Feste Burg ist unser Gott*. As he retired from office, he felt that "the time may come when our cities will be beautiful in their spirit, and in the common lot and the individuality of their citizens. Is it, in this old and moody and nervous age, too much to hope? . . . It is the dream of America, at any rate, the goal of democracy and the purpose of civilization." [8]

In 1912, wanting to do more writing, Whitlock refused to run for another term, and President Wilson named him minister to Belgium. He did write the autobiographical *Forty Years of It* before World War I turned his concern to practical politics and diplomacy. He remained in Belgium until 1920, when President

6. Whitlock, *Forty Years*, p. 217.
7. Brand Whitlock, "City and Civilization," *Scribner's Magazine* 52(1912):624.
8. Whitlock, "City and Civilization," p. 633.

Harding asked him to resign in order to make room for a member of the Republican "regulars."

During his years in Toledo Brand Whitlock sometimes went over to Cleveland where another Independent group had challenged the city bosses. At the center of the group was Tom L. Johnson, a chubby, hearty, immensely energetic leader. Like Golden Rule Jones, Johnson was a wealthy businessman who took up the cause of the working poor. Though he had an ivy-covered stone mansion set in spacious lawns on Euclid Avenue, he was often in the sooty flats, among immigrant families and laboring people. In street meetings he was simple, direct, and positive, quickly declaring his views and asking for questions and objections. He was at his best under the flaring lights with a cheering and jeering crowd around him. Though he meant not to forgive his enemies but to vanquish them, he always seemed to Whitlock a blood brother of Golden Rule Jones.

As a boy in Evansville, Indiana, Tom Johnson had three short years of schooling. At fifteen he began work for a Louisville streetcar company. He invented a new fare box that brought him enough money to invest in a street railway in Indianapolis. When his colleagues would not replace mules with electric power, he sold that interest. He had accumulated half a million dollars when he came to Cleveland in 1879. There he bought a debt-ridden streetcar line—two and a half miles of bumpy track, four cars, thirty mules, and a barn. That winter he put stoves in the cars and straw on the floor, and business picked up.

With that small start Johnson acquired other lines, despite the opposition of a strongly entrenched man, Marcus A. Hanna. Johnson introduced transfers without additional fare, an innovation fought by the Hanna organization. Johnson acquired more companies and merged them; Hanna did likewise. Then it was the Big Consolidated against the Little Consolidated, Johnson controlling Cleveland's East Side streetcars and Hanna controlling the West Side. Behind the driver's tinkling bell and the clip-clop of the little mules was a grim struggle of two determined men. When restless Tom Johnson sold that business and began steel making in Pennsylvania, Hanna united the two com-

panies. With that entrenched monopoly—Clevelanders called it
ConCon—Johnson would later fight a long and bitter political
war.

Tom Johnson was not a bookish man, yet a book, sold to him
by a railroad newsboy, shaped the rest of his life. The book was
Henry George's *Social Problems*. In New York he became a
friend of Henry George, heard discussions of tax reform, and
learned about public speaking. Back in Ohio he built a steel
plant at Lorain, paying $1.50 a day against the going rate of $1,
and hundreds of Cleveland workers rushed to the Lorain mills.

In 1888, back in Cleveland, Johnson ran for Congress on the
Democratic slate. Defeated at first try, he ran again in 1890 and
was elected. As a congressman he drew the nation's attention to
Henry George's *Protection or Free Trade* by reading it into the
Congressional Record. After two terms in Washington he lost his
seat and joined his brother in a streetcar venture in Detroit.
There he tried to bring the car lines into public ownership,
proposing to reduce the fare or even make it a free ride. When
the reform failed, he sold his Detroit interest at a substantial
profit. With a fortune of several million dollars he returned to
Cleveland when the street railway franchise was up for renewal.
Announcing candidacy for mayor on a platform of three-cent car
fares, he won the industrial districts. On an April morning in
1901 he took office in the City Hall, just in time to kill an ordinance that would give Cleveland's lakefront to the railroads. Already Johnson had a vision of a redeemed lake shore, with parks
and esplanades around a civic center.

During four terms as mayor, Johnson lost some battles and
won others. The building of a new City Hall and a high-level
bridge over the Cuyahoga gorge were rejected by the voters as
too costly. Tax reform after revaluation of property was partly
successful. But street maintenance and lighting were brought
under municipal control, garbage collection became a city func-
tion, and two electric-lighting plants went into public ownership. Other successes were a greatly improved water system, an
honest and efficient police force, a public parks development,
and a humane program of social welfare.

In charge of Charities and Corrections the mayor placed a

magnetic and social-minded clergyman, the Rev. Harris R. Cooley. Under his leadership the dismal old poorhouse was replaced by a farm colony—2,000 green and airy acres, with halls, houses, and cottages under the trees. Inmates of the old city workhouse were moved to the farm, where they lived in bright, clean quarters and worked in the open air. One part of the colony became Boyville, replacing the city reform school. Those sunlit acres had room for vagrants and derelicts in an Outdoor Relief Department, and a Brotherhood Home where discharged prisoners were prepared for a fresh start. While crime rates fell in Cleveland, officials from other places in America and abroad came to see this redemption of a city's castaways. Johnson wrote: "If service of a higher order on humanitarian lines has ever been rendered to any municipality than that rendered by Mr. Cooley to Cleveland, I have yet to hear of it." [9]

Mayor Johnson attracted a following of younger men who caught his energy and enthusiasm. Brand Whitlock, on a visit from Toledo, remembered him "in the great hall of his home on Euclid Avenue, one short, fat leg tucked comfortably under him, his cigar in his aristocratic hand, his friends and admirers around him." [10] One of the young men, Peter Witt, an iron molder who had gone hungry when on strike, had been a Johnson opponent, badgering him in street meetings and in the press; he became city clerk in the Johnson administration and, later, street railway commissioner. Of quite different temperament was scholarly Newton D. Baker, still boyish-looking at thirty-five, courteous, soft-spoken, seemingly distant from the others until he cut in with incisive fact and reason. As city solicitor he fought repeated lawsuits brought against the city. He was equally effective outside the courtroom. In tent meetings he preached free trade, home rule, tax reform, and he denounced all privileged interests and monopolies. "His diction," said a listener, "was too beautiful for a revolutionist and his manner too gentle. Yet there he stood, advocating the destruction of the old political structures and preaching the redemption of the

9. Tom L. Johnson, *My Story* (New York: B. W. Huebsch, 1911), p. 173.
10. Whitlock, *Forty Years,* p. 171.

people." [11] Still different was Frederick C. Howe, a Republican council member from a wealthy ward. Won over to Johnson's program, he was renominated on the Democratic ticket and later was elected to the Ohio senate. His book, *The City, The Hope of Democracy,* so lucidly expressed the philosophy and the program of civic reform that Johnson sent a copy to every member of the Ohio legislature.

These men, and others, worked together with infectious ardor and energy. Brand Whitlock once went over to Cleveland for a weekend of relaxation from his problems in Toledo. Instead of rest, he found himself working day and night with the Johnson team on an amendment to the municipal code. They all shared Johnson's unflagging ambition to make Cleveland a city set on a hill.

In the end Johnson lost his fortune and his health. From the Euclid Avenue mansion he moved into the Knickerbocker apartments. There he died in the spring of 1911, leaving both enemies and admirers. But the municipal debt that opponents called his monument did not lessen the loyalty of common citizens. In 1915 they dedicated his statue in the Public Square. It shows a sturdy, seated figure, one foot forward as though about to rise up from his chair, above the chiseled words:

He found us groping leaderless and blind
He left a city with a civic mind.

During the turbulent turn-of-the-century years, Lincoln Steffens of the *New York Post* and *McClure's Magazine* went from one American city to another—St. Louis, Chicago, Minneapolis, Providence, Newark, Philadelphia—as an investigating reporter. He saw a struggle going on, as crucial and mortal as the Revolution of 1776. His report on the revolution was given to the American people in *The Struggle for Self-Government,* a book dedicated to the Czar of Russia. In the dedication letter he explained:

11. Carl Lorenz, *Tom L. Johnson* (New York: The A. S. Barnes Company, 1911), p. 74.

Without permission but with the best of private intentions, I, a
sovereign American citizen, fearful for my crown as you are, Sire,
for yours—I lay this book at the foot of your throne. . . . It is a
description of something you dread, popular government, and I
write it for the encouragement of my own people, but they do not
see much to encourage them in it. Maybe your Majesty will.[12]

His pages, he said, describe a revolution going on everywhere in the United States, though few Americans were aware
of it. They thought of revolution in terms of civil strife—the
kind of revolution that created the American nation, when people demanded self-government. "And I do not doubt that your
people, knowing of our days of 1776 . . . are looking to us, to
the history and happenings of the American people, for inspira-
tion, example, and comfort. Sire, so shall you." [13] In a deepening irony the journalist compared the czar, a faltering sovereign,
on the edge of his uneasy throne, with Lincoln Steffens, a faltering sovereign citizen. American representative democracy, he
explained, does not represent the public; it protects the interests
of private businessmen. "We have czars, too. . . . We call them
bosses." [14]

Early in his investigations Steffens came to Toledo, and
Brand Whitlock took him to see Mayor Jones. When they left
City Hall, the visitor seemed depressed. They walked down St.
Clair Street in silence, and at last Steffens said, "Why, that
man's program will take a thousand years." [15]

Steffens went on to Cleveland, Whitlock recalled, with dis-
tinct prejudice against Tom Johnson—the wealthy businessman
reaching for political power. But the story he wrote portrayed
Johnson as the best mayor in the best-governed city in the nation. Some months later Steffens repeated that judgment, and
added another one. "The story of latter-day politics of Ohio, as
I understand the State, can best be told as a tale of two of her

12. Lincoln Steffens, *The Struggle for Self-Government* (New York: McClure, Phil-
lips & Co., 1906), p. v.
13. Steffens, *The Struggle,* p. vi.
14. Steffens, *The Struggle,* p. vii.
15. Whitlock, *Forty Years,* p. 164.

cities . . . Cleveland the best-governed city in the United States, Cincinnati, the worst." [16]

On Steffens's first trip to Cincinnati the train ran through morning sunshine into a band of mist and smoke "where the Queen City broods in gloom." [17] Postponing a visit to City Hall, he went straight to the sign of the Mecca saloon and climbed a dark stairway to a grubby office overlooking Central Avenue. There sat burly George B. Cox, ruler of the city. A saloon keeper who had entered politics to get police protection for his pub, Cox became a councilman (his only elected office) and an oil inspector who dispensed patronage throughout the city and county, taking the Democratic grafters into his Republican ring. Conventions were held according to plans outlined ahead of time; Cox named the ward leaders, and they delivered the votes. When a small-circulation weekly raised a protest, it was drowned out by the Cox-bossed dailies. Shrewd as well as autocratic, Cox appeased opponents with a good appointment, throwing the man out later. He personally handled tax assessments, contracts for street paving and lighting, and public-service franchises. His interest in schools was confined to cutting their budgets in favor of fatter departments. For twenty-five years this closemouthed, heavy-handed man was the czar of Cincinnati. "The city," wrote Steffens, "is all one great graft; Cox's system is the most perfect thing of its kind in this country, and he is proud of it." [18]

Behind Steffens's blunt indictment is a complex social scene and a complex story. Cincinnati, always the most attractive and sophisticated city in Ohio, has three levels—riverfront, basin, hilltop. In 1850 it was a compact, busy, and prosperous city with a basin area of market and commercial district flanked by residential neighborhoods, all under an arc of hills. When rapid streetcars came, a generation later, people could live at a distance from their work. Then the riverfront was taken over by railroads, livery stables, and warehouses, business spread in the central basin, and the former residential districts swarmed with

16. Steffens, *The Struggle,* p. 161.
17. Steffens, *The Struggle,* p. 172.
18. Steffens, *The Struggle,* pp. 199–200.

an ethnic mix of laboring people while airy new suburbs grew over the highlands.

What has happened in the twentieth century in other cities of Ohio and the nation happened earlier in Cincinnati. The diffusion of substantial families to the periphery left the inner city without a solid middle class. Deterioration brought crime and violence, culminating, in March 1884, in a mob clash with state militia, the killing and wounding of three hundred people, and the burning of the finest courthouse in Ohio. There were then two communities, one safe but helpless on the heights, another seething in the basin. No political party was strong enough to bridge and govern the divided city.

Into that vacuum moved Cox the tavern keeper, making his own rules, organizing his henchmen, bossing the city, and commanding a tacit assent from the newspapers and the elected officials in City Hall. With a perspective lacking to Lincoln Steffens, some recent historians see Cox as, at worst, a necessary evil. He kept the lid on an explosive city in years of bewildering change. Cox himself had said that a boss was "not necessarily a public enemy." [19]

Actually, Cincinnati had passed the crisis point when Steffens visited there, and he saw some signs of promise. A cadre of veteran reformers was finding recruits willing to line up against the machine. In 1905 the voters overthrew Cox, electing a reform mayor on a fusion ticket. Cox made a comeback, but was soon tarred in a banking scandal. When the Ohio legislature finally passed a home-rule act, removing state politics from city governments, the redeeming forces gathered momentum. In 1925, with a victory by the reform charter party, Cincinnati became the first major city to install a professional city manager, unbound and unobliged to any platform or party, responsible to a city council. Under a coalition of Republicans and Democrats the Queen City emerged from gloom into a cheerful sunlight.

Though it is glad to forget the domination of Boss Cox, Cincinnati has a long memory. It likes to recall the landing at Yeatman's Cove where the first boatload of settlers came ashore on a

19. Zane L. Miller, "Boss Cox's Cincinnati," *Journal of American History* 54(March 1968):838.

winter day in 1788. Now the historic site is a riverside park, green and tranquil, with a leafy river esplanade. Adjoining it is a concrete platform crowned by the Riverfront Stadium where the Reds and the Bengals play. At night the stadium blazes while channel buoys wink on the dark river and heavy-breathing towboats push long trains of barges. Cincinnati likes to remember the steamboat years; the mile-long landing lined with tall-stacked packet boats is handsomely pictured in the public library.

The city faces south, looking across the curving river to the hills of Kentucky. For a hundred years the Dixie Terminal was a station for streetcars, hacks, and busses that crossed the suspension bridge to Covington and Fort Thomas, on the Kentucky side. Now there is little public transportation, but the old name holds on. The new Dixie Terminal houses brokerage and travel offices.

Twentieth-century Cincinnati has been slow to change. After the canal basin had become a motor parkway, the German district beyond it remained "Over the Rhine," as it is today. The century-old Music Hall was not replaced but restored at the cost of a new structure, and the May Music Festival endures, as does the Findlay Street market a few blocks away. From the Music Hall a parked mile of urban renewal leads to the monumental Union Station, the most handsome railroad terminal anywhere. In 1933 it replaced, at last, the dingy old riverfront station that was frequently invaded by high water.

Approached by malls and gardens is the terminal's great dome that surmounts a huge rotunda once arced with ticket windows, shops, theater, restaurants, and a children's playroom. Faith in the future, a reporter wrote in the familiar Ohio style, had erected the 45-million-dollar structure. Inside the dome a series of mosaic murals reviewed the nation's development from Indian times to the industrial era. One segment showed stevedores loading a riverboat at the Cincinnati landing. Another, above the lighted schedule of departing trains, pictured a track gang laying rails for the transcontinental railroad. During the 1940s the terminal served 216 trains and 17,000 people daily.

The last train departed October 29, 1972, and the great terminal was silent. Its "future" had lasted thirty-nine years. Where a hundred million people had boarded limiteds and locals, no one would take a train again.

In 1973, while City Hall debated the future of the structure—a transportation museum, an exhibition center, a high-rise apartment block, a technological institute, an urban transit terminal—the mosaics were removed to the Greater Cincinnati Airport. Twelve miles south, in Boone County, Kentucky, the airport occupies high ground above the river hills. Often the highway bridge is choked with Cincinnati traffic, but there is another way to the airlines. Under Cincinnati's western hills is the Anderson Ferry. Two battered, unroofed, chuffing transports, *Big Boone* and *Little Boone,* capacity twelve cars and eight cars, shuttle across to drowsing Constance, Ky., where the road winds up through slopes of maple, oak, and redbud. The Anderson Ferry, says the homemade sign, has been operating since 1817. Where else can you take a 160-year-old ferry service, past creeping barge tows and shantyboats, to a jet landing field?

One morning in 1971 a photographer from Vermont got off a Cincinnati train and spent the day admiring the terminal. He returned sixteen times to study the structure and photograph the mosaics. His interest helped to save the murals, though they had to be separated. The airport has no dome to display the whole historical panorama.

Downtown Cincinnati remained dingy in the 1950s, while other cities were rebuilding. When renewal began in Cincinnati a continuity was preserved. Fountain Square has been the heart of the city ever since 1872 when a grateful immigrant citizen, whose success had far surpassed the hopes he had brought to Ohio, presented to Cincinnati the Tyler Davidson Fountain. "The Genius of Water," spraying a cascade from hundreds of jets, it symbolized the river that carries Cincinnati's commerce with the southern states.

The Fountain had spurred Cincinnati's first urban renewal. Its original location, in 1872, fixed by the City officials, was that of the noisy and odorous Fifth Street Market, between Walnut and Vine. The old market sheds were replaced by an esplanade with trees and gaslights framing the goddess of water. Lined by shops, hotels, and dining rooms, with carriages and horsecars parading past, the Square was an island of grace and repose in the midst of a changing city. One hundred years later, in 1972, the old buildings were replaced by soaring façades of glass and steel. But the goddess of water remained. The new Fountain Square is a tree-dotted plaza where people lunch at a sidewalk cafe and on stone terraces and benches. Often the place is filled with music—rock bands, folk concerts, the Cincinnati Symphony. From the plaza elevated walkways link department stores, hotels, and restaurants to the Convention Center and to Riverfront Stadium on its cement platform lapped by the river. The most historic of Ohio's cities has combined change with continuity.

As Cincinnati faces the river and the South, Cleveland faces Lake Erie and reaches toward Lake Superior and the St. Lawrence. Once the Forest City, it has little left from the early years. Cleveland's dominant feature is the Terminal Tower, another monument to transportation in plentiful Ohio; railroad and urban rapid transit come together there. People stream into the tunnels for "the rapid" to Shaker Heights and to the western suburbs, with a much-envied fifteen-minute run to Hopkins Airport. But the lofty passenger concourse for the vanished railroad trains now supports a canvased enclosure from which comes the gutty ping of tennis balls. Businessmen from the tower can drop down for a tennis break. Meanwhile the long ore carriers creep around the bends of the rusty Cuyahoga River toward the gleam and glare of mill sheds and blast furnaces.

Superior Avenue, bisecting the Public Square, is a constant reminder of Cleveland's tie with the great northern lake ringed in hills of iron rock. Cleveland men developed the iron ranges and emptied the open-pit mines. Then, giving a hopeful Ohio try, they quarried the mother rock—the mineral strata called taconite—that contained minute granules of iron. With new technologies they pulverized the rock, extracted the iron particles by magnetic separation, then balled and baked that heavy dust into iron ore pellets ready for shipment to the blast furnaces. Now lake vessels, longer, deeper, and wider than ever, bring fifty-thousand-ton cargoes into Cleveland harbor. Since 1950 Cleveland's commerce has reached through the St. Lawrence Seaway to harbors around the world. Grain and farm machinery are Cleveland's leading exports, while glassware, building materials, and food products come ashore. Deepwater docks in the outer harbor can berth eleven ocean-commerce freighters. In bounteous Ohio foreign trade is knocking at the door.

It is a gloomy assumption that technology has outrun humanity, and a gleam of hope appears in Cleveland. In 1963 a group of Clevelanders began welcoming foreign seamen to their city. Since then the Cleveland Seamen's Service has greeted many hundreds of foreign ships and made friends of thousands of foreign sailors. From the rich mix of Cleveland's population the society draws volunteers who can speak to diverse visitors in their own tongues. Local theaters, museums, churches, sports and cultural organizations have co-operated. For low-wage foreign seamen, American pastimes are mostly out of reach, but they are all cost-free in Cleveland. Instead of a few waterfront bars these men see the many attractions of an American city.

To Cleveland's original New England population many other strains are added. Irish construction crews built the canals and railroads, and they remained to work in Cleveland industry. Later came a great influx of peoples from eastern Europe, and most recently a black migration from the states of the Deep South. The new strains began at the bottom and worked upward. Success was expected in Ohio. It came, in varying measure, to the Irish on Whiskey Island, and it came, in turn, to the Serbians, Czechs, Hungarians, Croatians, and Lithuanians in the Cuyahoga flats—the second generation moving upward toward the growing middle class.

From those ranks came new political leaders. In the 1880s an immigrant family from a mountain village of Slovenia arrived in America. Their son, born in Cleveland in 1895, became mayor of the city, served an unmatched five terms as governor of Ohio, and capped his career in the United States Senate. A big, buoyant, athletic, and magnetic man, Frank Lausche radiated

Ohio's vigor and confidence. He was a walking, talking embodiment of "With God all things are possible," the state maxim adopted under the governorship of Michael DiSalle, another ethnic leader, who went from the mayor's office in Toledo to become President Truman's director of economic affairs. Anthony Celebreeze, born in sea-washed Anzio, Italy, in 1910, studied law at Ohio Northern University and became an Ohio state senator, mayor of Cleveland, and secretary of Health, Education and Welfare under President Kennedy. When Carl Stokes moved into Cleveland's City Hall in 1967, he was the first black mayor of a major city. The newest figures in this line are a father and son: Frank Palm Celeste, native of Calabria, Italy, recently mayor of Lakewood, and his son, strapping Richard Celeste, honor graduate of Yale and Oxford Rhodes Scholar, now lieutenant-governor of Ohio. Presiding over the Ohio senate where the action moves from a bill regulating hog feed to one empowering an urban municipality to issue revenue bonds, Dick Celeste gets the kind of political experience that few other states can offer.

"Columbus is a depressing place," [20] announces a biographer at the beginning of his life of James Thurber. That statement would have amused Thurber, at least, and it expresses a reluctant feeling shared by a good many Ohioans. Seventy years ago Columbus was a neighborly place, quiet streets under arching trees, people sitting on front porches and looking up at an occasional motorcar. Well before midnight the downtown streets were silent and empty. Now with half a million people and a constant rush of traffic, it still seems an overgrown country town. While Cincinnati, Cleveland, and Toledo look away toward distant places, Columbus looks in all directions at Ohio, and it rarely reaches beyond the eighty-eight counties represented in the state legislature.

An inland city, flat as a hayfield, Columbus grew up on the National Pike (now U.S. 40) with a traffic of freight wagons and stagecoaches. For many years its landmarks were the state-

---

20. Burton Bernstein, *Thurber* (New York: Dodd, Mead and Company, 1975), p. 3.

house, the Ohio penitentiary, and the state asylums in their wooded grounds on West Broad Street. Not till after the Civil War did High Street get its first pavement. The Gallery of Fine Arts has never competed with the State Fair—midway, race track, arena, sheep and cattle pens, and displays of Ohio cheeses, tractors, plows, and pumpkins. The Ohio State University, founded as the Ohio Agricultural and Mechanical College in 1873, on the far edge of Columbus, is now surrounded by the expanding city, with forty-five thousand students hunting parking space. State basketball tournaments bring crowds from all over Ohio, and the Ohio State Buckeyes make national headlines during the autumnal football frenzy. Thurber scored the institution, which he could also remember kindly, in *The Male Animal*. Up to his time the university stressed agriculture and stinted the arts, and he enjoyed recalling a complaint of Professor James V. Denney: "Millions for manure but not one cent for literature." [21]

The second largest city in Ohio, Columbus has the largest population of native-born Americans; less than three percent of its people are foreign-born. A German influx in mid-nineteenth century was absorbed more readily than the black migration a century later. Shopping centers interrupt long streets of fading frame houses, a black population occupies the city's core, and leafy suburbs spread over miles of Franklin County.

Transportation, so evident and important in past and present Ohio, has been a base of Columbus industry, from buggy factories and wagon works to railroad shops, automotive-parts and airplane plants. Other fortunes have been made in paper, beer, and patent medicines. Its central location made Columbus a pioneer airport. Soon after World War I Port Columbus was an important terminal in the first transcontinental air service. The 1913 flood carried off slums along the Scioto River, making way for development of the Civic Center and state office buildings in the heart of the city.

For a multitude of readers on both sides of the Atlantic, Columbus and environs are Thurber country. "Half my books,"

21. Bernstein, *Thurber*, p. 39.

James Thurber said, "could not have been written if it had not
been for the city of my birth." [22] Columbus sometimes calls itself an All-American city, a not surprising term for the capital
of the most American state. It now has a bustling vigor and enterprise that didn't appear in Thurber's stories. His Columbus
was a place of quirky, self-occupied people, quite unworldy and
defenseless, more inclined to look backward than ahead. Ironi-
cally, those stories made a provincial town known to the world
and so diminished its provincialism. Thurber is Ohio's most
surprising success story—the man whose doodling became col-
lector's items and whose blindness led him into his own memory.

If James Thurber could drop into Columbus now, he would
soon bump into his own name. On Neil Avenue toward the university are Thurber Village and Thurber Towers. There is the
Thurber Elementary School on Thurber Drive, along with
Thurber Manor, hard by the Thurber Square Apartments. It will
be a long time before Columbus forgets Jim Thurber.

22. *Ohio Authors,* p. 633.

11

The Smoldering Fire

$\mathcal{A}$ CENTURY and a half ago Washington Irving proposed replacing the cumbersome "United States of America" with a shorter and more expressive name. "Columbia," both musical and appropriate, was pre-empted by a country in South America. Looking further, he suggested "Appalachia," a native name of interesting origin. It goes back to Spanish soldiers in Florida, searching for rumored treasure. They found only a poor Indian village called Apalchen, but they remembered its name, using it to designate a vague interior region. In time the name was lengthened to "Appalachia" and attached to the Eastern mountain system, which extends into a portion of Ohio.

Ohio's southeastern counties are a foothill region. Unsuited to extensive agriculture, it proved to contain riches underground. The hill farmers with flocks of sheep and patches of corn and potatoes clinging to the slopes had no interest in minerals. But after the Civil War industrialists and railroad men came in. By 1880 a new day had dawned in those knobby hills. A local historian wrote:

> The Columbus, Hocking Valley and Toledo Railroad runs through a very rich and inexhaustible mineral region . . . which is to a great extent undeveloped. It has already a heavy freighting business . . . but this is not a tithe of what the future promises when the production of coal and iron shall receive from capital

that assistance which is required to uncover the hidden wealth and bring it forth for the use of man.'' [1]

Along with that bright promise the future held the first fatal clash of labor and capital in Ohio. From near the center of the state the Hocking River winds southeastward for a hundred miles, joining the Ohio at Hockingport. Along the way coalfields underlie whole counties, and coal seams honeycomb the hills. Scratch Perry, Hocking, and Athens counties and find coal. A shallow digging uncovers two strata, four to six feet thick, of gleaming coal, the second seam twenty-five feet below the first.

A hundred years ago the mining began. For $2,000 a shaft could be tunneled into a hillside, fitted with track and dump cars, powered with men and mules; but no air and water pumps, no escape shaft, and no light except the dim lamp on a crouching miner's cap. It was dangerous work. In 1873 more than 250 Ohio miners were killed and 750 injured. From an average wage of $490 a year the miner paid his own expenses—60 cents a gallon for lamp oil and 75 cents a month for tool-sharpening. For a few years small, independent mines pitted the hills. Then the coal companies came, with new machinery and equipment, merging scattered mines in unified operation. At Brush Fork the mines produced 2,000 tons per day, a steam engine hauling out creaking trains of bank cars. At the Straitsville mine mouth coal was loaded by chute into gondolas and by steam shovel into boxcars. The mechanical shovel replaced four sweating men. Railroad crews worked night and day, hauling coal to the hungry mills and docks on Lake Erie.

Straitsville lay in the heart of the richest coal district, and much of its life was underground. A visitor to the place would find two winding, close-built streets in the valley and scattered houses on the ridge. "He is scarcely ready to think," wrote a reporter, "that there is a population of nearly three thousand in the town, but if he went into many of the houses he would find them packed with people, and very often one roof shelters half-

1. *History of Hocking Valley, Ohio* (Chicago: Inter-state Publishing Co., 1883), p. 143.

a-dozen families." [2] While machines were replacing manpower on the loading platform, men continued toiling underground, stooped men hacking at the coal face and loading dump cars for seventy cents a ton.

In 1884, with coal stockpiled on the sidings, operators cut the wage to fifty cents a ton and four thousand Hocking Valley miners went on strike. The Knights of Labor, an early union, brought in some food and clothing, but the strikers hadn't a chance. In the 1880s immigrants were pouring into America, more than half a million every year, and crowding the employment agencies. The Hocking Valley owners brought in thirty-five hundred aliens to keep the coal cars full. While bitterness grew, one Ohio owner who had not slashed wages declared that the American laborer was entitled to wages that would afford him decent food and shelter and a share in the comforts of civilization. His voice was lost in clamor and violence. On a summer night Straitsville men attacked the aliens. A mine boss was killed, and several mine hoppers and railroad bridges were set on fire. The strikers dumped barrels of oil onto coal cars and sent them, blazing, into the tunnels. When Governor George Hoadley ordered state militia to the Hocking Valley, the mines resumed operation. Next spring the strike was settled, but at Straitsville smoke seeped up from fires spreading underground.

That year, 1885, saw organization of the Ohio Federation of Labor and the beginning of labor legislation in the state. In Ohio, as elsewhere in the northern states, workers called for an eight-hour day, a demand that in 1886 brought twenty-five union leaders to a Columbus convention. Then and there was born the American Federation of Labor, with Samuel Gompers at its head. Two years later, in Columbus, separate miners' organizations forgot their differences and formed the United Mine Workers of America.

As a central state, Ohio once more had a central role in social evolution and revolution. To look backward for a moment— freedom of enterprise and the availability of raw materials enabled businessmen to make Ohio a leading industrial state; a

2. Howe, *Historical Collections,* 2:399.

corresponding freedom of action and a rapidly growing population permitted labor organizers to develop a strong labor movement in Ohio. Early in the nineteenth century workers' groups were formed in Dayton and Cincinnati. These were mutual aid societies, providing sickness and death benefits for their members. Cincinnati was in the forefront here. With a population of 10,000 in 1820, Cincinnati had thirty societies of craftsmen, and they all marched together in a Fourth of July parade in 1821. That march was prophetic. A growing concern about long hours and low wages drew the craft groups together on common ground. In 1831 Cincinnati printers began publication of the *Working Man's Shield,* a pioneer labor newspaper, and in 1850 these printers joined with those in other cities to form the first permanent national labor union. Cincinnati, the wonder city of the West, had in 1850 a population of 150,000, while no other Ohio city had yet reached 20,000. During the railroad boom of that decade Cincinnati trainmen formed a pioneer body of the Brotherhood of Locomotive Engineers. With these beginnings it is not surprising that Ohio labor organizations took the lead in the turbulent 1880s.

Meanwhile, like the smoldering labor-capital conflict, that Straitsville mine in the Hocking Valley continued burning, as it does today. In 1937 the federal Works Projects Administration (WPA) put hundreds of men to work there, digging trenches and ditches, building barriers along the coal seams. But the fire kept on burning, smoke leaking from the hillsides and seeping from the valleys. It is estimated that $50 million worth of coal has been destroyed, and the fire still smolders.

At the World's Fair in Chicago on the last day of October, 1893, the sunset gun boomed its final salute and the Exposition flags came down. In the Court of Honor workmen were crating the Ohio Memorial Monument for its return to Columbus. As they trundled it off, yellow leaves blew over the plaza and paint was flaking from the domed pavilions. Something had ended in Chicago, in Ohio, and in the nation. During 1893 U.S. revenues decreased because of the McKinley Tariff Act, the gold reserve had shrunk and foreign capital fled the country, on the New

York Stock Exchange prices fell like a broken kite. Over the wide land went news of economic crisis. Coal and iron production was halted, hundreds of banks were closing, thousands of firms faced failure, one fourth of the railroads passed into the hands of receivers. After twenty years of rampant growth, America seemed prostrate.

That winter half the people of Pittsburgh were in want. In New York and Boston strikers patrolled silent factories while militiamen patrolled the strikers. On one day in Chicago 22,000 waited in line for food tickets, and the city hall was opened for people to sleep on the floor. In Cleveland wealthy families loaned their art works for a benefit show to feed the hungry.

In that panic year, 1894, Jacob S. Coxey of Massillon, Ohio, a prosperous farmer, horse breeder, and quarry owner, wearing a standup collar and gold-rimmed glasses, had no money problems but a troubled mind. The thought of three million unemployed in a half-built country led him to plan a "living petition"—a march of hungry men to Washington to ask for government help. Coxey was a "free silver" man, and as he drove his carriage over the mud roads of Stark County, ideas were merging in his mind: idle workers and inadequate roads, bottom showing in the national treasury while western silver mines were shutting down. Early in 1894 a son was born in Coxey's home at Paul's Station; Coxey christened him Legal Tender.

The previous summer Coxey had been at the World's Fair in Chicago and there he met a young Californian named Carl Browne, an eloquent and visionary man. Now Coxey sent for Browne, proposing a partnership in good works. During the winter at Paul's Station Browne fell in love with Coxey's twenty-year-old daughter; they were married shortly before Easter. Meanwhile Coxey had formulated a "good roads" bill to benefit rural districts and a companion "community improvement" bill to launch public works in the cities. Both programs would be funded by the printing of $500 million in greenbacks, and the sale of municipal bonds to be repaid, without interest, in ten or twenty years. Senator Peffer of Kansas introduced the twin bills in Congress on March 19, 1894.

A religious man, like many of the Populists, Coxey had gathered a few zealots, some fervent Socialists, and a larger number of Ohio workmen who wanted jobs they couldn't find. A bulletin had been circulated around the state: "We want no thieves or anarchists—no boodlers and bankers—to join us. We want patriots, not bummers; no firearms, but manhood." [3] Coxey called his recruits the Army of the Commonweal.

On Easter Day, March 25, under a cold, damp sky, the army lined up on Tuscarawas Street to begin the thirty-five-day march to Washington. It was Coxey's fortieth birthday. More than a demonstration of misery, the march was meant to mobilize public support for the relief bills in Congress. There was an undeniably Ohio flavor in this daft campaign—its zeal linked to organization, compassion paired with publicity, warm heart joined to impulsive and expectant mind. In short, Coxey had an offbeat idea and was giving it a try.

As press agent, Browne had made a front-page story of the movement. Sixteen reporters were on hand when the ragged army began to march. At the head rode Browne, mounted on the stallion Currier from Coxey's Dixiana farm. Coxey rode in a phaeton, its matched team driven by a Negro groom. With him were his wife and the infant Legal Tender. Behind the leaders came a hundred shabby and silent men. Others filled six wagons drawn by twelve horses from Coxey's farm. Banners on the wagons proclaimed: "The Commonwealth of Christ," "The Kingdom of Heaven Is At Hand," and "Peace on Earth, Good Will toward Men, but Death to Interest on Bonds." A tent wagon carried poles and canvas, stoves and stores. Townspeople on the line of march brought in straw for the men to sleep on and food to augment the army rations.

In gray March weather they trudged through the mill town of Canton, the pottery town of Alliance, the Quaker town of Salem, and on into Pennsylvania. The army had grown, some men dropping out but more joining in; there was food three times a day for this shuffling column. In the Pennsylvania mountains more men fell out than were added. At Cumberland

3. Rose, *Cleveland*, p. 551.

on the Cheseapeake and Ohio Canal, Coxey put the whole outfit into a few coal barges. For ninety miles they rested around the cooking stoves before hitting the road again at Williamsport. In the last seventy miles to Washington the numbers doubled. A Washington reporter tramping out to meet them on April 29 tallied 336 bedraggled men, many not yet twenty years old. He marched the last miles with them. Their pockets were empty, but not one asked him for a cent.

Coxey's comrade Browne, at work by mail and telegraph, had enlisted several hundred men in Los Angeles and San Francisco; they were to join the army in Washington. When the railroads threw them off freight cars, they commandeered trains for St. Louis and Chicago. There, amid rising hostility, the West Coast phalanx scattered, though many found their way to Washington where Coxey was encamped. Campground was the old Brightwood Driving Park on the northern edge of the city. From Philadelphia came a new contingent led by bearded Christopher Columbus Jones in a plug hat and dusty suit of clothes. They were accompanied by reporters on bicycles.

In that uneasy season Coxey's army had been headlined in the press, *Harper's Weekly* editorialized, "until some timid folks are almost persuaded that the republic is in danger of mob rule and that society is on the brink of rebellion." The actual number gathered in Washington, said the editor, was less than six thousand, mostly unemployed workmen with a sprinkling of tramps, adventurers, and criminals. The talk of the leaders was a vague denunciation of corporations, with a hint of distribution of property. The movement, he concluded, was foolish. "Its chief support is the newspaper reports, which magnify the number of recruits, describe great additional armies which are always about to be formed, and gratify petty seekers after notoriety by recording their silly deeds and words." [4]

Seven days later the *Weekly* added to the publicity by running photographs of Coxey and Browne at the head of a procession and giving the cover to a cartoon of "The Original Coxey Army"—a procession of men in frock coats and silk hats

4. *Harper's Weekly* 38(1894):411.

marching from a train of Pullman cars to the Capitol plaza with drums, horns, and placards: "Help the Feeble Steel Industry," "Help the Poor Plutocrats," "Please Assist the Tin-Plate Infant," "Help a Poor Sugar Refiner," "Help a Poor Coal Baron." [5] The rich asked more than the poor from their government; these supplicants wanted higher duties and larger profits. They were met on the Capitol steps by deeply bowing Congressmen.

For Coxey's army May first was the day of demonstration. Under bright noon sun Coxey and Browne led a parade up Pennsylvania Avenue, sidewalk crowds watching four thousand men in a straggling line. At the Capitol building they merged with twelve thousand petitioners already assembled there. A cordon of police barred the way up the broad steps. When General Coxey asked permission to make a speech, the police chief told him not to. Looking like a congressman with his silk scarf and ribboned glasses, he then read a formal protest, which Browne passed out to the reporters. Led by the police across the street to the Library of Congress, Coxey was released, and from there he watched the confrontation.

Striding onto the Capitol steps Browne waved an arm, and the ragged army pressed forward. At that moment mounted police whirled in, and police ranks scattered men across the lawns in all directions. Fifteen minutes later the banners of protest and petition lay trampled on the empty plaza.

In a courtroom Coxey and Browne were given a twenty-day jail term for demonstrating on the Capitol grounds. An unnamed Washington woman bailed them out. A week later, while the army sat around the big mess tent at Brightwood, both leaders were taken to court again. They were fined five dollars each and sentenced to twenty days' imprisonment for walking on the grass and spoiling the Capitol shrubbery.

After all their foreboding, the Eastern papers had a laugh, but back in Ohio Coxey's cause still shone. While sitting in the Washington jail, he was nominated to Congress by the People's party in the eighteenth Ohio District. When his twenty

5. *Harper's Weekly* 38(1894):433.

days were up, he had his campaign planned. With a three-pole circus tent drawn by forty horses he crisscrossed the Ohio district, speaking twice a day to cheering crowds. In the election he polled twenty-six percent of the votes, second best of the three parties. But the panic was past, and populism faded when Coxey's neighbor William McKinley, from Canton, just seven miles away, went to the White House on the slogan "A Full Dinner Pail." In 1932, when depression again darkened the land, the people of Massillon elected 78-year-old Jacob Coxey their mayor. He died there in 1951, at the age of ninety-seven.

Industrial Massillon, maker of iron and steel, was also the birthplace of woman's rights in Ohio, unless that distinction belongs to Oberlin, founded, 1833, as the first coeducational college in America. At Massillon in 1852 was organized the Ohio Women's Rights Association. From a slow start that movement gained momentum through the years, so that historians have ranked Ohio second only to New York in woman's-rights legislation. In 1919 Ohio ratified the national woman-suffrage amendment. In 1933 six women became members of the Ohio legislature, and with the election of Florence Allen to its supreme court, Ohio was the first state to seat a woman on its highest bench. Since then increasing numbers of Ohio women have won places in business managment, on health and welfare boards, and in college faculties and administration.

The most striking of Ohio women campaigners was Victoria Claflin Woodhull. From the hamlet of Homer, on the edge of Licking County, the clairvoyant Claflin sisters, Victoria and Tennessee, moved to New York in 1868, where their spiritualism attracted the interest of the elder Cornelius Vanderbilt. With his support they established a prosperous brokerage business and in 1870 began publishing *Woodhull & Claflin's Weekly,* a journal demanding equal rights for women and the single standard of morality, and denouncing prostitution and abortion. In spreading their cause the sisters founded the Equal Rights party, which in 1872 nominated Victoria as its candidate for president. After Vanderbilt's death the sisters took their crusade to England. Victoria, a woman of striking beauty and presence, soon married a London banker who came to her lectures. Under the banner of woman's rights she made widely publicized visits to the United States. She died in England in 1927.

The labor movement in Ohio has filled many books, with many more to come. It is, over all, a remarkable success story, though a costly one. A prolonged strike of Ohio miners in 1914–1915 was finally arbitrated without violence. But the next winter was different. A Youngstown steel strike, beginning two days after Christmas and idling nearly fifteen thousand men, brought riot, death, and destruction. During World War I thousands of women began work in Ohio factories, a movement that has kept on growing ever since. Labor organizations swelled their rolls in the 1920s.

From the multitude of Ohio workmen there emerged a national leader. Like most Ohio leaders he began at the bottom. As a young man hacking at the coal face in Coshocton County mines, William Green learned about labor. As a two-term member of the Ohio senate he learned about legislation; he became the author of the Ohio Workmen's Compensation Law. As an officer of the United Mine Workers he learned about national labor legislation. In 1924 Green succeeded Samuel Gompers as president of the American Federation of Labor with its 200,000 members.

Ahead were a few years of labor progress, then a long, dark decade of depression. With its large agricultural population and its diversity of business, Ohio suffered less than some other states. Yet nowhere did depression leave more scars than in the one-industry city of Akron.

In 1870 when Akron was a canal and flour-milling town on the canal, Benjamin Franklin Goodrich watched a neighbor's house burn down when the fire hose burst. Goodrich then started making Anchor Fire Hose, and so began Akron's rubber business. In the village of Columbiana, watching stagecoaches grind through on the way to Pittsburgh, young Harvey Firestone thought of making rubber rims for buggy wheels; in 1900 he came to Akron and organized the Firestone Tire & Rubber Company. Meanwhile in Akron the Seiberling brothers were making pneumatic bicycle tires; they named their rubber business for Charles Goodyear, who first vulcanized rubber. Goodyear never saw Ohio, where success was waiting. He died in debt in New York in 1860; though he took out many patents on rubber products, he never thought of rubber tires. Rubber was long considered an odd and useless substance, though Joseph Priestley, the English chemist and clergyman who first isolated oxygen, had found that it would rub out pencil marks: hence the name "rubber." It waited for Akron men to find it profitable beyond belief. By 1910 Akron was the rubber capital of the world.

Between 1910 and 1920 the rubber industry stretched itself. Through Appalachian hills and hollows, and in far-off Latvia, Albania, and Greece, went word of plentiful work and high wages in Akron—"the City of Opportunity." In ten years its population expanded from 69,000 to 209,000. Business ballooned in the 1920s, and then collapsed. In 1931 great mill yards were empty, and a third of Akron's workmen were unemployed. On a January day in 1932, the cruelest year of the depression, the vice-president of the First Central Trust Company put a revolver to his head—Ohio's first banker-suicide. A few weeks later Stanley Mikolajcsk, a laid-off tire builder, jumped to his death from the North Hill viaduct. In June eighty-five Akron war veterans climbed into five small trucks and drove off toward Washington to demand an army bonus. Part of the "bonus army" from all over, they left without a day's food supply and with no idea of what to do if they ever reached the Capitol.

While Akron banks and loan companies went out of business, workmen's families were evicted from mortgaged homes. One family was portrayed by Ruth McKenney, a young reporter on the *Beacon-Journal*. In years ahead Ruth McKenney wrote the Broadway hit *My Sister Eileen* and a dozen other books. The one she preferred was *Industrial Valley*, a compilation of her depression stories in Akron. Of all the people in that tense and troubled book a reader is least likely to forget the Miachiaroli family and union organizer Alex O 'Lari.

On a winter afternoon in Moon Street in falling mist mixed with smudgy flakes of rubber smoke, the eight Miachiaroli children watched strange men clumping through their house and lugging out the stove, the washtub, tables, beds, and chairs. They stacked them in the street. Near the pile of furniture the kids built a little fire on the curb and warmed their hands around it. Some men came from the Unemployed Council, led by Alex O'Lari. They picked things up and carried them back into the house, and a neighbor woman brought a kettle of steaming soup. While the kids were eating, a police car dropped off Patrolman Emery Davis. He told the men not to move anything more. When the oldest Miachiaroli boy came up the porch steps with his arms full, the patrolman threatened him. O'Lari stepped between them, pushing the officer away. Told he was under arrest, O'Lari demanded a warrant. On the porch men pressed around the patrolman. Lunging with his night stick he fell to his knees. In that helpless posture he drew his revolver and fired. The councilmen scattered, all but O'Lari who, spitting blood, sank onto the porch steps in the sooty drizzle. It took him four days to die.

While he lay in the hospital, the newspapers blamed O'Lari for resisting arrest, but when he died, the *Beacon-Journal* stated: "Hunger cannot be clubbed down; neither can a destitute family's right to shelter be denied." [6] On the day of the funeral eight thousand silent people marched through a cold rain to the cemetery. Beside the open grave a friend bared his head and said, "This man gave his life for the working class." [7]

In the pinch of prolonged depression, with thousands of workers replaced by labor-saving machinery, bewildered tire builders and pit men turned from their helpless company unions to the United Rubber Workers, an organization resisted by the companies. The new union made a slow start in 1934, but in the face of further lay-offs its numbers grew. One sit-down followed another in the big plants as the URW organized Akron's factories. The last big strike ended with an arrangement of six-hour shifts and a twenty-four-hour week—sharing the work and the wages until there was full-time work for all. In 1937 with

6. Ruth McKenney, *Industrial Valley* (New York: Harcourt, Brace and Company, 1939), p. 43.

7. McKenney, *Industrial Valley,* p. 44.

70,000 members the United Rubber Workers broke from the slow-moving AFL and allied with the CIO.

In Ohio's steel industry 1937 was a crucial year. When the companies refused negotiation with the Steel Workers' Organizing Committee, 50,000 workers struck seven big plants in the Mahoning Valley—lines of pickets night and day patrolling lifeless mills. While a mediation board heard employee grievances and company rebuttals, two strikers were killed and twenty-seven were wounded. State militia troops sent to Youngstown found the station massed with chanting men. During the next week five more were killed and 307 injured. In the eventual settlement the Supreme Court upheld the right of workers to collective bargaining through representatives of their own choosing. It was a hard-won victory.

The story of Ohio embraces a dynamic industrial development and a massive labor movement. Throughout a century of management-labor contest, Ohio has been in the middle, with a gathering of forces on each side. A middle position was intended in the enactment of the Taft-Hartley Law in 1947. A complex law grappling with complex problems, its object was to balance the bargaining rights of labor and management. Senator Taft considered it his greatest accomplishment, but it had, perhaps inevitably, a controversial reception. While William Green of the AFL called it a slave-labor law conceived in hostility to the unions, some businessmen called it a surrender to labor. Probably that contention attests its middle stand. At any rate, withstanding repeated attempts at repeal, it has worked on the side of arbitration rather than against it.

By their very nature labor and management are yoked together; neither could exist without the other. Like the positive and negative charges in electricity, their tension creates an entity. Since World War II Ohio has seen fewer strikes and more arbitration. Yet in a free system the tug-of-war continues, as, at New Straitsville in the far corner of Perry County, hidden fires still eat into the coal face and smoke seeps up from underground.

12

To the White House

$\mathcal{W}$HILE touring Japan in 1920, Will Rogers sometimes heard a familiar word. Told that "O-hi-o" meant a friendly greeting, Will doubted he could remember that; where he came from it meant "president." Ohio has sent to the Capital eight presidents, three vice-presidents, three chief justices, eight associate justices and thirty-five cabinet officers. Also-rans from Ohio were Norman Thomas, perennial Socialist presidential nominee, and Virginia Claflin Woodhull, the first woman presidential candidate. She lost to an Ohioan, President Grant, who was already there. The first woman member of Congress to represent the United States in the United Nations was Frances P. Bolton, elected from a Cuyahoga County district in 1952.

Despite these break-throughs Ohio's political moves have generally been cautious. The conservatism of an agricultural population made an odd alliance with wealthy industrialists. Yet that alliance was characteristic of Ohio, a state made up of opposites. America's first shopping center is said to have been created in Columbus; its name—Town and Country. In the political shopping center, Ohio has elected about as many Democratic governors as Republican, though all its presidents, except the Whig William Henry Harrison, have been Republican. Ohio men were active in the Republican party from its beginning, helping to build a national organization that embodied policies of broad potential appeal. Within some fifteen years after its in-

154

ception in 1854 the party lost its crusading radiance in a growing pragmatism. But for more than half a century it proved to be a consistent elector of presidents. Eight Ohio presidents in sixty years—Harrison, Grant, Hayes, Garfield, Harrison, McKinley, Taft, Harding. What do they have in common? The first thing that comes to mind is misfortune. Four of them died in office, and two of those, though men of generous good will, were shot by assassins. Two of the Ohio presidents were in office too briefly to leave a record. Of those who lived out a full term, two were re-elected, two were defeated for a second term, and one relinquished office without regret.

Another thing in common was moderation. Ohio had a broadly varied population and a balanced and stable economy. Its political leaders avoided extremes. There have been radicals in Ohio but not in high places in Ohio politics.

Five of the presidents—all the list up to McKinley—were generals, with military records that bespoke patriotism and the command of men in strenuous situations. Old William Henry Harrison was the General throughout his campaign and could never have been president without the popular appeal of frontier warfare and battles long ago. The others were more recently generals. In a little-noted season of his life, the winter of 1862, Nathaniel Hawthorne put away his literary notebooks and took the train from quiet Concord, Mass., to turbulent and troubled Washington. He wanted to see what the war was doing to America. He found the capital a-swarm with office-seekers, wire-pullers, would-be inventors, gloom-and-doom editors, railway directors, and mail contractors. Through the cigar smoke of Willard's Hotel he glimpsed the future of his country—"one bullet-headed general will succeed another in the presidential chair; and veterans will hold the offices at home and abroad, and sit in Congress and the state legislatures, and fill all the avenues of public life." [1] He saw the old America receding while new populations surged onto the prairies and the interior country

1. Nathaniel Hawthorne, "Chiefly About War-Matters" *Atlantic Monthly,* 10(July 1862):45.

dominated national politics. What to Hawthorne had been hinterland would become the heartland of the nation.

The romancer was a realistic prophet; except that "bulletheaded" does not describe the presidents from Ohio. They were practical men, not a martinet or a crusader among them. Not even a really strong leader. They were politicians more than commanders. They knew the art of compromise and the prudence of bending with the wind. Geography more than statesmanship or military reputation—with the exception of Grant— made them presidents.

In the half century after the Civil War Ohio became the heart of the nation. Through it flowed an ever increasing commerce. To it came people and ideas from both East and West, so that Ohio grew national in mind and character. The prospering state nourished a great variety of colleges, theological and technical, scientific and literary, in tranquil villages and strident cities. There was no preponderant industry to overshadow the state. The four great pursuits—agriculture, commerce, mining, and manufacture—were remarkably balanced in Ohio. With one in seven Ohioans of foreign birth in 1890, the state had neither the greatest nor the least admixture of immigrants. Its ethnic strains were richly various—Czech, Danish, Dutch, Finnish, German, Greek, Hungarian, Irish, Italian, Polish, Russian, Scottish, Serbian, Swedish, Swiss, Ukrainian—along with significant numbers of blacks. That remarkable range and balance added to the "national" character of the state. Altogether, Ohio made an advantageous background for a president. To any other part of the nation an Ohio candidate could not seem alien.

By 1840 the roads to Ohio had brought men of many voices: federalism and republicanism, abolition and states' rights, high tariff and low tariff, pro-Irish and anti-Irish, paper currency and hard money, high taxes and low taxes and no taxes at all. Many doctrines sounded in town halls and taverns and in the closeprinted columns of the Western press. Election time was a season of huge rallies, festive parades, fist fights and barbecues and shouting in the shade of the courthouse square. The election of 1840 was the noisiest of all.

There were things to shout about. Financial panic had swept the country in 1837, and it was hardly past when a new depression struck in 1839. There were rent riots in New York, banks falling apart, states going broke. While President Van Buren drove through the streets of Washington in a maroon coach with outriders, nobody knew what to do about the chaotic national currency. But the loudest shouting said the least about the nation's troubles. It echoed a border battle on a November morning in 1811, a small battle soon ended, on a frontier creek with an unlikely name. In 1840 an uproar rose over a "Log Cabin and Hard Cider" candidate, and "Tippecanoe and Tyler too!" went like a March wind over the wintry land.

In this 1840 extravaganza the young nation, like a mixed-up adolescent, was venting energy without much aim. Boisterous, gangly, fast-grown Ohio was sounding its own untried voice and feeling its muscle. To the surprise of the whole expanding country the center of American gravity had moved into the Ohio Valley.

William Henry Harrison had been a territorial governor, army general, U.S. congressman and senator. The inchoate Whig Party nominated him for president in 1836. When he lost to New York's Van Buren, Harrison, age sixty-three, retired to his farm at North Bend on the Ohio River. He seemed a man whose public life was past. But the panic of 1837 buffeted Van Buren, and Western newspapers, most notably those in Ohio, described a homespun Harrison, who tilled his own land, as the man to replace the effete New Yorker. Harrison was nominated by the Whig convention in December 1839. No platform was adopted, and instead of principles and policies, the campaign was waged with rallies, songs, and slogans. In 1840 the United States was a nation of seventeen million hard-working people, glad to forget financial panic in a free-swinging campaign.

In 1840, for the first time, two nationally organized parties contested for the White House. In Ohio the Whigs had the stronger leadership, and they showed greater spirit and drive than their rival Democrats. The public was attracted by party myths and emblems, and on that score the Whigs had a winner—a blue-blooded Virginian who had gone to the frontier and, like so many voters, had a part in the winning of the West. Harrison's "log cabin" lifestyle and his life story made for appealing songs and slogans. Even voters who had never crossed the Appalachians were susceptible, as all American generations have been, to the myth of the West. In England to go West was to die, but in the New World the West was a realm of venture, striving, and hope. Harrison was a potent symbol.

Early in 1840 the Ohio state convention assembled in Columbus to ratify the Harrison nomination. In a remarkable demonstration some ten thousand supporters converged from all over the state. In the crowd were some 950 from Ross County alone. After days on the way delegations vied for attention; the big parade included a simulated Lake Erie brig mounted on wheels, a log cabin swarming with "Mad River trappers," an Ohio River steamboat spouting smoke and steam, and a replica of Fort Meigs with thirty men at the gun posts. Finally came an immense ball covered with political graffiti from a dozen states. It was pushed by men singing:

> What has caused this great commotion
> All the country through?
> It is the ball a-rolling on
> For Tippecanoe and Tyler too.[2]

While Van Buren toured the East, speaking from an open carriage, Harrison let the people come to him. For editors and party leaders the old General had a ready welcome, though he would not discuss politics on Sunday. When an Indianapolis paper called for a great rally on the Tippecanoe battlefield, Harrison stayed home. But 40,000 came—with bands, banners, and wagonloads of pork, cider, hominy, and cornmeal. A reporter counted badges from all over Ohio and Indiana and from as far away as Massachusetts, Missouri, and the Iowa Territory.

Labeled "General Mum" by the Democrats, Harrison was said to be too old and tired to face the people. Proving his vigor he traveled to big rallies at Fort Meigs and Greenville. In hourlong speeches he reviewed past struggles and recalled the

2. E. D. Mansfield, *Personal Memories* (Cincinnati: Robert Clarke & Co., 1879), p. 318.

comradeship of the frontier. Though he offered no program for 1840, he voiced the feelings of people who had tamed a wilderness. Powerful memories and emotions, powerful to American people everywhere, clustered around the old General. The greatest rally came in September at Dayton, a town of 6,000, where Harrison spoke in a field massed with 50,000 people. To that celebration went the Cincinnati editor Edward Deering Mansfield, driving a buggy on roads streaming with wagons, carts, carriages, and families on horseback and afoot. Years later Mansfield remembered crossing the last high ground above the Miami Valley. "As we looked down upon the city below . . . Dayton was literally covered with flags. Every house seemed to have a flag, which waved in the breeze while the bright sun shone upon it." ³ When he reached the meeting ground, bands and processions were pouring in from all directions. Only a few, of all those thousands, heard Harrison speak, but all joined in the great choruses of shouting and song. In the election a few weeks later, Harrison carried all the states but seven. In Ohio the turnout of voters was an astonishing eighty-five percent.

On inaugural day, March 4, the new president gave thanks for a fine new coach presented by the Whigs of Baltimore, and then mounted his favorite horse, Old Whitey. At the Capitol he spoke for an hour in raw March air, bareheaded and without gloves or overcoat. In the next days he met with department heads, committeemen, and endless office-seekers, and he led a delegation of Indian chiefs to the War Office. With his judicious cabinet appointments and a prospect of congressional support, the future looked bright. But at the end of March Harrison fell ill of pneumonia, and on April 4 he died. He was buried above the Ohio River at North Bend. Eventually a sandstone shaft was erected there, with a beacon light to guide river pilots. For years they saluted Old Tip with a soft, hoarse whistle as they passed.

When Grant was buried beside the Hudson under an ornate dome supported by six Ionic columns and surrounded by the

3. Mansfield, *Memories,* pp. 319–320.

city tumult, it seemed out of keeping for the rumpled, slump-shouldered, sad-eyed man who never lost the memories of an Ohio farm boy. Over the entrance to the tomb are his four words *Let us have peace;* an almost ironic rubric for a man whose greatness was called forth by war. His life was all paradox—the many years of failure suddenly yielding to years of fame; the fame abruptly darkened by adversity and slander; the scrubby brigadier dismissing the magic of his leadership: "The men only wanted someone to give them a command;" [4] the iron-willed general baring his head to a commander he had defeated; the war-famed president dismissing the military guard at the White House; the laconic man in a cruel illness filling two big volumes with a great *Memoirs*.

On May 19, 1868, a Soldiers and Sailors Reunion, forerunner of the American Legion, paraded through Chicago and in a mock caucus named U. S. Grant for president. The next day eight thousand Republicans, converging on Chicago, crowded into Crosby's Opera House. Speaking for the Illinois delegation John A. Logan, who had served at Vicksburg, nominated General Ulysses Simpson Grant, and the assembly chorused acclamation. At his desk in the army headquarters in Washington, Grant received the news in silence. His brief acceptance speech the next day concluded with "Let us have peace." [5]

During the campaign Grant remained at home and made no speeches, but across the country Grant Clubs marched, cheered and sang:

> So boys, a final bumper
> While we all in chorus chant,
> For next President we nominate
> Our own Ulysses Grant.
> And if asked what state he hails from,
> Our sole reply shall be
> From Appomattox Court House
> With its famous apple tree. [6]

4. Dorothy Burne Goebel and Julius Goebel, Jr., *Generals in the White House* (Garden City: Doubleday, Doran and Company, 1945), p. 169.
5. W. E. Woodward, *Meet General Grant* (New York: Horace Liveright, 1928), p. 396.
6. Goebel, *Generals,* p. 185. Reprinted by permission of the publishers.

Grant must have heard the song, but he never mentioned it. He had no ear for tune or tempo; even at West Point he was often out of step.

Brown County, bordering the Ohio River halfway between Portsmouth and Cincinnati, has fertile fields and rolling pastures. In Grant's boyhood it was famous for steamboats and horses. From shipyards at Ripley came the *Paragon* in 1827, the *Banner* and the *Companion* in 1828, and a dozen vessels topped by the big six-boiler *Conqueror* in the 1830s. In those years the county's chief export was horses. Draft horses went east, stamping in the main deck and whinnying at passing steamers. Matched pairs were shipped downriver to Southern planters and liverymen. On the last Saturday of each summer month the Ripley horse fair drew buyers from as far as St. Louis and Philadelphia.

As a Brown County boy Grant loathed his father's tannery but liked to work with horses—plowing, furrowing, hauling wood and hay, bringing in the harvest. All his life he was a shrewd judge of horses and helpless in money matters. At eight years old he rode to a neighbor's farm on a happy errand. To the owner of a clean-limbed colt he announced: "Papa says I may offer you twenty dollars for the colt, but it you won't take that, I am to offer twenty-two and a half, and if you won't take that, to give you twenty-five." [7] Fifty years later he was no better prepared to deal with the plunger Ferdinand Ward, gold speculators Jay Gould and James Fisk, and railroad magnate William H. Vanderbilt. The Gilded Age, high, wide, and heedless, made him a dupe and a victim.

In the last years in New York, when he had lost everything but a viselike memory and a tenacious will, the man of few words called on language to pay his creditors. For *The Century* he wrote accounts of three Civil War battles, and circulation of the magazine soared by 50,000. Then his friend Mark Twain brought a contract for two volumes of memoirs, to be published by the Charles L. Webster Company and sold by subscription throughout the country.

7. *Personal Memoirs of U. S. Grant* 2 vols. (New York: Charles L. Webster & Company, 1885), 1:30.

While he relived the battles of Chattanooga, the Shenandoah, and the Wilderness, Grant fought another battle. In the summer of 1884 there began a soreness in his throat. The doctor forbade cigars and spoke of "serious epithelial trouble." [8] Grant himself named it—cancer. There were no more carriage drives behind fast horses, no more trudging through fresh snow in Central Park. But he kept at his task, dictating till his voice rasped to a whisper, then writing with a pad and pencil. In the spring of 1885 came massive hemorrhages and excruciating pain, but his will held on. In June he was taken to an Adirondack health resort. On the cottage porch, head in a woolen cap, scarf wrapped around his throat, a shawl over his knees, he worked through the gruelling campaign for Richmond. When his voice gave out, he made notes for his doctor. In an Ohio schoolroom he had learned "A noun is the name of a thing;" [9] now his tired hand scrawled: "A verb is anything that signifies to be; to do; or to suffer. I signify all three." [10] On July 10 he wrote: "Buck [Ulysses S. Grant, Jr.] has brought up the last of the first vol. in print. In two weeks if they work hard they can have the second vol. copied ready to go to the printer. I will then feel that my work is done." [11] He died thirteen days later.

The life that led to a tomb above a river in the city's never-ending roar had begun beside a river, in a two-room cottage at Point Pleasant where the Ohio rolls in silence under the Kentucky hills. In early pages of the *Memoirs* Grant recalled Georgetown, Ohio, a few miles inland, "where my youth had been spent and to which my daydreams carried me back as my future home if I should ever be able to retire on a competency." [12] Now the people come to see the two-room cottage by the river and the two-room schoolhouse in drowsy Georgetown where a farm boy wondered about the long road that lay before him.

8. Horace Green, *General Grant's Last Stand* (New York: Charles Scribner's Sons, 1936), p. 287.
9. Grant, *Memoirs,* 1:25.
10. Green, *Last Stand,* p. 47.
11. Green, *Last Stand,* p. 320.
12. Grant, *Memoirs,* 1:40.

When Henry Howe rode into Lower Sandusky (now Fremont, Ohio) in 1846, a young lawyer told him of an odd and interesting character who deserved a place in Howe's Ohio book. The historian replied that Ohio had more odd people than he had time and space for. In his later edition, in 1890, Howe gave time and space to the young lawyer, though not in 1846. "In those days," Howe wrote, "there was nobody around to tell him that he would become three times governor of Ohio and then president of the United States—Rutherford B. Hayes." [13]

Grant's election owed everything to his accomplishments in war and nothing to Ohio. He was succeeded by another Ohio general whose war record, though more than creditable, had not made him known to the nation. Hayes owed his election to his record as an Ohio governor and to the vigor and determination of the Republican party.

The two presidents began life in Ohio in 1822. Five months after Grant's birth at Point Pleasant, Hayes was born in Delaware, Ohio, near the center of the state. His parents had come from Vermont, and his father died shortly before the son was born. The boy's uncle, Sardis Birchard, already established in Ohio, sent his nephew to Connecticut for schooling. From there Hayes wrote to his uncle: "I have an aversion to Yankees." [14] He made himself a crest, showing a scythe, a rake, and a pitchfork, crossed, and a haycock [for Hayes] in the background, and signed it "R.H.B., Buckeye." [15] He informed his uncle that rather than Yale he would prefer a college in Ohio.

From Kenyon College, where he excelled in scholarship, chess, and ice-skating, he went to Harvard Law School. After two years' practice in his uncle's town of Fremont, he was taken with a throat and bronchial ailment. Doctors advised "an entire change of life, diet, climate, etc.—such as going to sea or something of that sort." [16] Although he had divided feelings about the War with Mexico, he thought of enlisting for army

13. Howe, *Historical Collections,* 2:523.

14. *Diary and Letters of Rutherford Birchard Hayes.* Edited by Charles Richard Williams. 5 vols. (The Ohio State Archaeological and Historical Society, 1922), 1:16.

15. Hayes, *Diary and Letters,* 1:24.

16. Hayes, *Diary and Letters,* 1:203.

service. Instead he took a summer outing in New England, in a surprisingly robust style. "I visited the highest mountain in Massachusetts, Greylock; the highest in Vermont, Ascutney; and the highest in the United States, Mount Washington." [17] After three months he was back in Ohio with health restored.

In 1849 Hayes moved to Cincinnati. There he married, had children, built a prosperous practice, was made city solicitor, became an active Republican and a leader in the select Literary Club. On Christmas eve in 1859 he wrote:

> Ten years ago tonight I came to Cincinnati. Arrived at Pearl Street House about 9:30 P.M., a cold, clear night, a stranger seeking room among the brethren of the greenbag. Without any extraordinary success, without the sort of success that makes men giddy sometimes, I have nevertheless found what I sought. [18]

This balanced man was destined to have some extraordinary success; indeed, the kind that makes some men giddy. His success came because he was steady, conscientious, industrious, and dependable, and it would never carry him off balance.

At the outbreak of war in 1861 he entered army service, being elected captain of a company formed from the Literary Club. Commissioned major of the 23rd Ohio Infantry, he spent a year in West Virginia. When his unit was transferred to the Potomac, he saw more fighting and was wounded at South Mountain. Though urged to resume civilian life, he stayed in uniform, serving throughout Sheridan's campaign in the Shenandoah Valley. At bloody Cedar Creek he was mistakenly reported killed; though his horse was shot from under him, he limped out of that battle and into the rank of brigadier general.

Elected to Congress from the Cincinnati district in 1864, Hayes did not take his seat until the war's end. After a congressional term he was elected governor of Ohio. In that office he improved the state's financial management and its welfare agencies and helped to establish the Ohio State University and the Ohio Geological Survey.

After two terms as governor Hayes returned to Fremont,

17. Hayes, *Diary and Letters,* 1:216.
18. Hayes, *Diary and Letters,* 1:547.

where he practiced law and managed the estate left to him by his uncle. Three years later, though he had not chosen to re-enter public life, he was nominated again for governor. His opponent was the old war-horse ex-Senator and ex-Governor William Allen, the thundering "Alanno" of Melville's *Mardi.* Though reluctant to set a third-term precedent, Hayes campaigned with all-out energy and was elected in a close ballot. The campaign had focused on the integrity of the national currency, Hayes standing for sound money and against inflation.

Hayes held the nation's attention when he returned to the governor's office in January 1876. That spring he sent state troops into Stark County to quell riots over a mine strike. Though sympathetic with labor, he declared that grievances could not be settled by violence. This balanced attitude came natural to a man who belonged to a state that had nurtured labor unions along with industrial development. In private practice and public office Hayes had seen the forces at work in Ohio— new techniques in farm and factory, wealth increasing, population growing, natural resources being converted into products for use in Ohio and other states and lands. Ohio was a place of progress. One could see that the present was better than the past, and could believe that the future would be better than the present—if only moderation and stability were maintained.

In June 1876 the Republican national convention in Cincinnati nominated Hayes for president. During the presidential campaign he remained in Ohio except for an official visit on Ohio Day to the Centennial celebration in Philadelphia. But an all-star cast of speakers was stumping for him—James G. Blaine, John Sherman, Benjamin Harrison; Carl Schurz of Wisconsin, Robert J. Ingersoll of Illinois, and Mark Twain.

The historic Hayes-Tilden standoff kept the presidential choice in doubt long after the November election. On January 2, 1887, Governor Hayes made his annual address to the Ohio legislature, and the entire nation searched his message for some reference, direct or sidelong, to the disputed presidency. There was not a syllable. With characteristic tact and restraint Hayes confined his words to Ohio matters. Wrote the *New York Times:* "This modest message is businesslike, free from flourish and flurry, and reveals an utter unconsciousness in the author of being today the most conspicuous and interesting character in the nation.'' [19] On the first day of March, with the electoral commission about to announce his election, he resigned as governor and boarded the train for Washington.

Early in the campaign Hayes had declared himself a one-term man; if elected, he would not seek nor accept a second term. On that basis he made appointments without regard to party interests. He opposed senatorial control of patronage and forbade assessment of federal employees for party funds. In an age of sellout he proposed reform, and despite congressional opposition he strengthened the civil service system. Hoping for the best, he withdrew federal troops from the Southern states and restored their autonomy. Sound financial management and the resumption of specie payment encouraged business activity. Still, there was agitation in the land.

In the first summer of the Hayes administration a railroad strike spreading westward from Pennsylvania brought on riots and arson in Ohio cities. At Newark, the old canal town that that had become a railroad center, workers reduced to three day's work a week at $1.58 a day grew desperate. When trains were derailed and sidetracked, the state militia was sent in. From New Straitsville six hundred coal miners started for Newark to battle the militia, but a committee of citizens dissuaded them from clashing with the massed troopers. From Washington President Hayes wrote that force could not bring a settlement; arbitration was the only way.

Into the White House the presidential family brought the friendly simplicity of its Ohio background. A self-contained man, Hayes had no close political friendships, though he was accessible enough. He received callers informally, shirt-sleeved in his strewn office, as he had done in Fremont. He had time for his family—morning prayers after breakfast, a carriage ride in late afternoon, sometimes hymns in the Blue Room on winter evenings. Lucy Webb Hayes was a poised, handsome, and hos-

19. Charles Richard Williams, *The Life of Rutherford Birchard Hayes,* 2 vols. (Boston: Houghton Mifflin Company, 1914), 1:412n.

pitable woman, devoted to her husband and five children, and to temperance, which to her meant total abstinence. She declined to serve wine at formal dinners, and the president assented. Early in their Washington residence Mrs. Hayes entertained a WCTU group from Ohio, where just four years past they had closed the thirteen saloons of Hillsboro by a sit-in—a kneel-in actually—with prayers and hymns. In Washington "Lemonade Lucy" was a jibe that failed. The American public, fed up with the indulgence and ostentation of the Gilded Age, respected the quiet respectability of this First Family. Its members were religious without sanctimony, upright without self-righteousness. From small-town Ohio they had brought values the nation needed and wanted. Their example would not harm the chances of the next Ohio candidate.

In January 1881, the *New York Graphic* wrote: "Hayes will step out of office on the 4th of March with more peace and blessing than any president in fifty-six years. Who since Monroe has gone out both *willingly* and regretted?" [20] Two months later the Hayes family willingly exchanged the White House for Spiegel Grove.

In 1885 historian Henry Howe, approaching his seventieth birthday, proposed to make a second tour of Ohio to expand and update his *Historical Collections*. President Hayes, whose copy of Howe's first edition was well worn, invited him to Fremont. This time the historian arrived by train rather than on horseback, carrying a camera in the place of sketching pads. He spent two autumn weeks at Spiegel ("Mirror") Grove. The spacious mansion, set in twenty-five acres of forest, ponds, and brooks, was a place of comfort and character. The library held eleven thousand volumes, and the halls and parlors were lined with portraits, busts, and landscapes. In the president's study, with two greyhounds dozing by the hearth, Howe planned his Ohio travels. The dogs followed him outside, stirring up noisy geese, guinea hens and peacocks, and a fluttering of pigeons and turkeys. Mrs. Hayes showed the visitor her Cashmere goats and Jersey cattle. The president led him to the carriage house, filled

20. Hayes, *Diary and Letters,* 3:637.

with gig, surrey, storm cart, sleigh, and phaeton, and to the paddock where colts were frisking. As he wandered on alone past mirror ponds in the golden October woods, the old historian must have had some interesting reflections. Thirty-eight years earlier he had threaded the Sandusky River swamps on a mud-stained horse, passing the charred circles of old Indian camps and stopping at half-cleared farms bought with a bounty on wolves' ears. "Those who would describe America now," wrote an English traveler in 1839, "would have to correct all in the short space of ten years." [21]

At the end of his visit Howe was taken to the train by President Hayes. He drove a roundabout way, and as they reached the depot, the express was pulling out. When the president stood with raised hand in the carriage, the train halted and the historian stepped on.

Now Spiegel Grove is a state park, a gift of the Hayes family, administered by the Ohio Historical Society. The mansion remains, with its furnishings, as it was in the 1880s. An added building, opened in 1916, is the Rutherford B. Hayes Memorial, the first presidential museum and library in the country.

At the close of the Hayes administration revived prosperity augured well for the Republicans. General Grant, completing his long tour around the world, found newspapers urging his return to the White House for a third term; the movement was led by Senator Roscoe Conkling, boss of the New York Republican machine. At the same time support was gathering for Senator James G. Blaine of Maine and Senator John Sherman of Ohio.

A brother of General William Tecumseh Sherman, Senator Sherman was a veteran legislator of both houses of Congress. As secretary of the Treasury in the Hayes cabinet he had directed monetary reform. In the Ohio delegation to the 1880 convention it was agreed that Sherman's name should be presented by James A. Garfield, the one-time mule driver on the Ohio Canal.

As a boy on some half-cleared acres in the Western Reserve,

21. Marryat, *Diary*, p. 5.

where his father had died of malarial fever, Garfield had a few terms of schooling and long seasons of manual labor. At Hiram Academy he doubled as scholar and janitor, before going East where he took class honors in Williams College. Returning to Ohio he taught at Hiram, was admitted to the bar, and was elected to the Ohio senate. Army service, in which he rose to major general, ended in December 1863, when he was elected to Congress and began eight terms in Washington. In 1880 the Ohio Republicans named him a candidate for senator. That spring he moved his family to a recently purchased farm—Lawnfield—at Mentor, Ohio, near the Lake Erie shore twenty miles east of Cleveland. There was barely time to direct the repair of fences and the plowing of fields before he took the train for Chicago and the Republican convention. "I go with much reluctance," he wrote, "for I dislike the antagonism and controversies which are likely to blaze out in the convention." [22] Though he had got on in both war and politics, Garfield was a noncombative man.

In Chicago antagonisms blazed out for ten days as fifteen thousand Republicans heard thirty-three roll calls: Grant and Blaine seesawing in the lead and Sherman a slowly gaining contender. Through the arena strode Garfield, tall, broadshouldered, with massive head and heavy beard, and through the clamor rose his clarion voice calling for party deliberation and harmony. On the thirty-fourth ballot the Wisconsin chairman, at the end of the alphabet, announced sixteen votes for Garfield. Though Garfield had held his own delegation in sustained support of Sherman, the unspoken will of the convention had found a voice. In the next ballot, when Ben Harrison of Indiana gave twenty-seven votes to Garfield, the avalanche impended. At the thirty-sixth ballot the huge hall rang with "Garfield! Garfield!" Not for thirty minutes was there order enough to make the vote unanimous. When the news reached Grant in New York, he took the cigar from his mouth and said, "Garfield is a good man. I am glad of it." [23]

22. Theodore Clarke Smith, *The Life and Letters of James Abram Garfield,* 2 vols. (New Haven: Yale University Press, 1925), 2:958.

23. Green, *Last Stand,* p. 266.

So an Ohio delegate who had gone to the convention to support an Ohio candidate became, himself, the nominee. If not one Ohio man, then another. Ohio seemed inevitable—another name for success. Again the national party placed its bet on the state that embodied so many of the features and facets of America. "Garfield of Ohio" was its candidate.

Returning to his Ohio farm Garfield kept an eye on the harvest while attending to a flood of correspondence and endless streams of visitors. A carriage shed behind the house became the "campaign building." In September the riven Republicans made a show of closing ranks; Grant and Conkling with some followers came to Ohio for Republican rallies. On the way to Cleveland their train stopped at the edge of Lawnfield, and the party walked through the barnyard to the house where, after lunch, Grant tried Garfield's large, thick cigars. That brief meeting reporters called the "Treaty of Mentor." Other visitors included the Fisk Jubilee Singers, the Women Suffragists, and seven cars of German-Americans. Special trains brought five hundred members of the Lincoln Club of Indianapolis, nine hundred women from Cleveland, an a hundred executives of the iron and steel business. On election day Garfield smoked his cigars in quiet and arranged for plowing and seeding the garden. Without elation he heard the outcome—214 electoral votes to 155.

On the eve of his inauguration, at a small dinner for some college classmates, he said, "This honor came to me unsought. I have never had the presidential fever, not even for a day, nor do I have it now." [24] He did not want the presidency, and he did not have it long. Four months later, in the Washington station where he was about to board a train to a reunion at Williams, an irrational office-seeker stepped up and fired two pistol shots. One bullet lodged near his spine and was never removed.

That night the doctors pronounced him dying, but Garfield's vitality refuted them. For nine weeks he lay in the White House, his strength ebbing but his mind clear and always considerate of others, while messages poured in from across the nation and

24. Smith, *Life of Garfield,* 2:1097.

abroad. Wrote the *New York Evening Mail:* "Lying patiently on
a bed of suffering he has conquered the whole civilized
world." [25] Early in September, longing for the sight and sound
of the sea, he was taken to a cottage on the New Jersey shore.
He died there September 19, 1881.

While eleven biographers hurried to tell his life story, Garfield's funeral train made the slow journey to Ohio, with bells
tolling in every village, town, and city. He was buried in the
Lake View Cemetery in Cleveland beside the wide waters of
Lake Erie.

Just beyond General William Henry Harrison's land at North
Bend on the Ohio River lay the farm of his son John Scott Harrison, whose son became the nation's president in 1889. Ben
was a chubby seven-year-old riding on his grandfather's lumber
wagon in 1840 when the Whigs were shouting for Tippecanoe
and rolling their campaign ball across the state. Forty-eight
years later in Chicago's Exposition Hall ten thousand Republicans chanted "Harrison for president!"

As a young lawyer Harrison had located in Indianapolis. Declining a post in Garfield's cabinet in 1881, he was elected to
the Senate where he favored augmenting Civil War pensions
and American expansion into the Pacific. At the Republican
convention in 1888 the leading candidate was Senator John Sherman of Ohio. After seven ballots Sherman was lost in a surge of
excitement for Benjamin Harrison. With his nomination the old
Tippecanoe songs were revived, log cabins sprang up in public
squares, and a campaign ball—bigger and brighter this time, it
was fourteen feet across, sheathed in red-and-white canvas covered with slogans—was rolled by boisterous bands from New
York and Maryland to Ohio and Indiana. After five thousand
zig-zag miles it arrived at Indianapolis on election eve. Less
noisy was the arrival of the Caroline Scott Harrison Club of Oxford College, Ohio, a procession of eighty young ladies led by
four members of their faculty. They addressed Mrs. Harrison on
behalf of the college town whose memories she shared with her

25. Smith, *Life of Garfield*, 2:1198.

husband. A few days later the victory came, as their college friend David Swing described it, "with a graceful sweep over hill and dale, along the lakes and from two oceans." [26] In little Oxford, however, the vote was Grover Cleveland 452, Benjamin Harrison 425.

Soon the presidential family belonged to history, but in Oxford the weekly *Citizen* asked: "Who can forget the young Ben Harrison and the charming Carrie Scott?" Caroline Scott was the daughter of John Witherspoon Scott, who had founded the Oxford College for Women, across town from Miami University where Ben Harrison was enrolled. They were married in 1853 when both had finished their college years.

Demure Carrie Scott had lace and iron in her makeup. In the White House she devoted herself to her household, which included her ninety-year-old father, her sister, a niece, and several grandchildren. She designed china, played the piano with near professional skill, and planned the White House gardens. In 1890 she headed the just-organized Daughters of the American Revolution with its avowed purpose "to cherish, maintain, and extend the institutions of American freedom." In a time before mass media the president made official travels around the country, and Mrs. Harrison was often at her husband's side.

The longest and most strenuous journey took them ten thousand miles through the South and West in the spring of 1891. In the South, where Harrison had served with Sherman's army, the presidential visit soothed the old ache of war. At Birmingham he was welcomed by the largest crowd ever gathered in Alabama, and Memphis was decked with flags and flowers for his parade.

Galveston, Houston, and El Paso gave the Harrisons a Texas welcome, and on April 23 they began a hectic week in California. At a San Francisco reception twenty thousand people passed through the Palace Hotel to shake the president's hand. Beside him stood his wife, who was holding a spray of roses, and Mrs. Leland Stanford with her dazzling diamonds and six strings of pearls. At the navy yard Mrs. Harrison christened the

26. Harry J. Sievers, *Benjamin Harrison, Hoosier Statesman* (New York: University Publishers Incorporated, 1959), p. 427.

USS *Monterey* and endured another reception crunch. A reporter wrote: "Like the fable, it was fun for the boys but death to the frogs." The president kept up the pace—nine speeches in one day—but his wife suffered a lung congestion that would prove fatal. Through Portland, Seattle, Salt Lake City, Denver, and Omaha, she went on nerve, though near exhaustion. Back in Washington in mid-May, her doctors diagnosed tuberculosis. Five months later Caroline Scott Harrison died in the White House.

During his wife's illness Harrison had become a reluctant candidate for a second term, being nominated at the Minneapolis convention in June. The nominee for vice-president was Whitelaw Reid, a native of Xenia, Ohio, and an 1856 graduate of Miami University—the only time in American history that two graduates of the same college headed a party slate. Reid was editor of the *New York Tribune* and had been the Harrison-appointed ambassador to France. It looked like a strong ticket. But as Harrison's wife weakened, he had neither mind nor heart for politics. "Indeed," he later said, "I was so removed from the campaign that I can scarcely realize that I was a candidate." [27] In November the Republican team lost to Grover Cleveland and Adlai Stevenson, and that month Harrison buried his wife and his father-in-law. Now in Oxford, Ohio, the original Women's College building is the Caroline Scott Harrison Memorial, and Benjamin Harrison Hall occupies a central place on the Miami University campus.

In the presidential contest of 1896 the struggle centered on monetary policy—this was the showdown on that stubborn question—the gold standard against free coinage of silver, Eastern industry against the agrarian South and West. Nebraska's windblown, silver-voiced William Jennings Bryan traveled thirteen thousand miles, speaking in twenty-nine states. Frock-coated McKinley, solidly seated on the gold platform, stayed at home in Canton, Ohio, where four bronze angels on the courthouse tower looked over the shops and mills of the city.

27. H. Wayne Morgan, *From Hayes to McKinley* (Syracuse: Syracuse University Press, 1969), p. 427.

In 1867 young William McKinley—he was just twenty-two and a major in the 23rd Ohio Infantry when the war ended—settled in Canton in a house facing the public square. After a term as prosecuting attorney, he was sent to Congress, where he made himself known as a high-tariff man. In the 1880s Ohio was booming with new business, and certain Ohio men were growing in wealth and power. None grew faster than Marcus Alonzo Hanna, the country boy from Columbiana County who became a president-maker. As a Cleveland businessman, his hands deep in coal mines, iron mines, shipyards, docks, street railways, blast furnaces, and banks, Hanna saw that businesses were interlocked. Beyond that he saw that all business was linked to politics. In a nation hurrying away from a simple rural society to a complex industrial order, politics acquired new measures of power. When McKinley sponsored a tariff bill in Congress, Hanna lined up beside him. In 1890 McKinley lost his congressional seat, but Hanna made him governor of Ohio. Four years later, labeling him the "advance agent of prosperity," Hanna powered the machinery that made McKinley president. They were an odd couple—Hanna blunt impulsive, hot-tempered, profane; McKinley logical, formal, guarded, a devout Methodist who, to set an example for the young, hid his cigar from the photographer.

After the presidential nomination McKinley made no effort to attract people, but Hanna's organization kept them coming. Special trains steamed into Canton from all directions. With bands and banners the visitors marched through a town ablaze with flags and bunting. On North Market Street they passed through the McKinley Arch and pressed around a white house under the summer trees. There, from his front porch, McKinley was making sixteen speeches a day to crowds massed on the lawns and sidewalks.

The noisiest delegation was a marching company of Confederate veterans who waved the stars and bars and woke the streets of Canton with the rebel yell. A free-silver parade paid McKinley a courtesy call when Bryan spoke in Canton. Gifts poured in—a polished tree stump from Tennessee; a plate of galvanized iron; a gavel carved from a log from the Lincoln cabin at New Salem, Illinois; a sixty-foot sheet of jointed tin bearing the names of Republican candidates; and five fierce-eyed eagles that McKinley promptly gave to the city park. By that time the front porch was sagging, and every scrap of fence and grape arbor had been carried off for souvenirs. Chauncey Depew, president of the New York Central Railroad, went on a speaking tour for McKinley; Henry Cabot Lodge and Theodore Roosevelt came to Canton for campaign planning; and John Hay, elder statesman and diplomat, found McKinley calmly discussing issues in an upstairs room while "his shouting worshippers" marched outside. Struck by McKinley's clear-minded deliberation and explicit answers, Hay wrote: "And there are idiots who think Mark Hanna will run him." [28]

Elected and re-elected, by substantial majorities, McKinley established the gold standard and maintained tariff protection for American manufactures. In the Ohio tradition he held moderate views, hoping that material progress and social harmony could be achieved together.

In the summer of 1901 the new century seemed bright with promise, and nowhere brighter than in Buffalo, where 35,000 electric lamps blazed over the grounds of the Pan-American Exposition. Pan-American then meant more than sea-to-sea; under a president from landlocked Ohio, the United States had annexed Hawaii and acquired Puerto Rico, Guam, and the Philippines. On September 6 the greatest crowd of the Exposition poured through the gates for the visit of the president. There, shaking hands with a line of people between the Fountain of Abundance and the Court of Lilies, he was shot point-blank by a young anarchist opposed to government, marriage, and religion. McKinley, who whispered the Lord's Prayer while doctors probed for the bullet, died eight days later.

In the fall of 1826 a rugged, rangy, sunburned youth of sixteen left a Vermont farm for Amherst Academy in Massachusetts, and from there he went to Yale College and the Yale Law School—always leading his class. Admitted to the Connecticut bar in 1838, he did not intend to stay in New England.

28. Tyler Dennett, *John Hay* (New York: Dodd, Mead & Company, 1934), p. 178.

Writing to his father that "Vermont is a noble state to emigrate from," he packed his law books and traveled by stagecoach and steamboat to Cincinnati. In years ahead the name he brought there would be known across Ohio and the nation. Since 1840 four generations of Tafts have built their lives into Cincinnati's civic order, its university and its law school; its newspapers, art museums, and churches; and into presidential cabinets, Republican councils and conventions, foreign embassies, and the halls of Congress. The Vermont heritage persisted; the Tafts had integrity rather than dash and daring, theirs was a fixed star and not a comet.

Soon after his arrival in Cincinnati Alphonso Taft strode into the political life of the Queen City. One of the founders of the Republican party, he became a delegate to the first Republican convention and a judge of the superior court of Cincinnati. Called to Washington, he served as Grant's secretary of War and then as attorney general. In diplomatic service he represented the United States in both Austria and Russia. While he lived abroad, his son William Howard Taft was appointed city solicitor in Cincinnati.

As a young man stalwart Will Taft excelled in both scholarship and athletics. He made football and baseball history at Yale, and according to an Ohio legend he turned down a contract as catcher with the Cincinnati Reds. Built, then, like Johnny Bench, with a strong arm and a rifling peg, he grew too heavy to run bases. Anyway, he loved law more than baseball; at twenty-nine he was appointed to the Ohio superior court. From there he moved up to the federal circuit, where he made firm, clear decisions, unvexed by the turmoil of politics. During a term as dean of the law school at Cincinnati he declined a nomination for the presidency of Yale, saying he was not prepared. Instead he accepted from President McKinley the presidency of the United States Philippine Commission. As civil governor he brought order and progress to the Islands and took a great liking to the Filipinos. Half reluctantly he sailed from Manila on Christmas eve 1903, to become Roosevelt's secretary of War.

Four years later he was Roosevelt's choice as a successor in the White House. On a warm June day in 1908 the big, easy man stood on the steps of a gracious mansion on Cincinnati's Pike Street—now the Taft Museum—and accepted nomination for the presidency.

Although all the Ohio presidents were Republican, there never failed to be a real contest in the state. Balanced in so many ways, Ohio was fairly evenly divided between political parties. The Republican candidates were not necessarily the better men, but they had a stronger party organization.

While Roosevelt went big-game hunting in Africa, Taft faced the hazards of politics. Surrounded by conservative advisers, opposed by labor, he traveled around the country without measuring the swelling tide of progressivism. Back at home with his hunting trophies, Theodore Roosevelt saw the gulf widening between president and people. "Taft means well," he said, "but he means well feebly." Renominated by the old-line Republicans in 1912, Taft carried but two states, Utah and Vermont. Without regret he heaved himself up from the presidential chair and began teaching constitutional law at Yale.

Eight years later the Republicans elevated another Ohio man, a politician this time, wholly different from the urbane and scholarly Taft. In one of his best appointments President Harding named Taft Chief Justice of the Supreme Court, a fitting seat for the deliberate man who could deal with concepts better than with the commotion of democracy.

In the fickle fortunes of politics some unlikely Ohio candidates have won the highest prize, and some who seemed more likely have been rejected. Robert A. Taft, son of a president and grandson of a cabinet officer and diplomat, was elected to the Senate in 1936. Unlike many Ohio leaders he did not bend with the wind. He attacked the fiscal policies of the New Deal, he opposed the growing centralization of government, he decried wasteful spending. In the Senate he won a place of sustained leadership. An expert in government finance, he was chief author of the Republican platform and himself a presidential candidate in four election years. He came close to nomination in 1952, when the party chose General Eisenhower. By training, experience, and character, Taft was well qualified for the presidency. Again, however, irony intrudes. In the spring of 1953 he was suddenly stricken with cancer. For a few weeks he went on crutches to his Senate duties, but the tumor cells were spreading. He died six months after Eisenhower's inauguration. Had Robert A. Taft been elected, he would have been another short-term president. Upon his death Herbert Hoover said: "He was more nearly the irreplaceable man in American life than we have seen in three generations." [29]

From the 1920 convention in Chicago, Will Rogers wrote: "The Republicans nominated Senator Warren G. Harding of Ohio. . . . Ohio claims they are due a president, as they haven't had one since Taft. Look at the United States, they haven't had one since Lincoln." [30]

Ohio's run of presidents was more notable in itself than in the caliber of the incumbents. In politics, as in industry and business, Ohio had the advantage of a central location. It was a bridge between East and West, and for 436 bending, twisting, turning miles it bordered on the South. It had a steadily growing population and a rich diversity of resources that its people knew how to use. It was a state of great and varied productiveness—hence wealth, stability, and what the politicians now call clout. No wonder the national parties looked to Ohio for vote-getting candidates.

For its bounty, Ohio's people, though second to none in vigor and inventiveness, were less accountable than was geography's gift of coal, oil, gas, and fertile soil, and of easy land and water transportation. In short, Ohio was so favored that its leaders got more than their share of national attention. Add to those strategic benefits the Ohio character—practical, industrious, self-confident—and it is not hard to see why "Columbus served as a stepping-stone to Washington." [31] Add, further, the democratic background and inclination of the candidates. Wrote the approv-

29. James T. Patterson, *Mr. Republican, A Biography of Robert A. Taft* (Boston: Houghton Mifflin Company, 1972), p. 614.

30. Will Rogers, *How We Elect Our Presidents*. Selected and edited by Donald Day (Boston: Little, Brown and Company, 1952), p. 9.

31. Hartt, "The Ohioans," *Atlantic Monthly* 84(1899):690.

ing observer for the *Atlantic Monthly:* "Out of the lair of the wolf came the founders of old Rome, and out of the Ohio forest came rulers for young America. . . . That splendid Cleveland newspaper is well named—the Ohioans are a nation of Plain Dealers. There is not a hundred silk hats in the state." [32]

From Morrow County, near the center of the state, came Warren Harding, the oldest of eight children of a country doctor. A big, strong boy, he worked between school terms in barnyards, brickyards, a printing shop, and on the track gang of the Toledo and Ohio Central Railroad. When the family moved to Marion, in the next county, he worked as printer, saved his money, and bought for $300 the weekly *Marion Star* with a circulation of five hundred. Tall, handsome, easy-going, he married a banker's daughter, joined the Elks and the Masons, and played cornet and tuba in the town band. Spurred by his shrewd, aggressive wife, whom he later called "the duchess," he made the *Star* into a daily and saw its circulation reach ten thousand. One of the delivery boys was Norman Thomas, who would become a durable Socialist candidate for president.

Harding was at home on Main Street. His paper carried his tolerable views throughout the rural county; he enjoyed public functions and could speak sonorously on short notice on appropriate subjects. Without any clear ambition, he was elected to the Ohio senate. In Columbus he fell in with Harry M. Daugherty, a young lawyer, lobbyist, and Republican organizer. Harding was by nature an ensemble man; his mellow voice, like his tuba, followed the written score. Columbus was a way-station to Washington, and in 1914, guided by Daugherty, Harding was elected to the United States Senate.

For six years the handsome, jovial, obliging man from Ohio followed the party line. He drank and played poker with his friends while supporting the Anti-Saloon League and the Volstead Act. He opposed high taxes on war profits, favored restricted immigration and high tariffs, and enjoyed a growing reputation as a Republican speech maker. In 1920, after the strenuous war years and the failing Wilson crusade for interna-

32. Hartt, "The Ohioans," *Atlantic Monthly* 84(1899):689.

tionalism, the Republicans expected to regain the White House. But Theodore Roosevelt's sudden death in 1919 had left the party without leadership. Into the void stepped the Ohio Republican Committee, with Daugherty building up Ohio's "favorite son" and on tireless travels lining up second- and third-choice pledges for his candidate.

When the delegates streamed into Chicago in the heat of early June, Harding seemed out of the running; he was almost as far back as President Nicholas Murray Butler of Columbia University. While the resolutions committee sweated over planks in the party platform and delegates seesawed between General Leonard Wood and Illinois's governor Frank Lowden, a discouraged Harding, fanning himself in his shirt sleeves, told Butler: "I am going to quit politics and devote myself to my newspaper." [33]

But the Ohio gang had not wilted. Daugherty, having infiltrated the larger delegations with Harding supporters, kept passing the word that Harding was the number-one dark horse. After four deadlock ballots the party leaders gathered at midnight. They were about to make political history in a sweltering, smoke-filled room.

Veteran old Henry Cabot Lodge took charge. He read a dozen names, from lead runners to men all the way back—names that had appeared in the seesaw balloting. Some had moved upward, some downward, half of them had hardly moved at all. Then he reminded the room of something. No Republican president had ever won without the electoral vote of Ohio. Ohio was a key factor. Ohio spelled success. Soon the Democrats would assemble in San Francisco. Their front-running candidate was James M. Cox, in his third term as Ohio's governor. With Cox's nomination would go the potent Ohio name. But the Republicans could claim it first. Name an Ohio man to beat an Ohio man. Name Harding. With that strategy the president-makers went off to bed.

Next day the balloting resumed. With the eighth count the galleries were chanting "Harding! Harding!" and on the tenth ballot the Ohio senator was in. When Chairman Lodge called

33. Francis Russell, *The Shadow of Blooming Grove: Warren G. Harding in His Times* (New York: McGraw-Hill Book Company, 1968), p. 376.

for a unanimous declaration, the "Nays!" of William Allen White and Harold Ickes were lost in the acclaim.

While reporters scribbled about long odds, outside chance, and stabs of lightning, Harding, half incredulous, put it in poker terms. "We drew to a pair of deuces and filled." [34]

Since 1865 when a German mechanic started a heavy-machinery business in Marion, the town was known as the home of the steam shovel. Its dredges and ditchers gouged mines and heaped roadbeds in Arizona, Chile, and Bolivia; its draglines and power shovels dug through the jungles of Panama. In 1920 Marion became known for the front porch where Harding conducted his presidential campaign. From the Union Depot a Victory Way, lined with white columns capped by gilded eagles, led to the white frame house under the maple trees of Mount Vernon Avenue. The house next door was made a campaign headquarters; its dining room became Harding's office. From there he sent a message to San Francisco where the Democrats had nominated James M. Cox of Dayton, with Assistant Secretary of the Navy Franklin D. Roosevelt as his running mate. Cox would campaign on a League of Nations platform while Harding called the people back to the "normalcy" of nationalism. Ohio, like the nation, was divided on that question, but Harding's telegram shared with his rival "the honor shown our great state." [35] During the campaign Governor Cox traveled twenty-two thousand miles in thirty-five states, but Harding stayed at home except for an autumn trip to a few cities in the East and the Midwest. On election day he voted after breakfast and then drove with Daugherty to Columbus for a round of golf. The next morning headlines declared a Harding landslide.

Inaugural day had generally been bad for Ohio presidents: a cruel wind for Old Tippecanoe, torrents of rain for Ben Harrison and McKinley, ice and snow driving Taft inside the Senate chamber for the swearing-in. For Harding the skies were cloudless; he had asked for a simple inauguration, and the sun shone on it. But very soon the skies would darken.

A month later Will Rogers reported: "Will Hays took me in

34. Russell, *The Shadow*, p. 396.
35. Russell, *The Shadow*, p. 398.

to meet President Harding. I said 'Mr. President, I would like to tell you all the latest political jokes.' He said 'You don't have to, Will. I appointed them.' " [36]

In fact, Harding had named some good men—Herbert Hoover, Charles Evans Hughes, Andrew Mellon, the elder Henry Wallace. But the rapacious gang was there, men over whom the kindly Harding, himself financially honest (and unlucky with investments) kept no watch. In the White House he was a likable, well-meaning man quickly surrounded by graft and corruption. Scandals were developing in the Veterans' Bureau, the Office of Alien Property, and the Departments of Justice, the Navy, and the Interior. The greatest graft underlay the leasing of Naval oil-reserve lands and the Ohio gang's control of the Department of Justice. To put off the showdown Harding made a presidential visit in 1923 to Alaska, but the abominations followed him. He was a harried, helpless man—on the Alaska steamship he asked Herbert Hoover what a president could do when friends betray him—unable to eat or sleep when a gastric illness prostrated him. He died on August 2 in San Francisco.

The political scandals would surface, one after another, in the years ahead, but at his death Harding was a popular president. When the funeral train arrived there, people streamed into Marion from across Ohio and the nation. Day and night they filed through the Harding house and past the casket. When the doors were closed, 20,000 stood waiting in the blazing August sun. A final procession led to the Marion Cemetery, where a girls' choir sang "Lead, Kindly Light," a Methodist bishop gave a benediction, a bugler sounded Taps, and a rifle corps fired a final salute over the flag-draped coffin.

Marion now manufactures road rollers and power shovels and, after every harvest, ships out mountains of popcorn, but the town is best known for the Harding Home, maintained as in 1920, and the Harding Memorial, a tomb of white marble encircled by classic columns. The Memorial was built by contributions from people near and far, funds that dried up as increasing scandals stained the memory of the fallen president. Beyond po-

36. Rogers, *How We Elect,* p. 12.

litical corruption there emerged the sorry tale of Harding's relationship with his obtuse wife and with infatuated women. One book followed another, gossipy and meretricious, heaping ignominy upon the entombed man. The marble mausoleum remained undedicated until the depression spring of 1931, when reluctant ex-President Hoover spoke of "a man whose soul was seared by a great disillusionment." [37]

In the only solid and searching biography yet written of him the author says that Harding with better luck might have gone into history as a later Garfield or McKinley, but "the mysteries of Harding's life . . . have proved more durable and persistent than politics." [38] The odium grew, there was no forgetting, new disclosures were seized upon by writers for personal gain and read by a morbid and mean-minded public. Now sadness and irony haunt the Harding Memorial, graceful and peaceful in its green Ohio lawns, where the dedication closed with a choir singing Mrs. Harding's favorite number, "The End of a Perfect Day."

37. Russell, *The Shadow*, p. 640.
38. Russell, *The Shadow*, p. xiii.

13

The Land and the People

WHEN white men entered Ohio, it was a forest realm containing 6,700 acres of lakes. Now its lakes cover 100,000 acres. Ohio has 3,300 named streams. The local word is "creek"; look on any county map and see them there, like the lines on a hand: Elm Creek, Sunday Creek, Paint Creek, Sugar Creek, Salt Creek, Owl Creek, Crow Creek, Brush Creek, Pipe Creek, Horse Creek, Cow Creek, and all the rest. They drain mostly southward, swelling the rivers that have kept their musical Indian names—Mahoning, Tuscarawas, Waldhoning, Muskingum, Hocking, Scioto, Little and Great Miami—and adding their tribute to the Ohio. With its gift of rarely failing rainfall Ohio is a well watered land. Occasionally the gift has been overwhelming, and never more so than in Easter week of 1913.

The great flood looms large in Ohio history, because of what it cost in death, suffering, and destruction and because of how it was surmounted. It has been memorialized in cities as far apart as Piqua, Columbus, and Zanesville; high-water line was marked like a badge of courage in scores of places. It made James Thurber's least amusing story of Columbus and surged through Allan Eckert's *A Time of Terror* fifty years after the event. It was, perhaps, a testing and tempering of Ohio character.

Things generally came easy in Ohio. Things kept getting better, just in the course of time. Scratch Ohio and find a success story, not only the great fortunes in iron, steel, oil, glass, and rubber, but odd, out-of-the-way success stories: Like Charles M. Hall's discovery, in a woodshed laboratory the year after his graduation from Oberlin, of the electrolytic process of making aluminum, and so transforming many industries and making his high-minded college an enviably rich one. Like Edward Mc-Clain of Highland County who, brooding on the chafing of the necks of horses, invented a pad for horse collars and started a one-room business that by 1900 had five hundred workers and turned out six million pads a year—sold everywhere a horse was harnessed. Like shy little Annie Oakley of North Star Township in Darke County, bowing in her cow-girl clothes before the Queen of England and welcomed to Paris by Ambassador Whitelaw Reid. Like George Barber, who began making matches in an Akron barn in 1847. With his son, whom he named Ohio Columbus Barber, he organized the Diamond Match Company. After a tax dispute in Akron, O. C. Barber founded Barberton, moved his company there, and turned out 250 million matches every day, while raising 75,000 Pekin ducks on the Barberton Reservoir. Even the Ohio presidents—front porch candidates—seemed carried into office by events or simple luck: "Drew to a pair of deuces and filled." Good fortune seemed the order of things in Dayton—the flying machine flew, the self-starter worked, the world seemed waiting for the electric money drawer and the electric icebox—until three days of downpour when Dayton became "the doomed city." It could be said that Ohio's tolerance for adversity had not been tested.

A popular misconception is that floods are caused by settlement and civilization. The Indians knew floods; they saw their villages washed away. After the Treaty of Greenville, when settlers came up the Miami River and built the beginnings of Dayton, the Indians warned them of flood waters. The land lay rich along the serpentine Miami, augmented there by the Stillwater flowing in from the north, Mad River from the east, and Wolf Creek from the west, and the settlers liked the place, thinking less of flood waters than of the southward-flowing Miami that would take their crops to market. In 1805 the waters rose, and the settlers built a levee. An 1814 flood washed out that embankment. Other inundations came, and each time the citizens enlarged their dikes and crossed their fingers. After a severe flood in 1898 the city made plans for a comprehensive project. By mid-March 1913, designs were complete, contracts let, construction equipment in place, and workmen gathering. Then, on March 23, the skies darkened and the rains began. In pleasant, prosperous Dayton three raging rivers swept over their banks and drowned the city.

Easter Sunday was dark with leaden clouds and intermittent downpour. On Monday the rain was ceaseless, and the lower streets filled with water. All that night the rain beat down. On Tuesday morning the blare of factory whistles and the clangor of church and fire-alarm bells sent people out of the basin streets. By noon water was lapping the residential districts. Along Monument Avenue the whole embankment gave way, and the tower of Steele High School toppled into the flood. Four hundred people were marooned in the Union Station tower. That night the rain turned to snow, and the skies were lit by fires of flooded buildings that exploded from intolerable air pressure. Some people clung to treetops; more huddled in gables and attics, peering out at floating and burning houses. Low-water flow at Dayton was 250 cubic feet per second. Now, a thousand times that volume, the Miami River was a mile-wide torrent raging and roaring through the city.

On Wednesday the sky cleared and a repaired telegraph line carried news of disaster. Headlines across the nation told of: FLOODED OHIO CITY AFLAME . . . MARTIAL LAW DECLARED . . . 200 BODIES FOUND IN RAGING WATERS . . . TENTH OF CITY'S 130,000 MAY BE DEAD.

The actuality was not that bad, but the misery could not be magnified. On Thursday the National Guard began rescuing people from rooftops and upper-story windows. The ten-blocks plant of National Cash Register Company, on high ground at the edge of the city, with its own heat, light, and power, was transformed into a relief center. Its pressroom kept in touch with the world, its kitchens fed endless lines of people, its hospital rooms treated illness and exhaustion and delivered babies—

three infants were named Cash. A tent city set up in the NCR park sheltered thousands of families.

By the end of the week the secretary of War and his chief-of-staff were in Dayton, and the Red Cross had mobilized relief agencies. New York was subscribing $100,000 for relief and a proclamation by President Wilson declared "We should make this a common cause." [1] A special correspondent for the *Outlook* reported that terror was past but there remained "crushed houses everywhere . . . trees torn up by the roots and jammed through second-story windows, pianos pasted about like postage stamps, dead horses sprawling along sodden streets." [2]

While the river sank back, thousands of households and establishments began the task of drying out, cleaning up, and returning to normal. In a remarkable community spirit Dayton people devoted themselves to each other. "Helpfulness," reported the *Daily News,* "was the one occupation. . . . There has never been a more striking example of the recovery of a city from disaster." [3] Ben Hecht, sent by the *Chicago Journal,* telegraphed that refugees in mud-stained clothes were dreaming of a New Dayton. The Indians had abandoned their village where the rivers meet, but the Ohio people meant to stay.

Early in April the *Outlook* stated: "The great lesson which has just shocked and terrified the country is the lesson of Conservation," [4] and in its pages Theodore Roosevelt called for national measures to prevent future disasters. But Dayton couldn't wait for national measures. Three weeks after the flood, crowds gathered at the water-stained courthouse under a sign: "Remember the Promises You Made in the Attic—Flood Prevention Fund." In a single day they subscribed $2 million for the planning of a flood-control system. Arthur E. Morgan of the Memphis Engineering Company was asked to prepare a comprehensive proposal.

A native of Cincinnati, Arthur Morgan had worked on flood

1. *Outlook* 103(1913):742.
2. *Outlook* 103(1913):805.
3. Arthur E. Morgan, *The Miami Conservancy District* (New York: McGraw-Hill Book Company, 1951), pp. 70–71.
4. *Outlook* 103(1913):750.

control in southern and western states. Now he drew plans larger than any yet undertaken anywhere. Spurred by Governor Cox, the Ohio legislature in special session passed the Conservancy Act of Ohio. Seventy-five thousand tracts of land were surveyed, appraised, and acquired by the Miami Conservancy District. The project called for five massive earth dams with concrete outlets and spillways. It involved 60 miles of levees, 32 miles of channel improvement, 35,000 acres of basin property, 200 floodgates and 58 observation wells, along with relocation of roads, railways, power and water lines. Twenty years later, when he was in charge of the Tennessee Valley transformation, Morgan said the TVA was an enlarged edition of the Miami project.

At each of the reservoir sites rose a clamor of construction—roaring of motors, creaking of cranes, pounding of pile drivers, the suck and throb of pumps and dredges. Each location had a construction village, complete with an English school for foreign workmen and a graded school for workers' children. Around the calendar men and machines hollowed the huge catch basins, heaped the levees and dams, leveled the cropland and graded the grass and forest slopes. In 1922 the system was complete. Since then the five dams have held back 857 cresting waters while life went on untroubled in the valley. This was a local project, paid for by Miami Valley property owners and public agencies in nine counties. The cost has totaled $40 million; direct benefits have come to $90 million. Another success story.

For the project Morgan had gathered a corps of college-trained engineers. He soon saw that they were long on theory and short on practical skill. That led to another gain for the Miami Valley. In 1920, while steam shovels gouged the watershed, Arthur E. Morgan was named president of Antioch College, at Yellow Springs, twelve miles east of Dayton. At the nearly defunct college (this man liked problems) he organized a curriculum alternating periods of study with on-the-job training. "Thinking plus experience," he said, "teaches us what thinking alone cannot." [5] This rugged man gave to Ohio original

5. Arthur E. Morgan, *Observations* (Yellow Springs, Ohio: The Antioch Press, 1968), p. 294.

designs of education as well as of conservancy. While president of Antioch—1920 to 1933—he helped to develop in Dayton the Kettering Research Laboratory for the study of photosynthesis and the Fels Institute for studies in human development. His basic belief seems akin to the "A for Ax" lesson in early Ohio readers: "American youth of today . . . is being robbed of those contacts with life that gave the salty savor of sanity and reality to his grandfather, and for which American pioneer life was especially noted." [6] Later in his career he set up educational projects in India and Africa. His last years were spent in Xenia, on the edge of the Miami District, where at age ninety-seven he died in 1975.

Since the 1920s the influence of the Miami Conservancy District has extended to many states and to foreign lands. The District was a training ground for hydraulic engineering, land reclamation, and river control. Men from Morgan's project went to jobs with the U. S. Reclamation Service and the Army Corps of Engineers as well as to the TVA. In Peru and Liberia they built water-supply systems, sanitary systems, and internal waterways.

In The Miami District conservation goes on with new measures for a new time. Since 1965 the agency has analyzed water pollution from municipalities and industries, and has conducted basic research in the improving of water quality. At Franklin, Ohio, ten miles below Dayton, it has developed an environmental control complex, a system that converts sewage into fertilizer and garbage into industrial resources. In place of the old town dump is a parked complex of tanks, towers, ramps, conveyors, chambers, and basins, from which are recovered aluminum, glass, fibers, and ferrous metals. Here is a light in the gloom of environmental distress.

In Dayton and other Miami Valley cities a current River Corridor program is making the long-feared river a public amenity. Miles of walkways and bikeways border the Miami. Landscaping and riverside parks bring the color of the changing seasons into the city center. In the heart of Dayton the District proposes to construct and maintain a riverfront plaza, with steps, ramps, and terraces leading to waterfront restaurants and cafés and a

6. Morgan, *Observations,* p. 183.

staging area for concerts, arts and crafts displays, and outdoor theater. Boat and bicycle rental will supplement a downtown water taxiway. In prospect is a greenbelt extending for fifty miles from Germantown to the upper District dams.

Out of calamity came far-reaching projects of conservation. The Ohio Conservancy Act, copied in Colorado and New Mexico, and in the National Conservancy Act, opened new horizons of regional co-operation in control and development of watersheds. In Ohio the Miami District was followed by other regional conservancy projects, built for programs of conservation and recreation as well as for flood control. Most extensive was the Muskingum Conservancy District in east-central Ohio. Editors and engineers have called it "the nation's Number One example of how a watershed may be developed and managed for the public benefit," [7] and "a shining example of local people and their state and national governments working together for the good of their community and the United States." [8]

In 1938, after five years of construction, fourteen flood-control dams were dedicated in a single ceremony, and the Muskingum Conservancy District was in operation. Lying in rolling and hilly country, the District embraces nearly one-fifth of Ohio's area. From Marietta on the Ohio it fans out northward and westward to Canton, Akron, Ashland, Mansfield, and Mt. Vernon, an extensive and diversified region containing forest and coal mines, sheep and dairy farms, hill towns and river cities. But it all runs downhill. With every flood went topsoil from the bottomlands and erosion from the hillsides, the riches of Ohio rushing away to the Gulf of Mexico. Trouble for farmers was also trouble for industry. In May of 1942 the steel mills of Youngstown were cutting production for want of water; twelve months later they were idled by flood. The Muskingum District was developed with a double aim: to restrain flood waters and to counter drought with retention reservoirs.

Of the District's fourteen retaining basins, ten are permanent

7. *Muskingum Country* (New Philadelphia, Ohio: Muskingum Watershed Conservancy District [1955]), p. 2.

8. *Muskingum Country*, p. 28.

lakes with a total shoreline of many hundred miles. Because of this watershed's relation to the capricious Ohio River, the system was built by the U. S. Army Corps of Engineers, while Ohio provided funds for the purchase of land and the relocating of highways. The balance sheet shows a cost of $48 million against benefits already nearing three times that amount.

In the middle 1930s, when winds from the dust bowl darkened skies many hundred miles away, the American people saw the result of careless and shortsighted agriculture. The land is sensitive, reflecting like a mirror the motives at work upon it. Overgrazing of grasslands, one-crop farming of prairie fields, and clear-cutting of wooded hillsides led to what famed conservationist Paul Sears described as "deserts on the march." The Muskingum project embodied a conception of land and water as public resources, whose misuse would impoverish a people and whose conservation would benefit all. With dams and power lines, planning boards and experiment stations, men could protect and reclaim land as effectively as past generations had plundered it. Where run-off was controlled and reservoirs held back flood waters, Ohio people could have a folksong like "Flow Gently, Sweet Afton" instead of "River Stay Away from My Door."

The Muskingum reservoirs doubled the area of Ohio's inland lakes. Nearly half the land in the District should never have been plowed. Where the soil is thin and slopes are steep, hill farms were soon worn out, thousands of acres of poverty grass replacing green woods and green pastures. Now the District began restoring old wood lots, planting new stands of forest, and selectively cutting mature timber. One sees huge logging trucks on the way to the mills, but they leave no cutover lands. On the larger lakes logging barges bring timber from isolated coves and inlets; water skiers skim past a pyramid of saw logs— beech, oak, maple—soon to become lumber. One of the lakes, Clendening, has been kept a wilderness. A single road leads to a small boat livery; the rest of the fifty-mile shoreline will remain woods forever. All the lakes and their shores are public property. The woods abound in squirrels, fox, grouse, and deer. In the waters are many kinds of fish, from succulent six-inch bluegills to big northern pike and three-foot muskellunge. Beaver, the first riches of the Ohio country and the first to be plundered, are here again. Beaver lodges in the coves and creek mouths catch the silt and hold back the water. Most of the Muskingum lakes are deep and clear, with rock and gravel bottom.

Recreation and reclamation go together in the District. It has been called the nation's model conservation laboratory. For thirty years its demonstration and research projects have drawn national attention. Ohio, once a destroyer of resources, now asserts some leadership in reforestation, soil-building, restocking of wildlife—a land use that is responsible to the future. As novelist-historian Louis Bromfield saw it: "The Muskingum Conservancy District is probably the greatest example up to now in all civilization of man's understanding of how to develop his natural environment to his greatest good." [9]

In the far northwestern corner of the Muskingum District lies Pleasant Hill Lake, its clear waters framed in the dense green slopes of the Mohican Forest. A few miles away is Malabar Farm, a venture in living and farming that became known afar.

Louis Bromfield was born and reared in the region that now is the Mohican State Forest. He left it for many years but he did not outgrow or forget it. Before he was thirty he had won a Pulitzer Prize for a novel that showed the older simplicities of Ohio giving way to the business order of the impersonal money-making mills. A visit to France in 1925 lengthened into thirteen years, including a stay in India, but in 1938 the rumblings of imminent war sent the family back to America. In Ohio Bromfield searched the back roads of Richland County for the scenes of his boyhood on his grandfather's farm. It was winter and the land lay white and still. Coming down into the Pinhook Valley he saw the ice-blue creek under the ridges where bare trees etched the fading amber sky. Suddenly he knew where he was. He had come home. He later wrote that he was grateful for having spent years abroad because "it made America a new

9. *Muskingum Country*, p. 4.

country to me, which I will never again take for granted as so many Americans do." [10]

There, in Pleasant Valley, he bought three adjoining farms— brushy pastures, ragged woodlots, eroded and depleted fields. Enlarging an old house for his family, reclaiming roomy barns and dredging a pond beside the road were first steps in a way of life in harmony with earth and seasons, rooted in the Ohio countryside. His venture meant protecting the woodland and rebuilding the soil, restoring meadow pastures, raising the water table, developing strong strains of livestock, and producing a variety of field, orchard, and garden crops. In his bow-windowed study, where his boxers lay at his feet, he wrote four books about Malabar Farm. He lived on a large scale, entertaining governors, conservationists, editors, and motion-picture people. Some of the visitors were farmers who admired his contoured fields, his prize cattle, and his rich, rolling pastures, but concluded that the farm supported the writer less than the writer supported the farm. Bromfield readily confessed that his venture needed help from beyond its fences.

From the study window, looking past his wooded hills, Bromfield pondered the American society he had come home to. It was like the three-legged milking stool in his dairy barn; one leg industry, another labor, the third agriculture. With any leg broken the other two are useless, the stool can't stand. If one leg is weak, the other two are insecure. In America he saw labor and industry supported by increasing legislation and public concern, while agriculture was neglected. The farmer needed more knowledge, better methods, improved seed and breeding stock. His land and water needed to become matters of public concern.

In the second year of Malabar Farm there gathered in Washington a group of writers, scientists, economists, businessmen, and government officials—people who shared an alarm over the nation's waste of resources. They organized a society called Friends of the Land. One-fourth of America's richest soil had been destroyed, another fourth was in danger. The Friends pro-

10. Louis Bromfield, *Malabar Farm* (New York: Harper & Brothers, 1948), p. 101.

posed to inform the American people of the threat to soil, forests, and water. They knew that a remedy could not be imposed by government; it would have to be accomplished by the people. Action in a democracy rests upon public information and public purpose. That was the platform of the Friends of the Land.

The first national meeting was scheduled in Columbus, because several of the founders were Ohio men and because Ohio had a unique balance of agriculture and industry. To the founders' surprise the meeting drew a standing-room crowd of concerned people. The newspapers were there, the labor unions, the chambers of commerce, the League of Women Voters, the Isaac Walton League, The Farm Bureau, the Grange, and the garden clubs. From a hotel meeting room the sessions overflowed into hallways, lobbies, and lounges.

Among my own heartening memories is a June afternoon with Bromfield, Russell Lord, Paul Sears, and some others, planning tours to devastated sections in Appalachian Ohio and to redeemed areas in the upper Muskingum District. The hotel room looked out at the Scioto River, sluggish and oily in the summer sun, but the planning committee saw it flowing clear and bright, as it once had been and might be again.

One year later two hundred cars, license plates from all over Ohio and neighboring states, wound over the hills of Knox County to the farm of Cosmos Bluebaugh. Oats, corn, alfalfa, and wheat lay in curving bands over the terrain, terrace ditches followed the slopes, and cattle stood knee-deep in timothy and clover. In seven years this richly productive farm had been reclaimed from eroded hills and boggy valleys. From there the caravan moved on, through green miles of the Mohican Forest, and down the Pinhook Road to Malabar Farm, its pond gleaming in a setting of willows and poplars, of corn and alfalfa and hillside pasture. In the farmyard five hundred people filled plates at long tables under the trees, and others joined them for a tour of Bromfield's contoured cover crops and highland forest.

During the 1940s the Friends of the Land established pilot farms, examples of sound conservation practice, in other states. They distributed 50,000 copies of a *Primer on Conservation* and developed a national circulation for their distinctive magazine *The Land*. The society's concern reached out to diet and nutrition, stream pollution and waste disposal. "The Friends," wrote Bromfield, "are not only serving the cause of conservation, they are also making good citizenship and love of one's country a practical reality." [11]

In Ohio four pioneer soil-conservation districts were organized in 1942. A product of local leadership in collaboration with agencies of government, the districts have now multiplied to eighty-eight, one in each of the state's counties. In the past twenty-five years they have helped in the building of 20,000 ponds, the development of 7,000 springs and 100,000 acres of reforestation, and the improvement of nearly a million acres of woodland and pasture. In a wholly voluntary program more than 70,000 landowners have used the Soil Conservation Service's counseling, technical help, and financial assistance. Two centuries after the first Ohio axmen began to attack the great forest, Ohio citizens are reclaiming and preserving their natural resources.

Malabar was just one farm, 700 acres in a state of 26 million acres. But Bromfield's venture dramatized, even glamorized, the conservation movement then gathering momentum in Ohio and the nation. In his last years Bromfield called himself a farmer rather than a writer, though the two were inseparable in him. As weathered lines deepened in his face, his writing reached deepening insights into man and nature. With a wondering reverence for life he loved all that was around him, from the big Angus bull in his dairy barn to the bright-eyed field mouse that nested in his bedside radio. At his death, of hepatitis, in a Columbus hospital in 1956, the farm was in debt, and there was talk of making Malabar a commercial resort. But the Friends of the Land saved it. On borrowed money the society operated the farm for ten years, while the debt increased. Then the Muskingum Conservancy District proposed to make it an Ohio memorial, and across the state newspapers, schools, and county agencies joined in.

11. Louis Bromfield, *Pleasant Valley* (New York: Harper & Brothers, 1945), p. 267.

In the summer of 1972 Malabar Farm became the property of Ohio, to be run in keeping with Bromfield's conservation program. Now the big house, the barns and barnyards, fields and forests, are all open to visitors—house tours, walking tours, wagon tours. Malabar Farm is an enduring demonstration of the kinship of people with the land.

Epilogue

AT the American Centennial Exposition in Philadelphia in 1876—a time of severe economic depression and political rancor—the Ohio Building occupied a focal point at the eastern end of State Row. A steep-roofed, five-gabled structure, built of stone from twenty-one Ohio quarries, it still stands in Fairmount Park.

Ohio Day, October 26, drew 135,000 to the fair, 30,000 of them Ohioans. They saw portraits of the survivors of Perry's 1813 victory on Lake Erie, an ornate organ case carved at the Cincinnati School of Design, and a Buckeye Table Rake Reaper and Mower. But the most enduring work was Archibald Willard's "Spirit of '76," which, a century later, became the ubiquitous emblem of the nation's Bicentennial.

Willard had begun in Wellington, Ohio, as a wagon painter, adding barnyard scenes to the wagons' sideboards and tailboards. Moving to Cleveland, he worked in a fourth-floor room of the Union National Bank Building, painting village scenes and characters in a pleasantly humorous vein. Recalling a Fourth of July parade, he produced "Yankee Doodle," showing an ancient white-haired drummer, a puff-cheeked fifer, and an excited boy rapping his own small drum—an early Norman Rockwell. The old drummer was drawn from the artist's father, a Baptist preacher who had come out to Ohio from Vermont. When his father died, Willard did the painting over, seriously

197

this time—battle smoke in the air, a bandage around the fifer's head, the boy drummer anxiously keeping time with the white-haired veteran. A Cleveland art dealer James F. Ryder, accustomed to showing Willard's comic chromos, put the painting in his window. It stopped so many people that the sidewalk was blocked until Ryder moved it into his back room.

At the Philadelphia Exposition Ryder sold small prints of "Spirit of '76." They were so popular that he sent for the original, and placed it in the Exposition's Memorial Hall. A reporter wrote that "Crowds stood before the picture, wrapped in silent emotion." [1] Many returned to study it again and again. From Philadelphia the canvas went to Washington, Boston, Chicago, and San Francisco. Back in Boston it was hung in the Old South Church on Washington Street.

In Cleveland the artist made several eight-by-ten-foot reproductions. One went to the Corcoran Gallery in Washington, another to Abbot Hall in Marblehead, Mass. In 1913, on commission of Mayor Newton D. Baker, Willard, then 76, made the largest reproduction for Cleveland's new City Hall. The work is said to have been copied more times and in more forms than any other in the world.

On Ohio Day, in Philadelphia, Governor Rutherford B. Hayes, about to be elected president, made a short speech and shook eight thousand hands. Then Edward Deering Mansfield, Cincinnati editor and civic leader, reviewed Ohio's development from savage country to a potent and prosperous commonwealth. His final words were of the future, as though addressed to a Bicentennial: "Long before another century shall have passed by, the single state of Ohio will present four-fold the population with which the thirteen states began their independence, more wealth than the entire Union now has, greater universities than any now in the country, and a development of arts and manufactures which the world now knows nothing of." [2]

The prophecy has been fulfilled; along with other Ohio developments the speaker did not foresee—urban decay, energy

---

1. Rose, *Cleveland,* p. 400.

2. *The Centinel of the North-Western Territory* (Ohio American Revolution Bicentennial Advisory Commission), July, 1975, p. 8.

crunch, environmental pollution, mass media purveying violence and crime; and the Boy Scouts, the 4-H Club, the American Federation of Labor, rural electrification, Dr. Sabin's polio vaccine, Jesse Owens's four gold medals at the Berlin Olympics, John Glenn's lift-off into outer space, and Neil Armstrong's footprints on the moon.

It is odd that "Spirit of '76" has survived the changes of a hundred years—in art and science, in manners and morals, in culture and economy. Apparently that primitive painting contains something time does not touch. It has been called a picture of the Minute Men, but Willard did not depict three soldiers marching toward the British lines. He showed three generations—eager boy, determined man, undaunted grandfather: past, present, and future joined in step and purpose. Perhaps the painting speaks of continuity in giving it a try.

Flag-shaped Ohio, with all the nation's problems, looks ahead without the assurance voiced in 1876. Yet it has unspent resources in its rich domain and inexhaustible capacities in its diverse people. In the depression 1930s Charles Allan Smart, after years away, returned to an ancestral farm near the old Ohio capital of Chillicothe. In *R. F. D.* he wrote of looking back at the virgin country of his forebears and then of looking forward "to a time when men can say, We nearly ruined this paradise but now it is restored and protected; it is invaded only for good farms and gardens, for clean, sunny houses and factories that are appropriate, and for inconspicuous, efficient tools." [3] Only then, one may conclude, can we exalt our local history.

3. Charles Allan Smart, *R.F.D.* (New York: W. W. Norton & Co., 1938), p. 26.

Suggestions for Further Reading

Anyone curious about the development of Ohio should become acquainted with the 1,900 double-column pages of Henry Howe's *Historical Collections of Ohio*, 2 volumes (Columbus: Henry Howe & Son, 1889). Based on two tours of the state, on horseback in 1846 and by train forty years later, the work is a compilation of history, geography, biography, and travel information. Organized by counties, it goes into every part of the state and tells something of lively interest about every city, town, and village. No other state has a historical grabbag like this. Its 1846 pencil sketches are supplemented by photographs from the 1880s.

The six-volume *History of the State of Ohio,* edited by Carl Wittke (Columbus: Ohio State Archaeological and Historical Society, 1941–1944) is a work of authoritative scholarship and comprehensive scope. The separate volumes are Beverley W. Bond, Jr., *The Foundations of Ohio;* William T. Utter, *The Frontier State, 1803–1825;* Francis P. Weisenberger, *The Passing of the Frontier, 1825–1850;* Eugene H. Roseboom, *The Civil War Era, 1850–1873;* Philip D. Jordan, *Ohio Comes of Age, 1873–1900;* and Harlow Lindley, editor, *Ohio in the Twentieth Century.* This series can be supplemented but not superseded.

The best single-volume general history is Eugene H. Roseboom and Francis P. Weisenberger, *A History of Ohio* (Columbus: Ohio State Archaeological and Historical Society, 1953). Written with vigor and clarity and generously illustrated, this book will reward any reader. The most comprehensive of all state histories of the Civil War is Whitelaw Reid's big two-volume *Ohio in the War* (Cincinnati: Moore, Wilstach & Baldwin, 1868). It includes detailed biographical sketches of the Ohio generals.

The approach of the regional historian, informal but informing, and more narrative than expository, is exemplified in Harlan Hatcher, *The Buckeye Country* (New York: Kinsey, 1940) and *The Western Reserve* (Indianapolis: Bobbs-Merrill, 1949); R. E. Banta, *The Ohio* (New

201

York: Rinehart & Company, 1949); and William D. Ellis, *The Cuyahoga* (New York: Holt, Rinehart and Winston, 1966). Philip D. Jordan, *The National Road* (Indianapolis: Bobbs-Merrill, 1948) shows Ohio in the yeasty years of the 1830s. This is also the period of Mrs. Frances Trollope's famous *Domestic Manners of the Americans,* edited by Donald Smalley (New York: Knopf, 1949), a graphic, caustic, and discerning book largely based on the English author's residence in Cincinnati.

Memoirs that make significant portrayals of Ohio background range from William Cooper Howells, *Recollections of Life in Ohio, from 1813 to 1840* (Cincinnati: Robert Clarke Company, 1890) and William Dean Howells, *A Boy's Town* (New York: Harper & Brothers, 1890) to Charles Allan Smart, *R. F. D.* (New York: Norton, 1938). Louis Bromfield, *The Farm* (New York: Harper, 1933) is a Western Reserve family chronicle that moves from a rooted provincialism to the restless commercialism that replaced it in the course of three generations. Like much of Ohio history and literature *The Farm* reveals forces at work not only in Ohio but in the nation generally.

Biographies of rewarding interest include Thomas Beer, *Hanna* (New York: Knopf, 1929); Forrest Wilson, *Crusader in Crinoline, Life of Harriet Beecher Stowe* (Philadelphia: Lippincott, 1941); Margaret Leech, *In the Days of McKinley* (New York: Harper & Row, 1959); and James T. Patterson, *Mr. Republican, A Biography of Robert A. Taft* (Boston: Houghton Mifflin, 1972). Ohio's large role in political history is examined in Richard P. McCormick, *The Second American Party System* (Chapel Hill: University of North Carolina Press, 1966); H. Wayne Morgan, *From Hayes to McKinley* (Syracuse: Syracuse University Press, 1969); and Hoyt Landon Warner, *Progressivism in Ohio* (Columbus: Ohio State University Press, 1964).

Engaging accounts of Ohio cities are George E. Condon, *Cleveland, The Best Kept Secret* (Garden City: Doubleday, 1967) and Clara Longworth de Chambrun, *Cincinnati, The Story of the Queen City* (New York: Scribners, 1939). Small-town Ohio is portrayed with humor, candor, and proportion in Helen Santmyer, *Ohio Town* (Columbus: Ohio State University Press, 1962), a leisurely recollection of county seat Xenia.

In historical fiction Conrad Richter traced the development of Ohio in terms of one family's rise from primitive life in the woods to prominence in a typical Ohio city. *The Trees* (New York: Knopf, 1940); *The Fields* (New York: Knopf, 1946); and *The Town* (New York: Knopf, 1950) combine distinguished writing with historical perception. The

Ohio wilderness of the eighteenth century is dramatically evoked in Allan W. Eckert, *The Frontiersmen* (Boston: Little, Brown, 1967) and *Wilderness Empire* (Boston: Little, Brown, 1969). These books use devices of fiction with material based solidly on historical records.

Yet to appear in this Bicentennial year is the *Pictorial History of Ohio* by George W. Knepper. With some six hundred illustrations and a comprehensive text, this book is a project of the Ohio American Revolution Bicentennial Advisory Commission.

Index

205

The University of Illinois Press
is a founding member of the
Association of American University Presses.

University of Illinois Press
1325 South Oak Street
Champaign, IL 61820-6903
www.press.uillinois.edu